Paul Lee Tan

THE INTERPRETATION OF PROPHECY

by

PAUL LEE TAN, Th.D.

Foreword by

DR. JOHN C. WHITCOMB, JR.

ASSURANCE PUBLISHERS
P.O. Box 420
Winona Lake, Indiana 46590

THE INTERPRETATION OF PROPHECY
Copyright © 1974
Paul Lee Tan

Second printing, 1976
Third printing, 1978

Library of Congress Catalog Card Number: 73-85613
International Standard Book Number: 0-88469-000-8

PRINTED IN THE UNITED STATES OF AMERICA
by Cushing-Malloy, Inc., Ann Arbor, Michigan

To
MOTHER
who brought me up in the nurture and
admonition of the Lord,
this book is affectionately dedicated.

TABLE OF CONTENTS

7

FOREWORD

It is impossible for us to know what our Lord Jesus Christ said to the two on the road to Emmaus when, ". . . he interpreted to them in all the scriptures the things concerning himself" (Luke 24:27). But we *do* know at least three things about this unique instructional experience.

First, we know that these disciples were typically slow to grasp the meaning of the prophetic Scriptures. "O foolish men, and slow of heart to believe in all that the prophets have spoken!" (v. 25). *Second*, we know that their slowness to understand cannot be attributed to the intrinsic obscurity of Biblical prophecy or to our Lord's inadequacy as a teacher. It was neither the Book nor the Teacher that fell short. The disciples alone were to blame, as Christ so pointedly asserted. *Third*, we know that God enflamed their hearts as Jesus expounded the Word and later opened their minds to understand it (vs. 32, 45).

What is our greatest need today? It is burning hearts and illumined minds, as God's prophetic Word is expounded by men who approach the exegetical skills of our Lord. But can we ever know *how* Christ handled the Scriptures on the road to Emmaus to bring about such remarkable effects? I believe we can know and must know. We *can* know because the Scriptures give us numerous examples of His literal, grammatical-historical use of the Old Testament. And we *must* know because otherwise we have no right to expect God in a similar way to warm and illumine the hearts and minds of men concerning His revelation in the Scriptures today!

19

This is why I am convinced that Dr. Paul Tan's book is vitally important. With amazing skill and clarity, Dr. Tan unfolds the methods of Bible interpretation employed by Christ and the apostles and shows why this literal method (which makes full allowance for all known figures of speech) is the only possible method of arriving at solid Biblical truth, whether in historical or prophetic passages.

Dr. Paul Lee Tan has proven himself to be a humble and diligent student of God's Word, "a workman that needeth not to be ashamed." It has been a personal blessing to fellowship with this man of God. I heartily recommend this volume to the Christian world as a fresh and powerful contribution toward the attainment of that level of spiritual discernment we must all diligently seek after, "handling aright the word of truth" (II Tim. 2:15 ASV).

John C. Whitcomb, Jr.

Grace Theological Seminary
Winona Lake, Indiana

PREFACE

While inside the library of the Dallas Theological Seminary some years ago, a fellow seminarian quietly approached and inquired, "Understandest thou what thou readest?" If I were up-to-date on the story of Philip and the Ethiopian eunuch, a proper reply would have been, "How can I, except some men should guide me?"

Although I did not give a quotable reply nor draft the grinning classmate to be tutor for the day, the question "Understandest thou?" has appeared time and again when the prophetic Scriptures are studied.

Most people know something about the teachings of prophecy, but a comparative few are acquainted with the hermeneutical principles and procedures on which prophecy is based. This is unfortunate, for hermeneutics is foundational and should be studied first. One possible cause for this situation is the paucity of hermeneutical works which specialize in the interpretation of prophecy. Admittedly, there are numerous works on general hermeneutics which deal with prophecy. But most of these, while condensed in their treatments of Bible prophecy, approach the subject in ways ranging from the moderately non-literal to the extremely allegorical. This has spawned a number of hermeneutical rules and procedures that are slanted to the non-literal eschatological systems.

This book attempts to narrow the gap in the field of hermeneutics. It is based on the proposition that consistent literal

21

interpretation of prophecy is good hermeneutics. Since consistent literal hermeneutics naturally results in the premillennial, pretribulational system of eschatology, the latter will also receive vindication. We have included a large number of illustrations and examples in this work. These serve not only to elucidate given points but also to point out and specify the various implications and applications which literal prophetic interpretation necessitates. These illustrations will inform regarding where it leads when prophecy is literally interpreted.

It is my earnest prayer that as the coming of the Lord draws near, God's people will possess a better understanding of the prophetic Word. Proper hermeneutics will enable the people of God to follow in the steps of the ancient Ethiopian who, after a better understanding of prophecy, "went on his way rejoicing" (Acts 8:39).

Paul L. Tan

ACKNOWLEDGEMENTS

The author wishes to express appreciation to the following persons whose assistance has made this work possible.

Dr. Edwin G. Spahr and Mr. Raymond W. Frame under whose teaching ministries my interest in Bible prophecy was first kindled.

Dr. Homer A. Kent, Jr., Dr. John C. Whitcomb, Jr., and Dr. James L. Boyer to whose committee at the Grace Theological Seminary this work was first presented as a doctoral dissertation; and the faculty of the Grace Theological Seminary by whose gracious permission this work is now published.

Dr. Charles Lee Feinberg of Talbot Theological Seminary, Dr. Herman A. Hoyt of Grace Theological Seminary, and Dr. John F. Walvoord of Dallas Theological Seminary for spending time over the manuscript and offering helpful suggestions.

Dr. Donald K. Campbell, Dr. J. Dwight Pentecost, and Dr. Charles C. Ryrie of the Dallas Theological Seminary for their counsel in certain areas of this study.

Dr. Benjamin A. Hamilton, Assistant Librarian, Grace Theological Seminary, for helping secure crucial reference materials.

Dr. John C. Whitcomb, Jr., Director of Post-Graduate Studies and Professor of Old Testament and Theology at the Grace Theological Seminary, for writing the *Foreword* and for his personal ministry in my life.

Mr. H. Roland Kincher who read the manuscript and made a number of critical notations prior to publication.

To all who have helped in the preparation and publication of this book, I am sincerely grateful.

INTRODUCTION

It has been said that every fourth verse in the Scripture was predictive when written. "There is hardly a book in the Bible," observes the interpreter Girdlestone, "which is wholly devoid of the prophetic element."[1]

Sooner or later, therefore, every reader of the Bible finds himself asking this question: "How is prophecy to be interpreted?" If the interpreter honors the Word of God and desires to delve into its total riches, he will find himself drawn into the study of prophecy, for it occupies a very large portion of God's Word.

Prophecy apparently can be approached differently. Liberal and neo-orthodox interpreters, depending on their intellects, approach the Scripture in a rationalistic and mechanical fashion. They reject anything that is supernatural and contrary to their reason. Bible prophecy is dismissed as pure speculation or written clandestinely after the event.

Pietistic interpreters, on the other hand, rely on the guidance of some *inner light* in their hearts during interpretation. Regular rules and usages of language are slighted. What takes precedence above all consideration is that the interpretation "fits" their feelings on the matter.

There is another group of interpreters which considers Bible prophecy so incomprehensible and full of dark meanings that interpretation must be aided by extra-Biblical sources,

---

[1] Robert Baker Girdlestone, *The Grammar of Prophecy* (Grand Rapids, Mich.: Kregel Pubs., 1955), p.8.

such as the popes and councils, religious founders and leaders, and theological presuppositions. Thus, Roman Catholics interpret by the pronouncements of their church, the Mormons depend on the Book of Mormon, the Seventh Day Adventists supplement Scripture with the revelations of Mrs. Ellen G. White, the followers of Christian Science interpret by *Science and Health with Key to the Scriptures*, and many Protestant theologians rely on the help of so-called theological interpretations. [1]

The only dependable approach to prophecy, however, is the *literal method of interpretation*. This method assumes that Bible prophecy, written in regular human language, should be interpreted according to laws governing written communication. It is a trustworthy and God-honoring method of interpretation which takes the Bible at its word.

The study of Bible prophecy, although made "more sure" (II Pet. 1:19) by literal interpretation, remains nevertheless a most demanding one. There exists no shortcut to true prophetic interpretation. The interpreter who wishes to enter into the study of God's written revelation must diligently prepare himself for this sacred task. At least four qualifications are necessary.

First, he must be *a spiritually sensitive Christian.* Since the Holy Spirit is the Author of Scripture, he who interprets the

---

[1] Daniel Payton Fuller in "The Hermeneutics of Dispensationalism" (Doctor's dissertation, Northern Baptist Theol. Seminary, Chicago, 1957), p. 147 frankly admits that "in Covenant Theology, there is the tendency to impute to passages a meaning which would not be gained merely from their historical and grammatical associations. This phase of interpretation is called the 'theological' interpretation."

Bible must possess the Spirit of God. In other words, he must be born of the Spirit (John 3:8). The apostle Paul explains this prerequisite:

> For what man knoweth the things of a man, save the spirit of man which is in him? Even so the things of God knoweth no man, but the Spirit of God. Now we have received . . . the Spirit who is of God; that we might know the things that are freely given to us of God. [I Cor. 2:11-12]

Since the Bible is a spiritual Book, he who approaches it must be spiritually in tune with it. He must have the spiritual capacity and sensitiveness of heart for the Holy Spirit to work in illuminating the Word.

Second, he must be *a sincere seeker*. God is doing the speaking in the Scripture. Interpreters who approach God's Word to prove their preconceived notions of how the future should be worked out or to slight that which does not fit their theologies will find themselves knocking at fast closed doors. As J. Sidlow Baxter says, "The Bible will no more speak to some minds than Christ would speak to Herod."[1] In His prayer to the Father, Jesus observes that "thou hast hidden these things from the wise and prudent, and hast revealed them unto babes" (Matt. 11:25-26). The spiritual equipment of the seeker of God's truth is child-like faith.

Third, he must be *knowledgeable in the original languages*. It is not unreasonable to ask that all interpretations of the Scripture be based on the original text. This does not mean that every interpreter of Scripture must possess the linguistic skills of specialists (who may lack other equally essential qualities). But interpretation of the Bible must not be at odds with the Hebrew and Greek texts. A love for the

---

[1] J. Sidlow Baxter, *The Strategic Grasp of the Bible* (Grand Rapids, Mich.: Zondervan Pub. House, 1968), p. 24.

original languages of the Bible, coupled with at least a working knowledge of their usages, will remove a veil which would otherwise exist between the interpreter and the Bible.

Fourth, he must be *a sensible exegete.* The writers of Scripture were sensible men who were not trying to bewilder and mislead their readers. They had a revelation to communicate and they wrote according to laws governing human comprehension and understanding. The interpreter "must not allow himself to be influenced by hidden meanings, spiritualizing processes, and plausible conjectures."[1] A sensible approach to the writings of Scripture is necessary.

---

[1] Milton S. Terry, *Biblical Hermeneutics* (New York, N.Y.: Eaton and Mains, 1911), p. 25.

I.
THE LITERAL METHOD OF INTERPRETATION

The literal method of interpreting God's Word is a true and honest method.[1] It is based on the assumption that the words of Scripture can be trusted. It assumes that since God intends His revelation to be understood, divine revelation must be written based on regular rules of human communication.

1. DEFINITION OF THE METHOD

To "interpret" means to explain the original sense of a speaker or writer. To interpret "literally" means to explain the original sense of the speaker or writer according to the normal, customary, and proper usages of words and language. Literal interpretation of the Bible simply means to explain the original sense of the Bible according to the normal and customary usages of its language.

In order to determine the normal and customary usages of Bible language, it is necessary to consider the accepted rules of grammar and rhetoric, as well as the factual historical and cultural data of Bible times. Therefore, the literal method of interpretation is also called the Grammatico-Historical Method.

---

[1] The science of interpretation is known as *hermeneutics*.

II. Description of the Method

It is proper for a word to have various meanings and senses. However, when a word is used in a given situation, it should normally possess but *one* intended sense or meaning. This is the regular law of linguistic exchange among sensible people.

Music lovers seek to understand music composers, not by out-thinking and out-sensing the composers, but by following the latter's choice and use of precise musical notes. Students of Music Appreciation courses do not go about trying to listen for something which is not there, but attempt rather to know the intended meaning and mood of a given composer through his use of the notes. Otherwise what the composer is trying to say is ignored and what the interpreter wants to say becomes the important factor.

Literal interpreters believe that Scriptural revelation is given to be understood by man. To "understand" a speaker or writer, one must assume that the speaker or writer is using words normally and without multiple meanings. This is what the literal method of interpretation assumes of God in Scriptural revelation. It believes the Bible to be revelation, not riddle.

III. Clarification of the Method

The literal method of interpretation is often held up for ridicule and written off as too foolish to be taken seriously. This unwarranted situation is the result of the following misunderstandings of the literal method.

A. Literal and Figurative

The word *literal* is often taken to mean that which is non-figurative. Interpreters often set the literal over against the figurative. This is a serious mispprehension of the method.

Everyone agrees that great literatures properly use both figurative and nonfigurative languages. Figures of speech are the legitimate, charming ornaments of language. They help to liven writing and conversing. Like all great literatures, the Bible contains both figurative and nonfigurative languages. For instance, Christ describes Himself as "the light of the world" (John 8:12). Figurative language helps make God's Word linguistically more interesting.

The presence of figures in Scripture, however, does not militate against literal interpretation. Since literal interpretation properly accepts that which is normal and customary in language—and figurative language is certainly normal and customary—literal interpreters are not hindered by that which is figurative. There is no necessity to change to a different method of interpretation.

As George N. H. Peters explains: "When employing the word 'literal,' we are to be comprehended as also fully acknowledging the figurative sense, the beautiful ornaments of language; we cordially accept all that is *natural* to language itself, its naked strength and its charming adornments, but object to *additionally* forcing on it a *foreign* element, and enclosing it in a garb that hides its just proportions."[1]

Although the Scriptures contain figurative language, the interpreter must be careful not to identify as a figure that which is actual. This is true especially of prophecy. The statement "Pray for the peace of Jerusalem" (Ps. 122:6) is a request concerning the earthly city of Jerusalem, not figurative of praying for the Christian church.[2]

---

[1] George N.H. Peters, *The Theocratic Kingdom* (3 vols.; Grand Rapids, Mich.: Kregel Pubs., 1952), I, 48.

[2] For a more extensive treatment of figurative language, see Chapter VI *THE LANGUAGE OF PROPHECY*, pp. 131–51.

B. Literal and Spiritual

The literal method is also often cast in the unnatural role of being against the spiritual. The argument is that literal interpretation misses the spiritual element. Non-literal interpreters therefore like to call their method "the spiritual method" or "spiritualization."

Spiritualizers believe that since the Bible is spiritual in nature, the interpreter should penetrate behind the speech to the living Spirit. They believe that the written words of Scripture simply can not contain all that is in the Spirit's mind, and that to interpret the words literally is to miss the true meaning of the Bible. "One may often feel, when reading the prophetic word, how much further the spiritual meaning reaches than the letter expresses; how prophecy struggles, as it were, to give its thoughts an adequate embodiment."[1]

Literal interpreters, of course, recognize that the Scripture contains spiritual truths which no uninspired Shakespeare could ever produce. The Bible is divine both in its origin and in its content, and, as such, it is certainly *spiritual*. The proper method of getting to know these spiritual truths, however, is not through *spiritualization*. Spiritual truths when revealed, are revealed as the written Word of God. Literal interpretation of that which is written brings out these truths.

Because of man's finiteness, God does not use an incomprehensible heavenly or 'spiritual' language to write the Scripture. He chooses to convey spiritual truths and principles through the medium of regular, earthly language. Scriptural revelation must therefore be interpreted according to regular

---

[1] Gustav Friedrich Oehler, *Theology of the Old Testament*, rev. and trans. by George E. Day (New York, N.Y.: Funk and Wagnalls Pubs., 1883), p. 491.

rules of earthly grammar and rhetoric. Being divinely intended for human comprehension, the Bible should be interpreted according to the normal mode of communication used among men.

Moreover, literal interpreters believe that the words of Scripture are adequate in conveying all that God wants man to know. The prophet Moses makes this quite clear in Deuteronomy 29:29, "The secret things belong unto the Lord our God; but those things which are *revealed* [Italics added] belong unto us and to our children forever." The proper bounds of research by Bible interpreters therefore should be truths revealed in God's Word. To overstep and trespass the bounds of written revelation for that which is unrevealed and hidden in God is contrary to the teachings of Scripture and mires the interpreter on uncertain ground.

Perhaps it is proper to describe what non-literalists mean by *'spiritual.'* Non-literal interpreters regard portions of Scripture to have secret meanings and mystical, hidden senses. This basic presupposition leads them to interpret mystically and allegorically. It therefore has nothing to do with spirituality or being spiritual. Actually the reverse seems more true to fact. By implying that the Scripture cannot say what it means, and then foisting on it a superadded, hidden sense, advocates of spiritualization are being irreverent to the Word they claim to cherish. The use of the word *spiritual* for such a method is therefore unfortunate.

John Peter Lange comments regarding this unhappy use of terms: "No terms could have been chosen more unfit to designate the two great schools of prophetical exegetes than *literal* and *spiritual*. These terms are not antithetical, nor are they in any proper sense significant of the peculiarities of the respective systems they are employed to characterize. They are positively misleading and confusing."[1]

C. Interpretation and Application

The literal method of interpretation is concerned with interpretation, not with application. The interpreter is primarily interested in what the Bible says; then he makes practical applications based on what has been interpreted. Applications are fair to the Bible when they are based on that which has been literally interpreted. To base interpretations of the Bible on applications is erroneous and will end in chaos.

As the reformer John Calvin says, "The Word of God is inexhaustible and applicable at all times, but there is a difference between explanation and application, and application must be consistent with explanation."

Incidentally, the devotional use of the Bible may be made through the literal or the non-literal method, but only in the literal exegesis of given passages will one be assured that his devotional exposition or application is anchored on solid Scriptural foundation.

D. Literalism and the Depth of Scripture

The literal interpreter, by insisting on the literal sense of Scripture, does not imply that the Bible has no depth or latent riches. God's Word contains truths, principles, and applications which every interpreter must fathom. Some of these are latent, inward, and hidden; others are patent, outward, and obvious. "In the Bible, which is simple and plain even to the

---

[1] John Peter Lange, *Revelation*, in *A Commentary on the Holy Scriptures*, ed. by J.P. Lange, trans. by Phillip Schaff, American editor, E.R. Craven (Grand Rapids, Mich.: Zondervan Pub. House, 1949-51), p. 98n.

wayfaring man, there is both the exoteric and the esoteric, both the open and the hidden, the public and the secret."[1]

For instance, Jesus' feeding of the five thousand (an actual, historical event) contains a number of spiritual truths and applications, one of which is mentioned by Christ Himself in John 6:25-59 (". . . I am the bread of life"). And during the subsequent storm which terrifies the disciples at sea, Mark comments that "they considered not the miracle of the loaves" (Mark 6:52)— another possible application.

The correlation of both the simple and the profound in God's Word is wonderful to behold. But this licenses neither a mystical approach nor a forced search for some superadded 'spiritual' sense. There is nothing clandestine about Christianity. The proper approach to God's Word is the reverent one of accepting what it says and then making applications to life.

John Milton in *Reformation in England* says: "The very essence of truth is plainness and brightness; the darkness and ignorance are our own . . . We would believe the Scriptures protesting their own plainness and perspicuity, calling to them to be instructed, not only the wise and the learned, but the simple, the poor, the babes."[2]

There are certain elements in the Scriptures which appear as types and symbols, and which would possess a *wider* or even *deeper* meaning.[3] But these do not introduce a mystical element or a different sense into the Bible. The interpretation of types and symbols springs from their respective literal bases.

---

[1] J. Sidlow Baxter, *The Strategic Grasp of the Bible* (Grand Rapids, Mich.: Zondervan Pub. House, 1968), p. 16.

[2] Cited by Milton S. Terry, *Biblical Hermeneutics* (New York, N.Y.: Eaton and Mains, 1911), p. 383.

[3] For instance, it is possible to see Satan and his career portrayed in Isaiah 14 and Ezekiel 28.

IV. The Need for a Word

The word *Literal* is often mistakenly thought to imply that which is actual, earthly, material, and substantial in opposition to that which is figurative, heavenly, conceptual, and abstract. This is unfortunate, for the literal method embraces *both* the actual and the figurative, the earthly and the heavenly, the material and the conceptual, the substantial and the abstract. Literal interpretation of the Bible may lead to any or all of the above concepts.

For this reason, it has been suggested that substitute words such as *plain*,[1] *proper, natural, or normal*[2] be used instead of *literal*. These words would convey more accurately the idea of interpretation according to *customary* usage of language, which is the basic meaning of *literal*.

While these substitutes words may help clear the air in some respects, they are in turn subject to misapprehensions in others. And the word *literal* has become so embedded in hermeneutical and theological discussions through the years that any effort to alter its traditional usage and implications would be quite in vain.

Alva J. McClain expresses the sentiment of many in this matter: "Perhaps it would help to clear the air if we could get rid of all the adjectives [literal, spiritual, etc.] and simply use the term 'interpretation' alone in its first and original sense, 'to give the meaning of.' We could then go on from there and talk about other things, such as types and applications. This is what we mean by literal interpretation."[3]

---

[1] James Oliver Buswell, *A Systematic Theology of the Christian Religion* (2vols.; Grand Rapids, Mich.: Zondervan Pub. House, 1963), II, 425.

[2] Lange, *Revelation*, p. 98n.

[3] Alva J. McClain, *The Greatness of the Kingdom* (Grand Rapids, Mich.: Zondervan Pub. House, 1959), p. 142.

V. OPPONENTS OF THE METHOD

In early church history, there arose a group of interpreters (known as the "allegorists") which saw a multiplicity of senses and meanings in the Scriptures. They regarded the literal words only as a vehicle for arriving at the hidden, more spiritual, and more profound sense of Scripture. "What was more natural, more in keeping with all of creation," reasoned the allegorists, "than that God should have concealed a spiritual message in crude material language . . . . Interpretation, therefore, lay in discerning the spiritual meaning of the text hidden beneath the letter, which could often for all practical purposes be discarded."[1]

The allegorists not only affirmed the concept of multiple sense in Scripture, but also decreed that the hidden, deeper sense is the *real* one. As we shall see under the chapter following, the Alexandrians and other church fathers practiced allegorism to the hilt, and the fanciful exegeses they produced "make one part of our mind laugh and another part groan."[2]

To cite a few examples: The journey of Abraham from Ur of the Chaldess to Haran is interpreted as the imaginary trip of a Stoic philosopher who leaves sensual understanding and arrives at the senses.[3] The two pence given by the Good Samaritan to the innkeeper has the hidden meanings of Baptism and the Lord's Supper. The river Euphrates means the outflow of manners and is not an actual literal river in

---

[1] Cited by Bruce Vawter, "The Fuller Sense: Some Considerations," *Catholic Biblical Quarterly*, XXVI, No. 1 (Jan., 1964), 87.
[2] Baxter, *Strategic Grasp*, p. 17.
[3] Cited by Frederic W. Farrar, *History of Interpretation* (London: Macmillan and Co., 1886), pp. 140-41.

Mesopotamia. Pope Gregory the Great's interpretation of the
Book of Job is equally disheartening: "The patriarch's three
friends denote the heretics; his seven sons are the twelve
apostles; his seven thousand sheep are God's faithful people;
and his three thousand hump-backed camels are the depraved
Gentiles!" [1]

It may thus be seen that when interpreters disregard the
normal signification of words, and go searching for all sorts of
supposedly hidden meanings, the eclipse of true Bible study
results. Imagination and speculation run wild as interpreters
place themselves out of all well-defined principles and laws,
appointing themselves as the arbitrator of what the Scriptures
say.

Because of the excesses which allegorization has produced
in church history, most conservative interpreters today have
rejected it. While this is commendable, the same interpreters
usually continue to allegorize the *prophetic* portions of the
Scripture. The basic technique and approach of allegorists of
general Scripture and spiritualizers of prophetic Scripture
however are similar.

For instance, allegorizers see Abraham as a Stoic
philosopher while spiritualizers see Israel as the church. Both
use the same approach to God's Word and assume the
existence of senses other than the literal. Thus when Floyd
Hamilton spiritualizes the first resurrection of Revelation 20
to be "the new birth of the believer," [2] he is allegorizing. In fact,
spiritualizers of prophecy occasionally slip and describe their
method as "allegorization." As non-literalist Bernhard Weiss
writes, "it is often by means of an *allegorical interpretation*

---

[1] Cited by McClain, *Greatness of the Kingdom*, p. 143.
[2] Floyd E. Hamilton, *The Basis of Millennial Faith* (Grand
Rapids, Mich.: Wm. B. Eerdmans Pub. Co., 1942), p. 117.

[Italics added] that this prophetic sense of the history and institutions of the Old Testament can be brought out."[1]

Conservatives who spiritualize the prophetic Scripture should therefore ruminate the fact that they are teaming with a method (albeit under a different name) which has been found wanting in church history. Gerald Stanton warns that "men who are prone to drift in their Biblical interpretations from the sure anchorage of the literal method would do well to consider the theological company in which they have chosen to travel, and the strange destinations arrived at by some."[2]

---

[1] Bernhard Weiss, *Biblical Theology of the New Testament*, trans. by David Eaton (2 vols.; Edinburgh: T.&T. Clark, 1885), I, 376.

[2] Gerald B. Stanton, *Kept from the Hour* (London: Marshall, Morgan and Scott, 1964), p. 284.

II.

HISTORY OF INTERPRETATION

The science of Bible interpretation is not a Johnny-Come-Lately. It has a history hoary with age and laced with excitement, as men down the centuries attempt to interpret the written revelation of God.

I. BEGINNINGS OF INTERPRETATION

For long centuries past, as the nation Israel progressively degenerated under wicked kings, the Scriptures were generally ignored and not widely used. During the reign of the godly king Josiah, the "book of the law" was discovered in the temple of Jerusalem, but the revival it provoked was short-lived. Soon God's Word was again all but forgotten as the Jews went into exile in Babylon.

After the Babylonian captivity and back in the land of Palestine, a bilingual situation existed among the Jews, for the postexilic Jews spoke mostly Aramaic while the Old Testament text was in the original Hebrew. There was need not only to translate but also to explain the Old Testament Scripture, for the peculiar nuances between the two languages were barricading real understanding of the text. In God's providence, the young priest Ezra, aided by a group of able men, arose to assume the leadership in explaining the Scripture. They expounded the law of Moses before the people from morning to mid-day (cf. Neh. 8:3). Herein lies the recorded birth of literal Bible exegesis and the formal exposition of God's Word.

II. The Jewish Rabbis Exalt Letterism

The splendid Bible study movement started under Ezra later deteriorated under the rabbis into a school which fanatically worshipped the bare letters of Scripture. The Jewish rabbis mistakenly believed that since the whole Massorah, even down to the verses, words, letters, vowel-points, and accents, was delivered to Moses at Mount Sinai, the very words and letters of the Law must be potent as magic. Some rabbis even supposed that God Himself spent three hours daily in the study of the letters of the Law!

A. Fathers of Rabbinism

The founder of the rabbinic system was Rabbi Hillel. Hillel systematized the chaotic mass of rules which had evolved from the Mosaic precepts. He set up seven hermeneutical rules by which the mass of Jewish traditions could (at least outwardly) be deduced from the Scripture.

Although some of Hillel's rules were valid and sensible, most opened the floodgates to excessive allegorization. Hillel's "rule of equivalence" affirmed that whenever identical expressions are found in the Scripture, some sort of relationship must be meant.

The rival of Hillel was Rabbi Shammai, a formalist of the narrowest school. Shammai interpreted every legal maxim with the extremest rigidity, while Hillel allowed modifying circumstances. Thus, Rabbi Hillel summarizes the entire law under the rule of love for one's neighbor. The Jewish proverb "Shammai bound and Hillel loosed" reflects the difference.

Rabbi Aqiba next systematized rabbinism and became the "Thomas Aquinas" of the Oral Law. He taught that a hidden meaning lies under every written peculiarity of the Law. He also taught the allegorical method of combining inferences and getting fresh inferences from the deduced inference.

Rabbi Juda committed the Oral Law into writing for the first time. This compilation of the Oral Law is called The *Mishna*. Ever since the time of Ezra, the Oral Law had been recognized among the Jews. It was supported by the Pharisees of Jesus' day, codified by Hillel, and systematized by Aqiba. Now Rabbi Juda put it all into writing. From now on, the entire theology and philosophy of Judaism would be molded by the *Mishna*.

B. Exegesis of Rabbinism

The rabbis of Palestine and of Babylon interpreted the Old Testament Scriptures through the methods of the Halakha, the Haggada, and the Qabbala. The method of Halakha tried to deduce rules and precepts not formally treated in the Mosaic Code by the use of analogies and combinations of the Law. It is confined to the Pentateuch. The Haggadic method extended over the entire Old Testament and was more practical and homiletical in nature. It aimed to stimulate the people to pious activities by means of legends, proverbs, quotations from famous men, and mystical interpretations of Bible narratives.

The qabbalistic method however is most significant to our discussion, for it is the method which led the Jews to the very worship of the letters of the Law. There are several variations of the qabbalistic method of Old Testament exegesis. These are the Gematria, Notarikon, and Temoorah.

The method of *Gematria* saw a mystical relationship between words and concepts which have the same numerical

values. For instance, the name "Eliezer" has the value of 318
in the Hebrew. Since Abraham also had 318 servants, the
rabbis interpreted this to mean that Eliezer was equal to all
the rest of Abraham's servants. Or, there must be 903 ways of
dying, because the Hebrew word   תוצאות   ("*issues* of
death") in Psalms 68:21 has a numerical value of 903.
Moreover, Moses did not marry an Ethiopian woman but a
"beautiful" woman, for the word "Kushith" yields 736 which
is equivalent to the Hebrew phrase מראה יפת ("fair of
form").

A more imaginative branch of *Gematria* speculated on the
sizes and shapes of letters. For instance, Since the ד in the
word אחד ("one") and the ע in the word
שמע ("hear") are lengthened in Deuteronomy 6:4, this
allegedly indicated three things: (1) to show the greatness of
the doctrine, (2) to show God's power in the four corners of
the world, for ד means "four," and (3) to show that
ע and ד make up the word עד ("witness").

Another qabbalistic method called *Notarikon* tried to form
words by combining initial and terminal letters of other words,
or by regarding the individual letters of a word as initial letters
of other words. For instance, *Adam* is interpreted to stand
for *"Adam, David, Messiah"* and this means that Adam's
soul passed into those of David and the messiah.

A qabbalistic extravaganza worthy of note, called
Temoorah, produced new meanings by interchanging letters
all around. Thus, the word   מלאכי   ("my angel") in
Exodus 23:23 is transposed into the name "Michael." The
commonest way of transposition, however, was to substitute
for each letter of a given word the letter which stands in
equivalent order in the other half of the Hebrew alphabet.
Thus, the word "Sheshach" in Jeremiah 25:26 and 51:41 is
thought of as a cypher for the word "Babel" (Babylon).

Another variation of *Temoorah* was to change the words of the text into some other words which resemble them either in form or even in sound. Under the Jewish rabbis, therefore, the Scriptures were forced to imply thousands of things which the original Bible writers certainly never had intended.

C. Observations on Rabbinism

Non-literal interpreters often cite the Jewish rabbis to illustrate "hyperliteralism"[1] or literalism at its worst. They parade the rabbis as extreme literalists who went overboard in their emphasis on the letters of the Bible. They infer that it is possible to err in being *too* literal. Are these suppositions valid?

It is true that the necessary first step in the literal method is to acknowledge and stress the written words of Scripture. This is why the doctrine of verbal, plenary inspiration and the literal method go hand in hand, and together they constitute an effective barrier against liberalism and modernism. Written words are the God-given conveyance of revelation and should properly be "fussed" over. Christ says concerning the written Word that not "one jot or tittle" shall pass away (Matt. 5:18).

Nevertheless, words and letters are not ends in themselves. The immediate step following the acknowledgment of the words of Scripture is the proper understanding of the revelation which the words intend to convey. Otherwise, one merely plays with letters and words.

The rabbis are to be commended for being scrupulous with the letters of Scripture. This is one reason why "unto them were committed the oracles of God" (Rom. 3:2). But they did not proceed to the meaning being transmitted in the use of the

---

[1] Bernard Ramm, *Protestant Biblical Interpretation* (3rd rev. ed.; Grand Rapids, Mich.: Baker Book House, 1969), p. 47.

letters. And this is where the rabbis went astray. The rabbis forgot that perfection of language points to perfection of revelation and message. They did not realize that, taken by itself, "the letter killeth, but the Spirit giveth life" (II Cor. 3:6). And, shutting themselves up with the bare letters of the Law, having nowhere else to go, they began to worship the very letters of the Sacred Text, and used letterism as a springboard to allegorization and spiritualization.

The Jewish rabbis did not really misuse the literal method. Literalism and letterism are two different things. It was the exclusion of any more than the bare letters of Scripture which set the rabbis on a tangent.[1] Letterism is the premature (not extreme) form of literalism. The interpreter who is properly conversant with the literal method of interpretation can never be *too* literal in interpreting God's Word.

III. THE ALEXANDRIAN JEWS COPY ALLEGORISM

For long centuries past, the Brahmins had given the Vedas a mystical interpretation, and heathen commentators were long used to allegorizing the poems of Homer and other ancients. The allegorical method of interpretation therefore did not originate with the Jews at Alexandria.

---

[1]Non-literal interpreters often point out that the Jews rejected and crucified Christ because they interpreted prophecy literally. As E. W. Hengstenberg charges: "The strongest argument that can be brought [against literalism] is this, it was this very method of interpretation which led to the crucifixion of Christ" (*Christology of the Old Testament* [4 vols.; Grand Rapids, Mich.: Kregel Pubs., 1956], IV, 382).

This is a mistaken affirmation. Literal interpretation of the Messianic prophecies would have enabled the Jews to recognize their Messiah. The Jews pinpointed Bethlehem as the exact town of Messiah's birth (Matt. 2:4-6). The reason why Christ was rejected

However, the dubious credit of being the first to use alle-
gorization on the Old Testament Scriptures belongs to the
Alexandrian Jews. This was about two hundred years before
Christ.

A. Allegorizing the Old Testament

In the Egyptian city of Alexandria, Jewish religion and
Greek philosophy were in daily and constant contact. The
Jews began to notice the ease with which the Greeks
allegorized away the uglier portions of their religious heritage,
such as the exploits and escapades of the Greek gods, explaining these as ethical and moral struggles.

Soon the Alexandrian Jews got the idea. "In the face of
such Old Testament problems as Lot's incest, the drunkenness
of Noah, Jacob's wives and concubines, Judah's seduction of
Tamar, minute distinctions between what was clean and not
clean in the animal kingdom, prohibitions against eating
vultures, anthropomorphic descriptions of God, etc., the
Alexandrians . . . resorted to allegorizing."[1]

In addition to the desire to explain away "oddities" in the
Old Testament, the Jews of Alexandria were also moved by
the charm of Greek literature and philosophy. To them, Greek
philosophy was inspiring, noble, and irresistible. And yet, they
could not leave their own Mosaic Law, for it was sacred,

---

is because the Jews steadfastly refused to accept and apply the
results of their interpretation to the person of Jesus Christ. The
rabbis generally interpreted prophecy in proper literal fashion. But
they refused to apply the Messianic expectations (the result of
literalism) to Christ. While Jesus often chided the rabbis for their
errors in Scriptural interpretation, He never corrected their interpretation of prophecy.

[1] Anton Berkeley Mickelsen, *Interpreting the Bible* (Grand
Rapids, Mich.: Wm. B. Eerdmans Pub. Co., 1969), p. 32.

binding, and eternal. There should be a way whereby the two might be united. Allegorism went to their rescue. Allegorism enabled the Alexandrian Jews to make Moses speak the beautiful philosophy of Plato and other Greek sages.

B. Philo of Alexandria

The pinnacle of Alexandrian allegorization rests on one person, Philo of Alexandria. A philosophical Jew who possessed both reverence for the Mosaic revelation and fondness for Grecian metaphysics, Philo aimed to explore the mystical depths of significances allegedly concealed beneath the Old Testament Scripture.

To Philo, the literal sense was "milk" and the allegorical sense "meat." Only the simple-minded does not aspire to reach the meaty, hidden, and inner levels of Scripture. Philo believed that something unusual must be lurking beneath the pages of Scripture when "expressions are doubled . . . when there is a repetition of facts already known. . . when words admit of a slight alteration; when the expression is unusual; when there is anything abnormal in the number or tense."[1] Thus, the repetition "Abraham! Abraham!" in Genesis 22:11 means that Abraham would live in the future life.

The allegorical method introduced by the Alexandrian Jews left deep and lasting scars on the study of the Scriptures. It lingered for more than fifteen hundred years on up to the time of the Reformation, vestiges of it continuing to the present.

The observation of J. Dwight Pentecost on allegorism is certainly apt: " . . the allegorical method was not born out of the study of the Scriptures, but rather out of a desire to unite Greek philosophy and the Word of God. It did not come out of

---

[1]Frederic W. Farrar, *History of Interpretation* (London: Macmillan and Co., 1886), p. 22.

a desire to present the truths of the Word, but to pervert them. It was not the child of orthodoxy, but of heterodoxy."[1]

IV. The Early Church Fathers Adopt Allegorism

The early fathers of the church, in their Bible interpretations, propounded "a chaos of elements unconsciously borrowed on the one hand from Philo and on the other from rabbis and kabbalists."[2] They therefore add little or nothing to our interpretation of Scripture in general. However, their interpretation of prophecy was overwhelmingly literal.

A. Allegorism in the Church

The Christian church did not adopt allegorism until well towards the end of the second century, A.D. Pantaenus (ca. A.D. 180), teacher of the school at Alexandria, was the first to adopt the allegorical method of interpretation. He was followed by Clement of Alexandria and other fathers.

The allegorization of the early fathers tended towards interpreting the Old Testament as a mysterious collection of isolated oracles all pointing to Christ.

Thus, the number of Abraham's servants who were circumcised is 318, expressed by the Greek numerals T I H, where T would stand for the cross by its shape, and IH for the first two letters of 'Iησοῦς ("Jesus"). The early fathers believed that this was the meaning the Bible had intended to convey. Moreover, the father Justin Martyr, assuming that Old Testament writers always speak in mysteries,

---

[1] J. Dwight Pentecost, *Things to Come*, with an Introduction by John F. Walvoord (Findlay, Ohio: Dunham Pub. Co., 1958), pp. 23-24.

[2] Farrar, *History of Interpretation*, p. 165.

types, and oracles, saw the cross in almost every Old Testament stick and piece of wood.

Milton Terry explains why most of the church fathers adopted the allegorical method: "The Church of this early period was too much engaged in struggles for life to develop an accurate or scientific interpretation of Scripture . . . and it was very natural that many of the early Christian writers should make use of methods of Scriptural interpretation which were widely prevalent at the time."[1]

B. Origen: "Mr. Allegorism"

Among the church fathers who allegorized the Scripture, Origen (A.D. 185-254) probably deserves the title "Mr. Allegorism." Origen so popularized the allegorical method that, in the eyes of church historians, he has become allegorization personified. Origen followed the path of Philo the Jew and assumed that the Old and New Testaments contain deep and hidden senses.

Origen said that like man who consists of body, soul, and spirit, the Scripture has a simultaneous threefold sense—the literal, the moral, and the spiritual. Nevertheless, in practice, he seldom referred to the moral sense, and scarcely at all to the literal.

Origen also taught that the Old and New Testaments contain not only absurb and unreasonable portions, but also fables which did not actually take place. Once Origen asked impatiently, "Of what use . . . is it to me who have come to hear what the Holy Spirit teaches the human race, to be told that Abraham stood under the oak of Mamre?"[2] and forth-

---

[1] Milton S. Terry, *Biblical Hermeneutics* (New York, N.Y.: Eaton and Mains, 1911), p. 35.

[2] Farrar, *History of Interpretation*, p. 199.

with dismissed this account in Genesis 18 as non-actual. He also called parts of the life of Rebecca a concoction of mysteries.

No wonder Charles Spurgeon warns his students: "Gentlemen, if you aspire to emulate Origen in wild, daring interpretation, it may be well to read his life and note attentively the follies unto which even his marvelous mind was drawn."

C. Augustine: Father of Dualism

The early history of allegorization also claimed the attention of the great church father Augustine (A.D. 354-430). Augustine modified allegorism by confining it to the prophetic Scriptures. That is, he interpreted the non-prophetic Scriptures literally and the prophetic Scriptures allegorically. This dualistic method of interpretation represents a new twist to the allegorical interpretation then on a rampage. Unfortunately for the church, Augustinian dualism was accepted without much debate into the Roman Catholic church, and later also by the Protestant reformers.

Augustine is best known among students of prophecy as the father of amillennialism. His view of the millennium was incorporated into Roman Catholic theology. Augustine rejected the literal millennium as too materialistic and carnal, and taught that "the millennium is to be interpreted spiritually as fulfilled in the Christian Church."[1] But for all his genius, Augustine never realized that the excessive materialistic elements then ascribed to the millennium were overstated and did not truly belong in the doctrine of the millennium. And so, the church father threw away the baby with the bath.

---

[1]Oswald T. Allis, *Prophecy and the Church* (Phila., Pa.: The Presbyterian and Reformed Pub. Co., 1964), p. 3.

Augustine, while rejecting the earthly, millennial kingdom accepted the literality of the 1,000 years of Revelation 20 and expected the second coming of Christ to occur around 650 A.D. This inconsistency in spiritualizing portions of Revelation 20 while literalizing its 1,000 years is an evidence that the church father did not give a reasonable exegesis to this subject.

Modern-day ammillennialists of course do not follow Augustine in seeing a literal thousand-year period, considering the latter as a symbol of life now in heaven. Others interpret the millennium to mean life in the future in heaven, although, according to Oswald Allis, this is not "ammillennial in the strictest sense of the word."[1]

V. THE SCHOOL OF ANTIOCH AFFIRMS LITERALISM

Among the early church fathers, apart from the afore-mentioned Origen and the allegorists, was a group of interpreters which stood firm on the literal method of interpretation against the oncoming tide of allegorism. Located in the Syrian city of Antioch (where the early disciples were first called "Christians"—Acts 11:26), this school of interpreters stood like a Gibraltar amidst a shifting sea of allegorism.

The School of Antioch was founded by Lucian (died A.D. 312). It soon produced a wave of illustrious alumni— Theodore, bishop of Mopsuestia (A.D. 350-428), also known as the "prince of ancient exegetes"; Chrysostom (AD.354-407) or "the Golden Mouthed"; and Theodoret (A.D. 386-458). Together, they produced some of the best exegetical literatures of ancient times. These Syrian church fathers totally rejected the fanciful exegesis of the allegorists and

---

[1] *Ibid.*, p. 5.

interpreted the Scripture on the basis of the historical reality of its events and personages.

The Antiochian school, however, became festooned with slander connected with the theological controversies of the 4th and 5th centuries (especially the Nestorian controversy), and was forced into an untimely recess. The hermeneutical historian Farrar sighs over the demise of the school: "Unhappily for the Church, unhappily for any real apprehension of Scripture, the allegorists, in spite of protest, were completely victorious. The School of Antioch was discredited by anathemas . . . And we soon descend to allegorical dictionaries of the threefold sense, like that of Eucherius, to the secondhandness of Cassiodorus (562), and the interminable tedium of Gregory the Great (604)."[1]

Despite the recess of the School of Antioch, the literal method of interpretation continued at Edessa and Nisibis, and later (in a roundabout way) touched the Reformation period.

VI. THE MEDIEVAL AGE PERPETUATES MYSTICISM

The period of the Middle Ages was not an age of original research. People were occupied with what the church and tradition had to say, not what the Scriptures say. And the allegorical approach was found most convenient for reconciling Scripture with church tradition.

The allegorism of the medieval churchmen was of the mystical type. The Scriptures were read mainly for instruction in morals and ethics; what was not devotionally useful was slighted or allegorized. The Scriptures were interpreted according to the mood of the moment. Victor of St. Hugo affirmed: "First learn what you are to believe, and then go to the Scripture to find it there."

---

[1] Farrar, *History of Interpretation*, pp. 239-40.

During the Middle Ages, the fourfold sense of Scripture was taught. Medieval scholars took Origen's threefold sense— the literal, the moral, and the spiritual—and subdivided the *spiritual* into the *allegorical* and the *anagogical*. As schoolman Thomas Aquinas affirmed, "The literal sense is that which the author intends, but God being the Author, we may expect to find in Scripture a wealth of meaning."[1]

An example of how the fourfold sense was worked out during the Middle Ages is Genesis 1:3, "Let there be light." Medieval churchmen interpreted that sentence to mean (1) Historically or literally—An act of creation; (2) Morally— May we be mentally illumined by Christ; (3) Allegorically— Let Christ be love; and (4) Anagogically—May we be led by Christ to glory.

The fourfold sense became such an accessory of medieval exegesis that it soon entered secular life and was widely used in astronomy and even for library classification. Thus, Mickelsen sums up: "Except for an oasis here and there, the Middle Ages were a vast desert so far as biblical interpretation is concerned . . . Amid the routine and drudgery of human existence the Church offered only another type of routine.[2]

VII.   THE REFORMATION REVIVES THE LITERAL METHOD

Under the Protestant reformers, the Bible was interpreted literally and the understanding of Scripture flamed up like the Aurora Borealis. Martin Luther declared in his *Table Talk:* "I have grounded my preaching upon the literal Word, he that pleases may follow me, he that will not may stay." And rejecting the fourfold sense of the medieval scholars as well as the allegorization of the preceding centuries, Luther took his stand on literal interpretation of Scripture.

---

[1] Quoted by Mickelsen, *Interpreting the Bible*, p. 37.
[2] *Ibid.*, p. 35.

John Calvin, in the Preface to his *Commentary on the Book of Romans*, lays down the golden rule of interpretation: "It is the first business of an interpreter to let his author say what he does say, instead of attributing to him what we think he ought to say."

The gift of the Protestant reformers to the Christian church thus consists not only in an open Bible but also in the literal method of interpreting that Bible. Unfortunately, however, the reformers refused to be involved in the issue of prophetic interpretation, and so the whole of Protestantism went the way of Roman Catholic amillennialism by default. This omission of the reformers is probably explainable by the fact that truths such as justification by faith and the problems of ecclesiology were claiming the immediate attention of the reformers as the latter sought to sift through the Roman debris.

VIII.   POST-REFORMATION SCHOLARS APPLY LITERALISM

A. Sixteenth Century

After the death of John Calvin (1564), the immediate post-Reformation period was an age of creeds and the formulation of various theological systems. The Council of Trent delineated the proper bounds of Roman Catholic theology and the Protestant churches came out in kind with theological statements. With the emphases of the age on creeds and church interpretations, there was little progress in sound Scriptural interpretation.

Nevertheless, after the Reformation, the literal method was firmly established as the proper method of Bible exegesis, and a large number of scholars and exegetes arose to follow in the footsteps of the reformers. F. W. Farrar describes the hermeneutics of this age as "a general agreement in principles, . . . a refusal to acknowledge the exclusive dominance of patristic authority and church tradition; . . . an avoidance of allegory; a study of the original language; a close attention to the literal sense . . . ."[1]

B. Seventeenth and Eighteenth Centuries

The seventeenth and eighteenth centuries were the period when *Reason* was considered supreme and final. Rationalists such as Hobbes, Descartes, Spinoza, Locke, Hume, and Kant propounded their rationalistic philosophies.

Rationalism's effect on Biblical hermeneutics may be seen in Semler's historical school, which taught that the Scriptures are human productions, fallible, and intended only for the particular periods of history in which they were written.

Despite its detrimental effects, the rationalistic spirit of the age did encourage orthodox and evangelical interpreters to a more scientific study of the Scripture. For instance, the rise of textual studies, concerned with investigations such as variant readings, authorships, and historical settings of the Scripture, occurred at this time. Scholars such as Johann Wettstein, and J. A. Bengel, renowned in textual critical studies, laid the foundation for much of later-day evangelical exegetical works.

The one man who exerts the most influence on the hermeneutics of modern times is John Augustus Ernesti. His *grammatical school* was founded on the principle that "the Bible must be rigidly explained according to its own language . . . . It must neither be bribed by any external authority of the Church, nor by our own feeling, nor by a sportive and allegorizing fancy."[2] Ernesti's classic work,

---

[1] Farrar, *History of Interpretation*, p. 342.
[2] Terry, *Biblical Hermeneutics*, p. 707.

Principles of New Testament Interpretation, published in 1761, was used as standard text by four generations of students of hermeneutics.

This period of history also saw the rise of a reaction movement in the church. Weary of seeing the Bible read from the unnatural glare of theological hatred and creedal controversies, the Pietists advocated the study of the Scriptures primarily for edification. During Scriptural interpretation, the emphasis was placed on the mystical, the psychological, and the personal feelings of the interpreter. Prominent men, such as Spener and Francke, were leaders of this movement.

C. Nineteenth Century

During this century, historical criticism came of age. Unfortunately, however, it appeared under the framework of naturalistic presuppositions. Adopting the attitudes of rationalistic investigators, critical interpreters handled the Bible as a human product without divine intervention in its production. The "Thus said the Lord" of the Old Testament prophet was explained as merely "a liturgical phrase or a psychological devise to impress upon the hearer the solemnity of what was being said."[1]   Julius Wellhausen, for instance, rationalistically hypothesized the Pentateuch into fragments written by writers J, E, D, and P.

The nineteenth century, nevertheless, saw the ascendency of brilliant conservative and non-rationalistic scholarship. Men such as Olshausen, Keil, Meyer, and Lange represented evangelical scholarship at its best. E. W. Hengstenberg, a professor at Berlin, was one of the staunchest defenders of orthodoxy at this time. A number of good exegetical commentaries were written by conservatives such as Carl F. Keil

---

[1] Mickelsen, *Interpreting the Bible*, p. 45.

and Franz Delitzsch, J. P. Lange, F. Godet, B. F. Westcott, Charles J. Ellicott, and J. B. Lightfoot.

D. Twentieth Century

The twentieth century may be defined in the history of interpretation as an age both of growth and of change. Before the Second World War, liberal theology in America was more imitative than creative. It reproduced almost faithfully the thinking of continental theologians. After the War, some pioneering strides were taken by American liberal theologians, as the dogmas and affirmations of nineteenth century European thinkers were re-examined and criticized even by continental theologians themselves.

Among evangelicals, however, inspiration was not found in nor solicited from the German theologians. The orientation was more on what the Bible teaches than on what great theologians had to say. Theological speculations were left mostly untouched. "It is noticeable that the best modern American exegesis, while not less thorough and painstaking than that of Europe, is more conservative and evangelical. There is less tendency to speculate and build up theories and hypotheses." [1]

Many of the evangelical writings of the twentieth century are based on such conservative scholars of the bygone century as Lightfoot, Westcott, and Alford. Evangelical works, such as *The Wycliffe Bible Commentary*, enjoy the happy balance of recognized scholarship and sound orthodoxy.

Finally, it should be noted that, although the battle for the interpretation of Scripture has largely been won in evangelical circles for the literal method, a hard and bitter conflict still looms over the interpretive method for the prophetic Scrip-

---

[1] Terry, *Biblical Hermeneutics*, p. 57.

tures. "There is no disagreement over the fundamental rules of interpretation—even though they spell literal interpretation," observes Charles C. Ryrie, "the disagreement is in the interpretation of prophecy."[1]

Modern day evangelicals generally subscribe to one of four prophetic systems: (1) dispensational premillennialism, (2) covenant premillennialism, (3) postmillennialism, and (4) amillennialism. These eschatological systems are the result of varying hermeneutical approaches and procedures. In general, dispensational premillennialists are the most consistent in the literal interpretation of prophecy; covenant premillennialists less so; postmillennialists much less so; and amillennialists the least so.[2]

---

[1] Charles Caldwell Ryrie, The Basis of the Premillennial Faith (New York, N.Y.: Loizeaux Bros., 1953), p. 47.

[2] Whenever reference is therefore made in this book to *literal prophetic interpreters*, we mean interpreters who adhere to the dispensational premillennial position. Adherents of other eschatological positions, being necessarily less consistent in their literal approach to prophecy, are generally referred to in this book—for reasons of facility—as *non-literal prophetic interpreters*.

III.
WHY INTERPRET PROPHECY LITERALLY?

When Alice in *Alice's Adventures in Wonderland* ran down the rabbit-hole, she stumbled into a world of fantasy, make-believe, and enigma—a world of talking caterpillars, rabbits, cabbages, and things. When the Bible interpreter steps into the prophetic portions of the Scripture, has he entered a world of make-believe, conundrums, and enigmas? Must he therefore interpret non-literally?

This chapter will show why prophecy, being part and parcel of the Word of God, should be interpreted like other portions of the Word. A four-fold reason exists for the literal interpretation of prophecy: (1) Scriptural authority, (2) Historical fulfillments, (3) Early church precedent, and (4) Logical necessity.

I. SCRIPTURAL AUTHORITY

A. Prophecy—Intended to be Understood

A lawyer once asked Christ, "What shall I do to inherit eternal life?" In reply our Lord asked two questions: "What is written in the law? How readest thou?" (Luke 10:25-26). From Christ's response, we may infer that for answers to eternal issues, the written Word read at face value is adequate.

On another occasion, our Lord mentioned "Daniel the prophet" (Matt. 24:15) and then inserted a parenthetical

59

statement—"Whosoever readeth, let him understand" (v. 15). This dramatic parenthesis points out the fact that God wants prophecy to be understood. "If God did not wish us to understand the Revelation," comments D. L. Moody, "He would not have given it to us at all." [1]

Christ reassured His disciples, when speaking about the future, that "if it were not so, I would have told you" (John 14:2). The apostle Peter called prophecy the "sure word of prophecy" (II Pet. 1:19).

A person is said to "understand" another when both of them fix the same meaning to that which is being spoken or written. This is the basic rule of human communication. For the speaker to say one thing and mean another is to immediately cut off communication and comprehension. If God really wants man to understand prophetic revelation, He must have had it written in words that are subordinated to this elementary rule of communication. As Charles Lee Feinberg observes: "God intended His revelation in prophecy to be understood as much as other parts of the Word. In that case He must have embodied His ideas in exact and specific terms which would accurately convey the meaning He originally intended when interpreted according to the laws of grammar." [2]

Non-literal interpreters affirm that the written words of the Scripture cannot convey all that is in God, for finite words cannot fully convey Infinite Mind. As Thomas Aquinas reasons, "God being the Author, we may expect to find in Scripture a wealth of meaning." [3]

---

[1] Cited by George N. H. Peters. *The Theocratic Kingdom* (3 vols.; Grand Rapids, Mich.: Kregel Pubs., 1952), I, 174.

[2] Charles Lee Feinberg, *Premillennialism or Amillennialism?* (Wheaton, Ill.: Van Kampen Press, 1954), p. 27.

[3] Cited by Anton Berkeley Mickelsen, *Interpreting the Bible* (Grand Rapids, Mich.: Wm. B. Eerdmans Pub. Co., 1963), p. 37.

Finite man, however, is never expected to fathom *all* that is in an infinite God. The consecrated interpreter is never commanded to plumb the unrevealed, hidden depths of God. He is simply required to comprehend and understand that which God has chosen to reveal. As Moses puts it so clearly, "The secret things belong unto the Lord our God, but those things which are revealed belong unto us and our children forever" (Deut. 29:29).

B. Language—Originated by God

Another reason why we should interpret prophecy literally is that human language originated from God. When God created Adam, He gave Adam the gift of intelligible speech and communication. Adam was immediately able to converse with God and even to name the created animals by identifying their essential characteristics (Gen. 1:28; 2:19). Later, the diversity of languages at the Tower of Babel also came about as a direct act of God (cf. Gen. 11:9).

God not only originated human language but went on to choose it as the medium of revelational communication. Scriptural revelation is not given in the form of an unknown, supra-human language or some unintelligible hieroglyphics. God used regular human language to write Scriptural revelation. The fact that God originated and then chose earthly language for divine revelation means that He considered earthly language an adequate revelational medium. "If God be the originator of language and if the chief purpose of originating it was to convey His message to man, then it must follow that He . . . originated sufficient language to convey all that was in His heart to tell man."[1]

---

[1] Charles Caldwell Ryrie, *Dispensationalism Today* (Chicago, Ill.: Moody Press, 1965), p. 88.

Thus, despite the admitted depths and infinite riches of truth in God, regular human language, written according to regular rules of communication, stands sufficient to convey all that God wants man to know.

The apostle Paul, facing an impending shipwreck, remembers God's promise to him that all lives will be spared and confidently assures his shipmates: "Wherefore, sirs, be of good cheer; for I believe God, that it shall be even as it was told me" (Acts 27:25). This is literal interpretation of God's Word.

II.   HISTORICAL FULFILLMENTS

A. The Case Presented

Before the invention of the rocket ship, scores of theories were postulated regarding the composition of the moon. Children believed it to be made of green cheese and adults theorized that anyone stepping on the moon would sink out of sight. It is now possible to test the validity of these theories.

In prophecy, however, one has no scientific way of checking on how prophecy will be realized. One cannot be rocketed from history into eschatology—and return with the news. There is nevertheless a practical way to determine whether future events will transpire as predicted. It is to look at *past* fulfillments of prophecy. The manner of past prophetic fulfillment indicates the manner of future prophetic fulfillment. "The only way to know how God will fulfill prophecy in the future," observes Charles Feinberg," is to ascertain how He has done it in the past."[1]   J. Dwight Pentecost adds: "From God's viewpoint, prophecy is a unit, indivisible on the time basis. Since it is a unit, . . . that method used in those

---

[1]Feinberg, *Premillennialism or Amillennialism?*, p. 18.

prophecies that are now fulfilled will also be the method used to fulfill those prophecies that await future fulfillment."[1]

How did God fulfill prophecy in the past? Sir Robert Anderson of Scotland Yard, making a scientific study of prophetic fulfillments in Scripture, reports: "There is not a single prophecy, of which the fulfillment is recorded in Scripture, that was not realized with absolute accuracy, and in every detail; and it is wholly unjustifiable to assume that a new system of fulfillment was inaugurated after the sacred canon closed."[2]

Thus, every prophecy that has been fulfilled has been fulfilled literally. On the basis of New Testament attestations and the record of history, the fulfillment of Bible prophecy has always been literal.

B. Messianic Prophecies

At the first advent of Christ, over 300 prophecies were completely fulfilled. We list a few of these.

1. "Behold, a virgin shall conceive and bear a son" (Isa. 7:14). The fulfillment of this prophecy is impossible without supernatural intervention. Christ fulfilled this prophecy in His supernatural, virgin birth.

2. "They weighed for my price thirty pieces of silver . . . and I took . . . and cast them to the potter in the house of the Lord" (Zech. 11:12-13). Jesus surely had no control over the fulfillment of this prophecy, and had even forewarned the betrayer Judas about the consequences of his act.

---

[1] J. Dwight Pentecost, *Things to Come*, with an Introduction by John F. Walvoord (Findlay, Ohio: Dunham Pub. Co., 1958), pp. 60-61.

[2] Robert Anderson, *The Coming Prince* (14th ed.; Grand Rapids, Mich.: Kregel Pubs., 1954), p. 147.

3. The crucifixion scene portrayed in Psalm 22:16-18. Crucifixion was unknown among the Jews whose method of capital punishment was by stoning. Rome popularized crucifixion around 200 B.C.

4. Peter's denial of the Lord three times—predicted by Christ Himself (Matt. 26:34). Peter actually thought of hindering its fulfillment!

C. Prophecies Concerning Ancient Lands

In addition to the Messianic prophecies, there are predictions in the Old Testament which describe judgments to be meted out to Israel's ancient neighbors—and these have all been literally fulfilled. For instance:

1. *Regarding Samaria.* Micah 1:6 predicts utter ruin to Samaria—even down to its foundations. During the time of Christ, Samaria was still a prominent city and was visited several times by Christ. But now, the old city stands no more. "Vegetation grows on the hillsides of Old Samaria. The stones of the palaces have been thrown down and many of them have found their way to the valley below."[1]

2. *Regarding Gaza and Ashkelon.* Predicted to ruin by the prophets Jeremiah (Jer. 47:5), Amos (Amos 1:8), and Zephaniah (Zeph. 2:4,6), these ancient cities are now covered under sand dunes and dotted with sheepfolds respectively— just as the prophets had foretold.[2]

3. *Regarding Babylon.* One of the heavily populated and greatest of ancient cities, but predicted to judgment by Isaiah

---

[1] Martin Jacob Wyngaarden, *The Future of the Kingdom in Prophecy and Fulfillment* (Grand Rapids, Mich.: Baker Book House, 1955), p. 20.

[2] In Bible lands today are cities and places with the same names as the cities predicted to judgment in the Old Testament. The former however are in the vicinities of these ancient sites.

(Isa. 13:19-21) and Jeremiah (Jer. 51:26, 43), Babylon is now one vast expanse of arid desert, a howling wilderness. Even traveling Arabs are superstitious about pitching tents there at night.

4. *Regarding Tyre.* The prophecy against the city of Tyre well illustrates literal fulfillment. Statistician Peter Stoner, using the principle of probability, assigns this prophecy a one-in-seventy five million chance of fulfillment. [1]

In Ezekiel 26:3-16, the prophet Ezekiel delineates seven steps relative to the destruction of Tyre, as follows:

(1) Nebuchadnezzar shall take the city of Tyre.

(2) Other nations shall participate in fulfilling the prophecy.

(3) The city is to be made flat like the top of a rock.

(4) It is to become a place for the spreading of nets (fishing).

(5) Its stones and timbers are to be laid in the sea.

(6) Other cities will fear greatly at the fall of Tyre.

(7) The old city of Tyre shall never be rebuilt.

This prophecy against Tyre was partly fulfilled in 586 B.C. when King Nebuchadnezzar took the mainland city of Tyre after a siege of thirteen years but was unable to take its nearby island to which most of the people had fled. In 322 B.C., Alexander the Great, by scraping up the stones and timber of the mainland city as building material, built a great causeway to the heavily-defended island, and so completed the conquest of Tyre.

Today, the site of ancient Tyre, has fresh water supply enough for a large modern city, but it has not been occupied for 2,300 years. However it is very popular with fishermen!

---

[1] Peter W. Stoner, *Science Speaks* (Chicago, Ill.: Moody Press, 1968), pp. 72-79.

D. Restoration of the Nation Israel

In 1948, before the astonished eyes of the world, the seemingly impossible occurred. Israel became a new state. Scattered throughout the earth as state-less wanderers for countless generations, the Jews now have their own land to be born in, to defend, and to enjoy.

Because of the obvious nature of this fulfillment, non-literal interpreters are divided on what to make out of the restored nation Israel. Some interpreters concede the fulfillment, saying: "If Israel's return to Palestine is compared with prophecy, we may say that this present-day return would seem to be a literal fulfillment of prophecy, if the prophecy may be thus literally interpreted."[1]

Other interpreters, such as John Wilmot, refuse to concede by explaining the phenomenon as a modern-day name change: "Today a resettled people has assumed the title ["Israel"] and applies it also to their country or state, but obviously the Israel first mentioned in this text is a specialized Israel . . . . The only entitlement to the name 'Israel' is from spiritual relationship to Jesus Christ."[2]

The restoration of Israel in modern times, however, is a foregone fact and cannot be gainsaid. The majestic doxology which the apostle Paul composes to climax his chapter on the restoration of Israel may conclude our discussion:

> Oh, the depth of the riches both of the wisdom and knowledge of God! How unsearchable are his judgments, and his ways past finding out! For who hath

---

[1] Martin Jacob Wyngaarden, *The Future of the Kingdom in Prophecy and Fulfillment* (Grand Rapids, Mich.: Baker Book House, 1955), p. 189.

[2] John Wilmot, *Inspired Principles of Prophetic Interpretation* (Swengel, Pa.: Reiner Pubs., 1967), p. 94.

known the mind of the Lord? Or who hath been his counselor? . . . For of him, and through him, and to him, are all things: to whom be glory forever. Amen. [Romans 11:33-36]

III. EARLY CHURCH PRECEDENT

There are at least two main early church beliefs which attest to the fact that early Christians interpreted prophecy literally. These two beliefs are on the earthly reign of Christ and the imminent return of Christ.

A. The Earthly Reign of Christ

That the early church believed in the millennial reign of Christ on earth is accepted by church historians. Phillip Schaff writes: "The most striking point in the eschatology of the ante-Nicene age is the prominent chiliasm, or millennarianism, that is the belief of a visible reign of Christ in glory on earth with the risen saints for a thousand years, before the general resurrection and judgment."[1]

And the liberal theologian Shirley Jackson Case testifies that "Christian hopes for the next two generations [after Christ] revolve about this primitive notion of the heavenly Christ soon to return to inaugurate a new regime upon a miraculously renovated earth . . . It was also a fundamental item in the early preaching to the Gentiles."[2]   Even George L. Murray, who set out to disprove the historical lineage of premillennialism, states: "Students of church history will

---

[1] Phillip Schaff, *History of the Christian Church* (7 vols.; New York, N.Y.: Charles Scribner and Co., 1884), II, 614.

[2] Shirley Jackson Case, *The Millennial Hope* (Chicago, Ill.: The University of Chicago Press, 1918), p. 117.

agree that if any premillennialism existed in the early church it was during the first four centuries of its history."[1]

The very fact that we have no record of controversy in the early church over the doctrine of the millennium, plus the phenomenon that this doctrine disappeared after the emergence of Alexandrian allegorism, are evidences that the reign of Christ on earth in the millennium was the prevailing belief of the early church. This doctrine is the natural outgrowth of the literal interpretation of prophecy.

Amillennial theologians, therefore, cannot rightly claim that theirs is the historic faith of the church, for amillennialism is simply not the belief of the first two centuries of the Christian church. Only towards the close of the second century and at the beginning of the third, do we find men who oppose the prevailing millennial position. The doctrinal vagaries of these early redactors as well as their allegorism, however, have shocked even present-day amillennialists.

In relationship to historical lineage, therefore, modern amillennialists have given the early church fathers a wide berth. As John F. Walvoord observes, "Usually like [Oswald] Allis, amillennarians abandon the early centuries as a lost cause and begin with Augustine."[2]

There are amillennial interpreters who attempt to downgrade premillennialists by pointing to some early fathers who were allegedly not premillennial. Aside from the fact that not much data on this exists, the most that amillennialists can prove is that some church fathers were careless or inconsistent in their premillennial eschatology.[3]

---

[1]George L. Murray, *Millennial Studies* (Grand Rapids, Mich.: Baker Book House, 1948), p. 192.

[2]John F. Walvoord, *The Millennial Kingdom* (Findlay, Ohio: Dunham Pub. Co., 1959), p. 123.

[3]D.H. Kromminga in *The Millennium* (Grand Rapids, Mich.: Wm.B. Eerdmans Pub. Co., 1948), pp. 36-38 cites the

Other critics of premillennialism are likely to point out that only a few fathers fully detailed the doctrine of the millennium. [1] Although the fathers may not have been clear-cut in their eschatology, whenever they mentioned the *kingdom* in their writings, it is always an earthly, apocalyptic one. Moreover, although the early church's premillennialism may vary in some details with that held by present-day premillennialists, its basic scheme has remained intact down the centuries.

It is therefore wiser for amillennial and postmillennial interpreters to conclude, as Boettner does, that the early fathers were simply mistaken in their beliefs: "It has also been a standard doctrine of Premillennialism in every age that the coming of Christ is 'near" or 'imminent,' although every generation of Premillennialists *from the first century until the present time has been mistaken on that point* [Italics added]." [2]

B. The Imminent Return of Christ

The early church believed that the coming of the Lord was imminent. The doctrine of imminency means that Christ may come at any moment and that no prophesied event stands between the Christian and that hour. A common greeting in the early church was "Maranatha!" or "The Lord is

---

church father Barnabas who interpreted Exodus 33:3, Ezekiel 47:12, and Zephaniah 3:19 figuratively. But the most this can mean is that Barnabas was inconsistent in the literal method.

[1] As George Eldon Ladd observes, "only a few Fathers expressly affirm the doctrine" *(Crucial Questions About the Kingdom of God* [Grand Rapids, Mich.: Wm. B. Eerdmans Pub. Co., 1952], p. 155n).

[2] Loraine Boettner, *The Millennium* (Phila., Pa.: The Presbyterian and Reformed Pub. Co., 1964), p. 16.

coming!" (I Cor 16:22). Even the non-literal interpreter Murray admits that "the early church definitely believed in the second coming of Jesus Christ, and seemed to cherish the conviction that His coming was imminent."[1]

Some detractors of pretribulationism observe that the early Christians could not possibly have expected the Lord to come at any moment for the Bible does not really depict the coming of the Lord as immiment. The key passage usually cited is John 21:18-19 where Jesus tells Peter, "When thou shalt be old, thou shalt stretch forth thy hands, and another shall gird thee, and carry thee where thou wouldest not" (signifying his death). The argument of critics is that as long as Peter was still alive, the early believers would surely not have expected the Lord's imminent return.

In reply, it must be pointed out that this text in the Gospel of John was written some 20 years *after* Peter's death. There was no grounds therefore for the early believers' use of this text to deny the Lord's imminent return. The early Christians actually expected their Lord to come *during* the life-time of John (cf. John 21:20-23). This is the whole emphasis of John 21.

Moreover, in Acts 12:15-16, the early believers (including Peter himself) expected that he would die that very night under the hands of Herod who had just killed James and had already seized Peter (Acts 12:1-3). Peter could have died suddenly without most people knowing it. The early church, therefore, was not waiting for the death of Peter but for the imminent coming of her Lord.

Since the early Christians expected Christ to return at any moment, it can be inferred that they did not expect any event (such as the Great Tribulation) to come in between. Since the

---

[1]Murray, *Millennial Studies*, p. 192.

early church accepted the return of Christ as imminent, she certainly was not expecting to go through a period of "great tribulation, such as was not since the beginning of the world to this time, no, nor ever shall be" (Matt. 24:21). The early church's doctrine of the coming of Christ must therefore have been pre-tribulational. "If imminent, then pretribulational."

A most interesting illustration of pretribulationism from early church writings is *The Shepherd of Hermas* (Book I, Vision Fourth, Chapter ii). This early church narrative describes the vision of the shepherd of Hermas who meets a wild beast but is not harmed by the beast. The shepherd reports his harrowing encounter with the wild animal to the heavenly interpreter, "I was met by a beast of such a size that it could destroy peoples, but through the power of the Lord and His great mercy I escaped from it." The heavenly interpreter explains to the shepherd that his escape from the beast means that the elect of God will escape the Great Tribulation, saying, "You have escaped from great tribulation on account of your faith, and because you did not doubt in the presence of such a beast. Go, therefore, and tell the elect of the Lord His mighty deeds, and say to them that the beast is a type of the great tribulation that is coming."[1]

Another illustration of pretribulationism may be found in Irenaeus' book *Against Heresies* (Book V, Chapter xix). After describing the sinfulness of the present age, the church father Irenaeus comments: "And therefore, when in the end the Church shall be suddenly caught up from this [evil age], it

---

[1] Alexander Roberts and James Donaldson (eds.), *The Ante-Nicene Fathers* (9 vols.; American reprint of the Edinburgh edition; Grand Rapids, Mich.: Wm. B. Eerdmans Pub. Co., 1951), II, 18.

is said, "There shall be tribulation such as has not been since the beginning; neither shall be.' "[1]

Thus, it may be seen that the Lord's coming before the Great Tribulation is a concept not unknown in the early Christian church.

It must be noted, however, that the early fathers did not refine and think through the doctrine of pretribulationism as a precise eschatological system. The church was then fighting for her very existence, and other more basic doctrines were clamoring for her attention and systematization. The question of whether the Lord's coming is to be before or after the Great Tribulation was not a main one at that time. In their common distresses, the early fathers did not have much concern for a yet-future Tribulation period.

Although the expectation of the early Christians is certainly pretribulational in its implication, it seems wiser to classify the early fathers as Premillennial rather than specifically Pre- or Post- Tribulational. The doctrine of the pre tribulational rapture—like many Bible doctrines—comes from the thorough exegesis of Scripture, not by polling the fathers.

In summary, we note that the early church was premillennial in her doctrine because she interpreted prophecy literally. Moreover, the early church expected the imminent return of the Lord, and this is the product of literal interpretation of prophecy.

IV. PRACTICAL NECESSITY

When the Alexandrian church fathers left the sure footing of the literal interpretation of Scripture in favor of the

---

[1] *Ibid.*, I, 558. Irenaues' later statements, however, negated the sequence of future events herein set forth. Like many church fathers, Irenaeus may have had a vague idea of the sequence of definite events, yet the method with which he approached prophecy was literal.

allegorical method, a runaway situation resulted. Taking flight from the literal Word, every father became virtually an authority to himself, and the sky was the limit. No concrete test of an acceptable interpretation was available. And exegeses differed from church father to church father, and even from time to time under a man.

A similar situation now exists in the arena of prophetic interpretation. Among non-literal prophetic interpreters, a state of virtual interpretive chaos exists. It is rare, for instance, to see a well-ordered and definitive work by an amillennial interpreter setting forth positively and consistently his prophetic interpretations. On the contrary, amillennial writings usually concentrate on attacking and ridiculing the premillennial position. This approach is probably one of necessity, for amillennialists seldom agree with each other in specific interpretations of prophecy except to be against the earthly millennium.

When Loraine Boettner, a postmillennialist, was attacking the *Scofield Reference Bible,* he made this observation: "Imagine the confusion that would result if other schools of thought put out Bibles with notes setting forth postmillennial, amillennial, historic premillennial [systems] . . ."[1] If this task were really attempted, however, the world would probably not be able to contain all the divergent opinions being set forth under the non-literal systems.

Whether it is the interpretation of prophecy or non-prophecy, once literality is sacrificed, it is like starting down an incline. Momentum speedily gathers as one succumbs to the temptation to spiritualize one passage after another. The ease in spiritualizing all and every "difficulty" is irresistible, and a runaway situation soon results. All objectivity is lost as

---

[1] Boettner, *The Millennium*, p. 370.

one method of interpretation appears, disappears, and reappears under the whims of the interpreter.

Moreover, under the method of spiritualization, there is no way for an interpreter to test the validity of his conclusions, except to compare his works with that of a colleague. Instead of "a more sure word of prophecy" (II Pet. 1:19), interpreters end up with an "unsure" Word and chaos in the ranks. Practical consideration demands that the literal method of interpretation be used for all of Scripture.

W.A. Criswell who has gone through the Scriptures verse by verse with the congregation of the huge First Baptist Church of Dallas (Texas) gives a very practical and logical reason for his dependence on the literal method: "If we preach the Bible literally, it is like telling the truth. You do not have to remember what you said. But if you spiritualize, . . . what you said about a passage yesterday may be diametrically opposed to what you make it mean today . . . . A man will find himself contradicting himself over and over again as he preaches through the years."[1]   And the congregation, we add, would be delivered bound hand and foot to the weekly caprice of the interpreter.

---

[1] W.A. Criswell, *Why I Preach that the Bible is Literally True* (Nashville, Tenn.: Broadman Press, 1969), p. 145.

IV

NATURE OF PROPHECY

The prophets and the nature of their prophecies are two areas crucial to any discussion of prophetic interpretation. A sound understanding in these areas will establish the interpretation of prophecy on solid foundation.

I. Introducing the Bible Prophets

The commonest designation of the Hebrew prophet in the Old Testament is the word נביא . Scholars differ as to the root meaning of this word. But, in general, it has two basic meanings: (1) An inspired person (passive), and (2) An interpreter of God's will to man (active). This two-fold meaning reflects the true function of a prophet. A Bible prophet is a man to whom the will of God has been revealed under inspiration in order that it might in turn be communicated to the people. Isaiah tells his contemporaries: "That which I have heard of the Lord of hosts . . . have I declared unto you" (Isa. 21:10).

Aside from the usual designation of נביא the prophet is also known as ראה ("he who sees with the natural eyes") and חוזה ("he who sees with the mental or spiritual eyes"). The prophet sees both contemporary issues and future events. His message is delivered through regular preaching and forth-telling as well as through supernatural

75

prognosticating and foretelling. The prophetic message may concern the present in the form of warnings, rebukes, promises, and exhortations. It may concern the future through prognostications and predictions. The popular picture of a prophet as a recluse who main concern is for things future is obviously one-sided.

Because God's will and revelation were communicated through the prophet, the prophet was authorized to use the formula "Thus said the Lord." His message was said to be the "word" of the Lord. Frequently, to emphasize its importance and reliability, a prophet would precede or conclude his message with the phrase "I, the Lord, have spoken."

For this cause, the Hebrew prophet was admired and sought after as the transmitter of God's will and word. King Zedekiah once sent messengers to ask of Jeremiah, "Is there any word from the Lord?" (Jer. 37:17). In Ezekiel 33:30, we see groups of people going to the prophet and saying one to another, "Come and hear what is the word that cometh forth from the Lord."

On the other hand, because of his pronouncements, denunciations, and accurate foresights, the Bible prophet was hated, terribly persecuted, and sometimes attempts were made on his life. The prophet Jeremiah, because of his stand and predictions, was hated, hounded, and often imprisoned. In one instance, God had to explain to Ezekiel that he must speak out regardless of "whether they will hear, or whether they will forbear" (Ezek. 3:11).

It is true that the message of the prophet may be either forth-telling or foretelling. But when the prophet is said to prophesy, foretelling rather than forth-telling is meant. Prophecy must technically be thought of in terms of the prognosticative, not the didactic.

Prognostications are subdivided into Predictions and Apocalyptics. *Predictions* involve events which will happen in the near future. *Apocalyptics* involve events which relate to the end time. While this subdivision of prophecy is justified on some occasions for purposes of emphasis, it should not be used when interpretation is under progress. Predictions and apocalyptics must not be separated during interpretation. Principles that are used to interpret near-future predictions should be used to interpret far-future apocalyptic prophecies.

Some modern interpreters categorize Bible prophets as ancient writers of ambiguous oracles, conundrums, and riddles. What the prophets wrote and said are not to be taken at face value, for their statements allegedly contained dark and hidden meanings. Such an apprehension is both unfair and reprehensible.

Under ordinary conditions, a writer would say what he means and mean what he says. He seeks to express his meaning in the clearest and simplest method at his command. Anything less would cast a shadow on the writer's sincerity and even question his sanity. Must we suppose that the writer of Scripture, apart from the sacredness of his task, departed from this way of simplicity and truth?

It is true that Bible prophets have been accused of being "mad" (cf. II Kings 9:11: John 10:20; Acts 26:24). But these were unjust charges made by infidels and skeptics of the day. As James Snowden affirms, the prophets "never spoke, after the manner of pagan oracles, in riddles that were inexplicable puzzles to their hearers, but always spoke unto their business and bosoms."[1] Of course there are scattered instances of dark sayings and riddles in prophecy. But these are given so sparingly in the Scripture, and are usually immediately explained or pointed out in the context, that the Scripture as a whole must be considered non-enigmatical.

---

[1] James H. Snowden, *The Coming of the Lord* (New York, N.Y.: The Macmillan Co., 1919), p. 45.

It should be noted that the prophets of Israel were often statesmen and political leaders of their day. Moses, Samuel, and David are good examples. Others such as Elijah, Isaiah, Jeremiah, and Amos were social and religious reformers. This is because in ancient Israel, "political and religious questions were so closely identified that the prophet could hardly be a religious teacher without being also a political leader."[1] It is natural to suppose that these men whom God saw fit to choose as religious, social, and political leaders of the nation would also be sensible communicants of divine revelation in the Scripture.

II. TRUE AND FALSE PROPHETS

Alongside the true prophets of Israel were the false prophets. Both claimed to be speaking for God (cf. I Kings 13:18; 22:24; Jer. 28:2), although their prophecies often contradict.

Thus, the false prophet Hananiah told the people that the Babylonian captivity would last only two years (Jer. 28:1-4), whereas the prophet Jeremiah had predicted that it would last 70 years (Jer. 25:11-12). The four hundred false prophets led by Zedekiah predicted victory at the Battle of Ramoth-Gilead (I Kings 22:11-12) in contrast to the defeat predicted by the prophet Micaiah (I Kings 22:17). How is one able to discern whether a prophet is true or false?

In the Scripture, we see many methods by which the genuineness of a prophet may be tested. No single method by itself sufficiently determines a true prophet. But when the aggregate of these tests is applied, the profile of a true prophet emerges.

---

[1] Willis Judson Beecher, *The Prophets and the Promise* (New York, N.Y.: Thomas Y. Crowell & Co., 1905), p. 94.

The following are five tests of a true prophet as found in the Scripture: (1) Moral character of the prophet, (2) Spiritual nature of the prophecy, (3) Authentication by signs, (4) Discernment by the people, and (5) Fulfillment in history.

A. Moral Character of the Prophet

During Old Testament times, false prophets were characterized by their low morality and unethical conduct. This was repeatedly pointed out to the people by the true prophets of God. False prophets were featured as drunkards (Isa. 28:7), adulterous (Jer. 23:14), treacherous (Zeph. 3:4), liers (Micah 2:11), and opportunists (Micah 3:11).

In contrast, true prophets of Israel, as a rule (Hosea is *not* an exception), were morally uncompromising and above reproach. Christ refers to this test in the New Testament, saying, "Beware of false prophets . . . Every good tree bringeth forth good fruit, but a corrupt tree bringeth forth evil fruit . . . By their fruits ye shall known them" (Matt. 7:17-20).

B. Spiritual Nature of the Prophecy

The theme and content of a prophet's message is another give-away to the true character of a prophet. In this respect, two sub-tests are possible.

First, if the words of the prophet cause people to turn from the Lord, the prophet is false, for it is patently impossible for one to be sent from God who seeks to turn people away from God. This test is set forth in Deuteronomy 13:1-3, "If there arise among you a prophet . . . [who] spoke unto thee saying, Let us go after other gods, which thou has not known, and let us serve them; Thou shalt not hearken unto the words of that prophet."

Second, if the prophecy tends to cover up sin and downplay the importance of repentance, it comes from an imposter.

False prophets are religious opportunists who say only what the people like to hear. True prophets disregard the acceptability of their messages, being unconcerned for any consequences to their own persons. In the Scripture, it is the first mark of a true prophet that he announces judgment. Thus, the prophet Jeremiah uses this test against the false prophet Hananiah, saying, "The prophets that have been before me and before thee of old prophesied both against many countries, and . . . of war, and of evil, and of pestilence" (Jer. 28:8).

As Lindblom comments, "The task of a true prophet was to intercede for the people and to bring them to repentance and righteousness in order to save them from the wrath of Yahweh and secure their existence. This task was neglected by the false prophets."[1]

C. Authentication by Signs

True prophets in the Old Testament were given temporary sign-gifts in order to authenticate their ministries. Perhaps in the ministries of the prophets Elijah and Elisha are to be seen the greatest display of signs and wonders accompanying true prophets in the Old Testament.

However, the working of wonders is not to be regarded as the exclusive prerogative of God's prophets. Satan's emissaries could work signs and wonders. One obvious instance are the magicians of Pharoah who duplicated many of the signs of Moses and Aaron (Exod. 7:11-12, 22).

Incidentally, the sign-gifts accompanying true prophets do not imply divinations, ravings, and excitations which false prophets commonly indulged in to induce and solicit their

---

[1] J. Lindblom, *Prophecy in Ancient Israel* (Phila., Pa.: Fortress Press, 1962), p. 212.

"revelations." Genuine prophecies are never self-induced nor are they the product of the prophets' own minds. "When God chose to speak His word to Israel, it would come through His prophets unsolicited, apart from divination and augury; . . . This appears as one of the greatest distinctions between the religion of Israel and the heathen religions. The nations sought to discover truth by means of divination and sorcery, whereas Israel received it by revelation."[1]

There were false prophets in Bible times who did not go into divinations and excesses and claimed to be speaking for the Lord. But they usually did this by "stealing" words from true prophets (cf. Jer. 23:30).

D. Discernment by the People

It is possible to fool some people at some time, but not all the people all the time. It was generally not difficult in Old Testament times for the people of God to discern false prophets. King Jehoshaphat, before the Battle of Ramoth-Gilead, saw through the ruse spread by the 400 lying prophets and asked, "Is there not here a prophet of the Lord besides . . . ?" (I King 22:7).

But this kind of spiritual discernment was evident only when the Israelites were in right relationship with God. In times of moral darkness, the people generally failed to discover the true prophets and acclaimed false prophets as true. "In times of moral darkness the false prophets predicting smooth things for the nation, independent of repentance, consecration and the pursuit of spiritual ideals, were honored above the true

---

[1] Hobart E. Freeman, *An Introduction to the Old Testament Prophets* (Chicago, Ill.: Moody Press, 1968), p. 103.

prophets who emphasized the moral greatness of Jehovah and the necessity of righteousness for the nation."[1]

E. Fulfillment in History

The final test which distinguishes a real prophet from an imposter is the fulfillment of his prediction in history. The prophet Moses warns: "And if thou say in thine heart, How shall we know the word which the Lord hath not spoken? When a prophet speaketh . . . . if the thing follow not, nor come to pass, . . . the Lord hath not spoken . . . (Deut. 18:21-22).

The prophet Micaiah proved his own genuineness by saying to the kings of Israel and of Judah, "If thou return at all in peace, the Lord hath not spoken by me" (I Kings 22:28).

Although history would ultimately tell a true from a false prophet, the true prophet felt no need to wait for historical confirmation before declaring himself true. The true prophet acutely knew that the Lord had spoken to him and that he would ultimately be vindicated.

III.   THE PROPHETIC STATE

The prophetic state is the God-given state of absolute concentration during which revelation is communicated to the prophet by God. God spoke to man through the prophets "at sundry times and in diverse manners" (Heb. 1:1), the usual method being visions and dreams. Numbers 12:6 states: "If there be a prophet among you, I, the Lord will make myself known to him in a *vision*, and will speak unto him in a *dream* [Italics added]."

---

[1] C.E. Schenk, "Prophesyings, False," *International Standard Bible Encyclopedia* (5 vols.; Grand Rapids, Mich.: Wm. B. Eerdmans Pub. Co., 1939), IV, 2466.

There are various levels of the prophetic state which may be classified as (1) revelational dreams, (2) direct encounters, and (3) ecstatic visions. Based on the intensity of concentration as well as revelational content, the lowest gradation of the prophetic state appears to be revelational dreams, while the highest belongs to ecstatic visions.

A. Revelational Dreams

A method of divine communication between God and the prophets is dreams which contain or are intended as revelation. Some of the remarkable revelational dreams in the Bible are those of Abimelech in Gerar (Gen. 20:3-7), Jacob at Bethel (Gen. 28:12), Joseph on the sheaves and luminaries (Gen. 37:5-10), King Nebuchadnezzar and his mammoth image (Dan. 2), and the prophet Nathan on the Davidic kingdom (II Sam. 7:4-17). While natural dreams may be used by God to reveal, it is not true that all dreams contain revelation.

Some non-literal interpreters equate the form and content of natural dreams with the form and content of divine revelation. In natural dreams, past or known experiences are dreamed into some unreal or fantastic situations and plots. The dreaming mind acts on objects, concepts, and ideas in ways instinctive, intuitive, and habitual. This phenomenon of dreaming is cited by non-literalists to bolster their non-literal approach to prophetic revelation. "Like a dream", reasons Lindblom "a vision is composed of different elements taken from the world of normal experience, but often caricatured and combined in a strange and unreal unity."[1]

It is of course true that some of the revelational dreams in the Bible involve familiar objects and concepts. Pharoah's

---

[1] Lindblom, *Prophecy in Ancient Israel*, p. 125.

dream in Genesis 41 figures river, cows, and ears of corn. God apparently uses the backgrounds and experiences of His servants when choosing figurative and symbolical representations. But God certainly did not allow divine revelation to be molded or structured by the human backgrounds—if these would misrepresent or contradict what He wanted to reveal. In a real sense, therefore, the form and content of revelational dreams originate from God, not from human minds.

Moreover, there are many revelational dreams in the Scripture which utilize figures and symbols *un*familiar to the prophets. These "signs" of the future come to the prophets devoid of what is contemporary, instinctive, and familiar. In Daniel 7, the prophet sees four beasts which appear so unfamiliar and unearthly that he has to use analogies (e.g. "like a lion"). But the fourth beast is so unlike anything Daniel has ever seen that he does not bother to use an earthly analogy in reporting to his readers. Surely these representations could not have originated from the prophet Daniel's own "imaginative" mind.

B. Direct Encounters

A direct encounter is a revelational encounter between God and the prophet where there is nothing to suggest that the prophet is being deprived of his wakeful, outward consciousness, and where revelation is relatively instant. Revelation is here divinely projected into the prophet's inner senses, and the message is received while the recipient is not necessarily under the state of ecstasy.

Thus, the prophet Isaiah, as he walks across the king's court, receives a new revelation concerning King Hezekiah (cf. II Kings 20:4-6). On another occasion, the revelation comes even as the prophet talks with the king (cf. Isa. 39:1-8; II Kings 20:12-19).

C. Ecstatic Visions

Ecstasy, the highest gradation of the prophetic state, is the elevation of the prophet above the sphere of outward sense, providing the deepest concentration of soul and clearest perception of revelation.

In ecstasy, the outward, natural eyes of the prophet are usually shut (as in a trance) in order that the process of concentration might be enhanced. Jeremiah calls this "sleep" (Jer. 31:26). With the closing of the outward eyes, the opening of the inner sense commences. Thus, while appearing to be asleep, the prophet inwardly focuses his inner eyes and ears on the message being conveyed by God. Moses describes this condition as "falling into a trance but having his eyes open" (Num. 24:4).

In this state of intense, perceptive consciousness (which only God can bestow) the prophet sees things which do not lie in the domain of the natural and hears things which human ears do not ordinarily receive. The mind of the prophet becomes so concentrated on the revelation being transmitted that the *natural* current of thoughts and senses breaks off and temporarily ceases to function. The prophet is conscious of what is going on, but he is like a rider who, having lost the reins, knows what is going on but cannot alter it. The prophet is conscious of being laid hold of by the Spirit of God to receive a message which he knows is not the product of his own reflective or imaginative mind.

It is not necessary to suppose that the ecstatic visions of Bible prophets are accompanied by excitations, convulsions, and ravings, for much of the revelation of the Old and New Testaments is made without any excitations. Ecstatic visions are anchored on I Corinthians 14:32— "the spirits of the prophets are subject to the prophets."

IV. Vision and the Imaginative Mind

A. View of Non-Literalists

Many non-literal prophetic interpreters believe that the prophetic state is a state of great *mental* activity with the mind careening along a course directed either by innate tendencies or by the laws of habitual association. Prophecy, it is alleged, is the product of the prophet's mind under the guidance of instinct. Objects seen in the vision are not actually perceived, but only thought of as perceived.

As non-literalist Kaplan says, "I am convinced that the prophetic visions like other visions are a species of mental illusion, due sometimes to the high mental activity and profound interest of the prophet, sometimes, perhaps, to external stimulus, and again, to pathological conditions of mind, . . . but always, it must be emphasized, built up from the elements already existing in the prophet's consciousness."[1]

As for God's part in prophecy, non-literal interpreters assign it simply as "an influence exerted on the mind so as to stimulate it to think, rather than materials of thought suggested to it."[2] Jacob Kaplan goes on: "The intense psychological experience coming with a force never before experienced makes it certain that it is the hand of God in visitation, and the clearness and profundity of thought makes it equally certain that the result is a revelation from God."[3]

Since prophecy comes from the operation of the prophet's mind, the *form* of divine revelation would naturally be colored

---

[1] Jacob H. Kaplan, *Psychology of Prophecy* (Phila., Pa.: Julius H. Greenstone, 1908), p. 125.

[2] A.B. Davidson, *Old Testament Prophecy*, ed. by J.A. Paterson (Edinburgh: T. & T. Clark, 1903), p. 129.

[3] Kaplan, *Psychology of Prophecy*, pp. 112-13.

by the backgrounds, experiences, and idiosyncrasies of the prophet. "The prophet's own imaginative mind," states Davidson, "will often present the truth in a dress . . . which itself is altogether the work of the poet's fancy."[1]

Because of their theory, non-literalists open the floodgates of speculations on the *extent* to which the form of revelation might have been manipulated by the prophet. C. von Orelli wonders how far the prophet "regarded his plastic description as symbolic, or unconsciously supplied a more sensuous conception as a substratum to the abstract idea."[2]   And Davidson theorizes: "The elements of the prophetic vision were drawn partly from the mind of the seer, partly from the circumstances about him, and partly from revelation from God."[3]

Moreover, the theory of mental activity pulls prophecy down to the level of a mere human phenomenon. As a non-literalist is led to conclude, "It cannot be emphasized too often that prophecy is a human process, a mind process, and must be studied from a human point of view as a branch of psychology."[4]

B. View of Literalists

Literal prophetic interpreters believe that the concept of the prophetic state as a condition of great *mental* activity is overstated and consequently in error.

---

[1] Davidson, *Old Testament Prophecy*, p. 143.

[2] C. von Orelli, *Old Testament Prophecy*, (Edinburg: T. & T. Clark, 1885), p. 32.

[3] Davidson, *Old Testament Prophecy*, p. 137. And Davidson manages to escape the impossible task of pinpointing these various elements by hedging: "In general... we cannot separate them, or assign distinct elements to each. . . . Where we cannot trace this reflection, we may assume that it is present though undetected" (pp. 137-38).

[4] Kaplan, *The Psychology of Prophecy*, pp. 143-44.

First, it is true that the connection between the mind of the Holy Spirit and that of the prophet, being miraculous, is very unclear and may probably never be determined. Nevertheless, to emphasize the working of the human mind to the extent of slighting or setting aside the operation of the Divine Author of Scripture is certainly erroneous. It is significant that in matters of revelational transmission, the Scripture stresses the Spirit's supernatural work.

For instance, the seer John was "in the Spirit" (Rev. 4:2) when the visions in the Book of Revelation were given. Daniel was supernaturally touched by "an hand" (Dan. 10:10) before he received his final vision. Ezekiel reported that "the Spirit entered into me" (Ezek. 2:2). The Bible abundantly shows how "the hand of the Lord was upon the prophets" and how "the Spirit fell upon the prophets." The apostle Peter certainly puts it in right perspective when he writes: "For the prophecy came not in old time by the will of man, but holy men of God spoke as they were moved by the Holy Ghost" (II Pet. 1:21).

Prophecy is not a deduction of the human mind. The prophets wrote what they saw and heard as revealed to them by God.

Second, it is clear from the Scripture that the prophets, without prior reflection, wrote down what they saw and heard, accepting them at face value. The prophets never took upon themselves to become redactors of divine revelation. The seer John started to write even while in the prophetic state (cf. Rev. 10:4 "When the seven thunders had uttered their voices, I was about to write . . ."). Other prophets registered the revelation right after the vision, as in the case of Ezekiel (Ezek. 11:24-25 "So the vision that I had seen went up from me. Then I spoke unto them of the captivity . . .").

Although the mind of the prophet during the communication of revelation could not have influenced the content of revelation, this does not mean that the prophets were mechanically used by the Holy Spirit. In God's foreknowledge of coming events, the backgrounds, faculties, and personalities of each writer of Bible prophecy were fully considered and utilized by God. Thus, only an apostle Paul, with his unique training and background, could have written the Pauline epistles. God ordained everything in the lives of His instrumental writers in order that they might become the specific individuals uniquely equipped and molded to write given books of the Bible.[1]

Third, the prophets participated in their visions by asking questions and responding to that which was being revealed. Such actions are proof that the prophets perceived objects and concepts as something entirely *apart* from themselves.

For instance, the prophet Zechariah repeatedly asked his revealing angel, "What are these, my lord?" (Zech. 4:4). The seer John reacted emotionally to the visions being shown him (e.g. Rev. 5:4 "I wept much"). And many prophets tried to compare the things they saw in the visions with those found on earth (e.g. Dan. 7:4 "like a lion" and Rev. 21:11 "like a jasper stone").

V.   Vision and Figurative Imagery

Some interpreters affirm that prophecy being transmitted through visions and dreams must necessarily appear under figurative representations. This affirmation is based on the concept that things make more of an impression on the envisioned mind when seen as figurative imageries. "As in vision,

---

[1] For a more detailed discussion of the "form" of prophecy, see below, *Prophecy in Supposedly Colored Form,* pp. 217-227.

it is the imaginative faculty that is more immediately called into play, images were necessary to make on it the fitting impressions, and these impressions could only be conveyed to others by means of figurative representations."[1]

This concept of prophecy allows interpreters to spiritualize almost any prophecy. Thus, Revelation 20 is considered figurative precisely because it was transmitted under a vision. "John did not actually see an angel come with a great chain," reasons Hoeksema, "he saw all this as it was represented in a vision."[2]   And Roderick Campbell uses this presupposition to spiritualize the Millennial Temple and the New Jerusalem, saying, "The visions which Ezekiel and John describe were seen in apocalyptic visions. The descriptions are *therefore* [Italics added] to be considered as highly pictorial and symbolic."[3]

It is true that in the ordinary sphere, figures and imageries are excellent devices to make more lasting on the mind any impression and concept. But the prophetic state transcends that which is natural and belongs to the realm of the supranatural. In Scripture, perception, not imagination, is enjoined on the prophets during the projection of the visions. The prophets accurately wrote Scriptural revelation, not because of the workings of their impressionable minds, but because they were under divine inspiration.

Actually, God could have revealed things to man in a state of prayer as in a state of ecstasy. But God used the mode of

---

[1] Milton S. Terry, *Biblical Hermeneutics* (New York, N.Y.: Eaton and Mains, 1911), p. 320n.

[2] Herman Hoeksema, *Reformed Dogmatics* (Grand Rapids, Mich.: Reformed Free Pub. Ass'n, 1966), p. 819.

[3] Roderick Campbell, *Israel and the New Covenant* (Phila, Pa.: The Presbyterian and Reformed Pub. Co., 1954), p. 147.

ecstatic vision in order to ensure supernatural concentration and in-depth perception. God did not choose the mode of vision to make prophecy unclear and ambiguous through figurative representations. The prophetic state is intended to help register more clearly and make more impressive the sacred revelations being given.

As J. Dwight Pentecost observes, "the interpretation of the prophecies given through dreams or prophetic ecstasy will present no special problems of interpretation. Although the method of giving the prophecy may have been unique that which was given did not differ from a prophecy stated in clear language."[1]

To sum up, it is true that prophecy is usually conveyed to the prophets in visions. But it is not true that objects seen and concepts perceived in visions are necessarily all (or nearly all) figurative representations. Prophecy does contain figures and symbols, but these are not the necessary upshoots of ecstatic visions. Figurative representations are God-given signs and concepts which depict future events and details.

VI.   PERSPECTIVE OF PROPHECY

A. Description of Perspective

The perspective of prophecy (also known as "the law of time relationship") means that two or more future events, widely separated in time, may be seen by the prophet in a single profile or side by side.

From the hint given in I Peter 1:11, we suppose that after the prophets had written prophecy, they sat down and tried to figure the time perspectives of their writings. This is because

---

[1] Pentecost, *Things to Come*, p. 59.

during the transmission of prophecy, the prophets are stationed in space and not in time. Since they stand royally above all conceptions of time, their prophecies naturally lack the perspective of time.

The prophets see future events in their visions just as a common observer would observe the stars, grouping them as they appear to his eyes and not according to their true positions in space. This phenomenon is therefore also called the "foreshortening" of the prophet's horizon. And since this is comparable to a series of mountain ranges observed at a distance, where the peaks would appear to be close together or even as one, when in reality there are valleys in between, the perspective of prophecy is further known as the "mountain peak" view.

Standing above all conceptions of time, the prophets feel free to couch their prophecies in the future tense (cf. Isa. 2), in the present tense (cf. Isa. 9:6), and sometimes even in the past tense (cf. Isa. 53). Moreover, parts of one prophecy may have reverse time sequences. Thus, Isaiah 65:17-25 introduces first the new heaven and new earth (eternal state), and then paints a picture of millennial bliss—whereas the reverse sequence would have been chronologically correct.

B. Determining Prophetic Foreshortening

Although many prophecies do contain the element of foreshortening, not all Bible prophecies possess this characteristic. Foreshortening is usually found in prophecies that bear some relationship to one another or are related to one future program. Charles Feinberg says that foreshortening "is particularly true of the predictions of the so-called major prophets, where many times prophecies concerning the Babylonian captivity, the events of the day of the Lord, the return from Babylon, the world wide dispersion of Israel, and their future regathering from all the corners of the earth, are grouped together seemingly almost indiscriminately."[1]

Because there is no definite way of knowing whether a given prophecy contains foreshortening, some interpreters conclude that only history will tell whether a gap exists in a prophecy. As C. von Orelli says, "only when they [gaps] emerge in history is it seen that an interval lies between."[2] This viewpoint makes the interpretation of prophecy enigmatical, for an interpreter is never quite sure of his interpretation until later history should prove him right.

The true guide to the determination of time gaps or foreshortening in a prophecy is to be found in the complete canon of Scripture, not in the unfolding of history. The complete revelation of the prophetic Scripture will show the element of foreshortening in a given prophecy.

It is true that because of the perspective of the prophets, there is an "unfolding" or "widening" import in some of their prophecies. Genesis 3:15 unfolds into the first advent of the Messiah who "bruised the serpent's head." Prophecies with such widening imports are usually referred to as *generic prophecies*. A generic prophecy is one which "regards an event as occurring in a series of parts, separated by intervals, and expresses itself in language that may apply indifferently to the nearest part, or to the remoter part, or to the whole—in other words, a prediction which, in applying to the whole of a complex event, also applies to some of its parts."[3]

Although generic prophecies exist in Scripture, the very possibility and even the process of the unfolding of a prophecy

---

[1] Feinberg, *Premillennialism or Amillennailism?*, pp. 17-18.

[2] C. von Orelli, *Old Testament Prophecy*, p. 33.

[3] Willis Judson Beecher, *The Prophets and the Promise* (New York, N.Y.: Thomas Y. Crowell Co., 1905), p. 130.

must be determined by the complete canon of Scripture. The interpreter must not automatically assume that a given prophecy is repeatedly and successively fulfilled (especially in the church). Generic prophecies are legitimate, but their unfoldings must be studiously determined.

C. Illustrations of Foreshortening

1. *First illustration.*—The following two texts of Scripture place the resurrections of saints and of sinners side by side:

> And many of those who sleep in the dust of the earth shall awake, some of everlasting life, and some to shame and everlasting contempt. [Daniel 12:2]

> Marvel not at this; for the hour is coming, in which all that are in the graves . . . shall come forth: they that have done good, unto the resurrection of life; and they that have done evil, unto the resurrection of damnation. [John 5:28-29]

Without the help of other portions of Scripture, the interpreter may well conclude that there will be but *one* general resurrection at the same time for all: the righteous to heaven and the unrighteous to hell.

However, when the parallel passage in Revelation 20 is consulted, it becomes apparent that when Christ comes, the righteous will be resurrected and shall reign with Christ a thousand years (v.4), whereas "the rest of the dead live not again until the thousand years were finished" (v. 5), and that this is the *first* resurrection. Thus, the two resurrections, placed side by side in the Gospel of John and in the Book of Daniel, have a time gap of at least a thousand years.

Moreover, although the resurrection of the righteous is called "first" in Revelation 20:4, it is not one event but embraces a series of resurrection events. "Every man in his own order: Christ the first fruits; afterward they that are Christ's at his coming" (I Cor. 15:23). Under the single profile of the *first* resurrection, therefore, is to be comprehended the resurrection of Christ, the rapture-resurrection of church saints, and the resurrection of tribulation saints (such as the two witnesses of Revelation 11). It also comprehends the resurrection of Old Testament saints at the end of the tribulation.

2. *Second illustration.*—On the basis of the analogy of prophecy, there is to be seen a time gap between the coming of Christ for the church saints and His coming to set up the millennial kingdom. The prophetic Scriptures make it clear that there will be mortals and even sinners (cf. Rev. 20:8) who will be subjects of Christ's reign on the earth. Since all saints will be in glorified bodies and sinners will be consumed in judgment at Christ's second coming (Matt. 13:30, 40-42; II Thess. 2:8-12; Rev. 19:15; etc), who then are going to be in mortal bodies and propagate children during the millennium?

An intervening period is necessary—after the rapture of the church but before the return of Christ to establish the kingdom—for a group of mortals to be born and / or born-again, who will enter the millennium in their mortal bodies. This period is the Tribulation. Because of the foreshortening of their horizons, the prophets did not clearly perceive these two phases of Christ's second coming. The complete revelation of Scripture, not the fulfillment of events in history, have supplemented this lack of time perspective in the prophets.

V

PRINCIPLES OF PROPHETIC INTERPRETATION

To interpret Bible prophecy properly, one must know something about the basic nature of prophecy, the principles of prophetic interpretation, and the language of prophecy, including types and symbols. We have already considered the nature of prophecy and the prophetic consciousness. The language of prophecy shall be considered in the chapter following. Now we come to one of the most important sections of this book—the principles of prophetic interpretation.

There are certain principles by which all conservatives interpret general Scripture. These are called the regular principles of hermeneutics. The question is, may these regular hermeneutical principles be used to interpret prophecy?

We affirm that the prophetic Scripture, being part of God's written revelation and intended for comprehension, must be interpreted according to rules governing regular literature. Milton Terry observes correctly: "While duly appreciating the peculiarities of prophecy, we nevertheless must employ in its interpretation essentially the same great principles as in the interpretation of other ancient writings."[1]

---

[1] Milton S. Terry, *Biblical Hermeneutics* (New York, N.Y.: Eaton and Mains, 1911), pp. 396-97.

The following are the regular principles of hermeneutics:

1. Follow customary usage of language.
2. Commit no historical-cultural blunder.
3. Make Christ central in all interpretations.
4. Be conscious of context.
5. Interpret by the analogy of faith.
6. Recognize the progress of revelation.
7. Grant one interpretation to each passage.
8. Choose the simplest alternative.

I. FOLLOW CUSTOMARY USAGE OF LANGUAGE

God chose the medium of language with its normal and grammatical usages of words and concept to write Scripture. The interpreter therefore should seek to master the language of the Bible in its customary, grammatical form.

A. Study of Lexicography

The interpreter should first be adept at lexicographical study or the study of individual words. He should be able to trace the etymology of single words and grapple with any rare words. For example, Isaiah 21 contains words such as Elam, Media, Babylon, Dumah, Seir, Arabia, Dedanim, and Kedar—all of which would need some clarifications. The synonymns of words with their shades of meaning must also be examined. Moreover, those fleeting *hapax legomena* (words used only once) should be learned.

Sometimes, a word may lose its primary significance in favor of an acquired sense. That is, words may change their meanings down the centuries. This is why interpreters should spare no effort in extracting the *current*, established usages of words in Bible times. The study of Bible idioms is significant in this regard.

Consider the prophecy of Isaiah 11:14, "But they shall fly upon the shoulders of the Philistines . . . and Ammon shall obey them." The phrase "shoulders of the Philistines" is a Bible idiom for the coast-lands of Philistia which slope like a shoulder towards the sea (cf. Josh. 15:11). This idiom is found also in Ezekiel 25:9 ("shoulder of Moab"), Numbers 34:11 ("shoulder of the sea of Chinnereth"), and other passages.

The immediate context of the prophecy of Isaiah sets the prophecy at the time when the Lord shall "recover the remnant of his people" (v. 11) and shall punish Israel's national oppressors. This will be at the setting up or the beginning of the millennial kingdom—not throughout the kingdom's duration. To paint a turbulent scene of millennial disharmony, with vengeful Israel getting on the literal *shoulders* of their former enemies, is to miss the point of this prophecy.[1]

B. Study of Syntax

From the study of lexicography, the interpreter must proceed to the study of syntax or word relationship. The position of words and clauses in sentences, significance of conjunctions, adverbs, and prepositions, as well as the unique usages of the tense, voice, mood, and case of a word, must be recognized.

When the etymologies, customary usages, and associations of words in a given prophecy are studied, the interpreter can be confident that he is on the right track in the discovery of the meaning of that prophecy. As Anton Mickelsen observes,

---

[1]Martin Jacob Wyngaarden *(The Future of the Kingdom in Prophecy and Fulfillment* [Grand Rapids, Mich.: Baker Book House, 1955], pp. 72, 74, 79, and 80) repeatedly refers to this prophecy to show the absurdity of literal interpretation of prophecy.

"Putting time and effort into language study is like putting money in the bank. As one's capital increases, so does the interest."[1]

C. Isaiah 66:23—an Illustration

When interpreters slight the study of language in the study of prophecy, this neglect often results in faulty exegesis and unfair allegations. The interpretation of Isaiah 66:23 is an illustration of the danger of hurried exegesis and skimpy treatment of prophetic language. The text reads:

> It shall come to pass from one new moon to another
> and from one sabbath to another, shall all flesh come
> to worship before me. (Isa. 66:23)

Non-literal prophetic interpreters jump on this Old Testament text as predicting—when literally interpreted—that during the millennium every person on earth will go to Jerusalem *every* Sabbath. James Snowden blinks unbelievingly: "All the people in the word are to go every week to Jerusalem to offer sacrifices in the temple! Many premillennarians do not balk or blink even at this, but some of them at this point abandon the *literal* . . . ."[2]

Charles Hodge similarly observes: "Another objection to the pre-millennial theory is the want of consistency in its advocates. . . . They profess to adopt the principle of literal interpretation. . . . Yet they are forced to abandon their literalism when they come to the interpretation of the prophecies which predict that *all the nations of the earth are to go*

---

[1] Anton Berkeley Mickelsen, *Interpreting the Bible* (Grand Rapids, Mich.: Wm. B. Eerdmans Pub. Co., 1963), p. 114.

[2] James H. Snowden, *The Coming of the Lord* (New York, N.Y.: Macmillan Co., 1919), p. 43.

up to Jerusalem every month, and even on every Sabbath [Italics added]."[1]

The usual non-literal interpretation of this passage is simply to accuse the prophet Isaiah of religious fanaticism. As T. K. Cheyne charges the prophet, "He cannot give up the idea of the religious supremacy of Jerusalem; . . . Hence the strange inconsistencies in his picture."[2]

The issue over Isaiah 66:23 would probably not have risen had the language of this prophecy been more studiously examined.[3] One glance at the original Hebrew text tells us that this passage is so idiomatic and peculiar that it does not admit of an exact translation. The original Hebrew text literally reads:

> From the fitness of new moon in its new moon,
> And from the fitness of sabbath in its sabbath,
> Shall all flesh come to worship before me.

It is virtually impossible to determine the exact meaning being conveyed by the prophet at this point.

Two ideas however are possible under the two usages of ב in the clause מדי שבת בשבתו ("from one sabbath to another"), as follows: (1) The idea of temporal exchange or succession—which would see millennial pilgrimages made *every* seven days; and (2) The idea of no strict time obligation; a usage found in I Kings 8:59 ("day by day") and Numbers 28:10, and which would allow pilgrimages to be made *whenever* fitting or due.

---

[1] Charles Hodge, *Systematic Theology* (3 vols,; New York, N.Y.: Charles Scribner's Sons, 1872), III, 865.

[2] T. K. Cheyne, *The Prophecies of Isaiah* (2 vols.; New York, N.Y.: Thomas Whittaker, 1895), II, 131.

[3] There is another prophecy in Zechariah 14:16 which predicts millennial pilgrimages. But the journeys there are said to be *yearly*.

Commentator Delitzsch justifiably prefers the latter alternative, basing his decision on grammar: "The meaning of change and not of a series might be sustained in the passage before us by the suffixless mode or expression which occurs in connection with it." [1]

Since Jerusalem will be the centre of Christ's earthly reign at the millennium, a stream of holy, sincere pilgrims will certainly be journeying there whenever fitting or due. These pilgrimages (not necessarily weekly) will be made up of those mortals who will populate and propagate on the millennial earth.

The question has been raised regarding the possibility of pilgrimages of such world-wide proportions. But if within the short span of a few recent years, supersonic transports have been developed which can carry hundreds of passengers, and circle the globe in mere hours, surely within the thousand-year period, much more efficient modes of transportation will be developed to serve the millennial inhabitants.

Even today, a sizable part of the world's population goes in an unending stream of pilgrimages to Mecca. A reporter for the *Reader's Digest* describes this modern-day scene: "Day in, day out, no place on earth gets as much attention as this sprawling city in the sand. . . . On any given day of the year, someone, somewhere among 500 million Muslims (about 14 percent of the world's population) is beginning the journey to Mecca." [2]

Thus, before an attempt to interpret a prophecy (or to spiritualize it) is made, it is imperative that the usages and

---

[1] Franz Delitzsch, *Biblical Commentary on the Prophecies of Isaiah*, trans. by James Martin (2 vols.; Grand Rapids. Mich.: Wm. B. Eerdmans Pubs. Co., 1950), II, 516.

[2] Edward Hughes, "On the Holy Road to Mecca," *Reader's Digest* (Oct., 1971), p. 27.

meanings of words in the given prophecy be carefully determined.

II. Commit No Historical-Cultural Blunder

A. Importance of Historical Study

The Bible is written in three different languages—Hebrew, Aramaic, and Greek. It spans hundreds of years and covers scores of historical backgrounds and cultural settings. Moses lived a millennium before the most ancient Greek sages; and the last writer of Scripture, John, lived 1,500 years after Moses.

It should be expected therefore that between the pages of Scripture, the customs, habits, language expressions, and sceneries of Bible lands and peoples would not remain static. The interpreter cannot afford to be sloppy in his research down the corridors of Bible times if he wants to avoid historical and cultural errors.

An advantage provided by the knowledge of historical backgrounds is the help it gives to the interpretation of figures. Figures used in the Bible are oftentimes drawn "from the physical features of the Holy Land, the religious institutions of Israel, the history of the Jews, and the daily life and customs of the various people who occupy so prominent a place in the Bible."[1]   Acquaintance with the lives and times of Bible writers is basic to the understanding and interpreting of Bible figures.

---

[1] Gerald B. Stanton, *Kept from the Hour* (London: Marshall, Morgan and Scott, 1964), p. 294. Non-literal interpreters of course say the same thing about figures being drawn from the institutions,

Non-literal interpreters of Scripture usually give slight attention to the historical factor in Scripture. In their zeal to see a deeper meaning in the text, the historical setting of the Bible is overlooked. Donald K. Campbell points this out in his observation: "If the teacher of the Scriptures ignores the historical element, he is in effect allegorizing, that is, seeking a deeper sense in the text on the ground that the natural historical sense is unsatisfactory or inadequate."[1]

B. Some Implications and Applications

It must not be surmised that since literal interpreters insist on interpretation geared to historical considerations, the Bible is to be confined to its early readers and hearers. This is the fallacious teaching of liberal interpreters who use the historical method to dismiss the relevance of the Word of God for today. By misunderstanding the concept of *Sitz im Lebem* (life situation of the prophets), liberals eviscerate the practical relevance of the Scripture on the altar of the historical.

The proper concept of the historical in Bible interpretation is to view the Scriptures as written during given ages and cultures. Applications may then be drawn which are relevant to our times. For instance, the subject of meat offered to idols can only be interpreted from the historical and cultural setting of New Testament times. Principles to be drawn are relevant to us today. Besides those Scriptures which relate to

---

customs, and times of the Bible writers and readers. The issue, however, lies in the determination of *which* prophetic elements are properly figurative (see below, pp. 131-47, for a discussion on this subject), as well as in the acknowledgement of the fact that revelational figures (although often couched in terms of the familiar) are, just the same, from God.

[1] Donald K. Campbell, "The Interpretation of Types," *Bibliotheca Sacra*, CXII, No. 447 (July, 1955), 253.

the historical situations of Bible times, a large portion of God's Word contains doctrinal teachings and spiritual truths which are ageless or directly applicable in any age. In these instances, historical and cultural factors would not assume as large a consideration.

Moreover, in the interpretation of the prophetic Scripture, it is a good rule to know first whether the prophet is mentioning a specific historical and contemporary event or is predicting something in the distant future. It is clear that although many predictions in Scripture relate to the prophet's own time, many others do not. Daniel is told by the revealing angel, "I am come to make thee understand what shall befall thy people *in the latter days*; for yet the vision is *for many days*" (Dan. 10:14—Italics added). The revelation which the angel is about to transmit to Daniel in this instance would be directly applicable to the future. In such cases, and during interpretation, historical and cultural considerations would not loom as significantly as in other predictions.

III. MAKE CHRIST CENTRAL IN ALL INTERPRETATIONS

Christ is the central figure and focus of all history and prophecy. The apostle Peter tells the household of Cornelius that all the prophets witnessed of Jesus (Acts 10:43). The angel tells John the Seer that "the testimony of Jesus is the spirit of prophecy" (Rev. 19:10). Christ Himself, on the road to Emmaus, explains to the two disciples "in all the Scriptures the things concerning Himself" (Luke 24:27). The centrality of Christ in prophecy is therefore an indispensable element in prophetic interpretation. Since Christ is the theme of prophecy and history, the interpreter must interpret prophecy Christologically.

To some interpreters, the concept of the centrality of Christ means that in Christ (and in the church) all prophecy and promises end. As John Wilmot puts it, "The covenants, promises, and prophecies reach their goal in Christ and His Church."[1]

This concept is a lopsided one. The proper concept of the centrality of Christ takes into consideration the *whole* aspect of the person and work of Christ in history and prophecy. In prophecy, Christ is not only the suffering Messiah and Saviour but also the glorious King who is coming again to reign on earth. Although Christ has instituted the church, His work as the Fulfiller of the whole prophetic program goes on. Neither the first coming of Christ nor His second coming exhausts the whole content of prophecy, which also portends a coming age (the millennium). Christ is central in the sense that in His person, prophecy and history come into fruition. His person enables all future events to eventuate and be realized.

Advocates of covenant theology are markedly vocal in affirming the centrality of Christ and the cross during interpretation. They see Christ's centrality under the whole context of their so-called Covenant of Grace. This covenant is said to extend from Adam to the end of the age, with *redemption* as its main theme. In the interpretation of prophecy, anything which cannot fit into the theme of "Christ and His redemption" is spiritualized to fit this theme. Thus, the prophecies of the Millennial Temple and the New Jerusalem are spiritualized as the Christian church.

We shall have occasion under Chapter X to discuss this in more detail. It should however be noted that by making the theme of Christ and redemption cover the whole of prophecy

---

[1] John Wilmot, *Inspired Principles of Prophetic Interpretation* (Swengel, Pa.: Reiner Pubs., 1967), p. 199.

and history, covenant theologians have greatly restricted the concept of the central position of Christ. The cross of Christ saves men of all ages, and Christ's redemption extends from eternity past to eternity future. This is one aspect of the whole program of God in Scripture. God's program also involves plans for the angels and Lucifer, the nation Israel, the Gentiles, and others. Christ is the central figure and focus of all these plans. The cross does not end it all as far as God's program is concerned. The apostle Paul defines the centrality of Christ as "all things in Christ, both which are in heaven, and which are on earth, even in him" (Eph. 1:10)

IV. BE CONSCIOUS OF CONTEXT

A. Case for Contextual Study

Some interpreters are able to make the Scripture prove almost anything. This is possible when the context of Scripture is slighted. During the temptation of Christ, the devil purposely quoted Scripture without regard to its context. As someone has observed, "A text without a context is only a pretext."

The study of context is a *must* in prophetic interpretation. Whenever the context is fully considered during interpretation, the Scripture will not hesitate to give its true meaning. Prophecy is not a hodge-podge of unrelated, piecemeal revelations but is one related, harmonized whole under the context of Scripture. Patrick Fairbairn says regarding this basic harmony of Bible prophecy: "The testimony of prophecy . . . is a chain composed of many links, each running into others before and after it, and by the introduction of some fresh particulars, or some different aspect of the truth, contributing at once to the elucidation of the past, and to a more explicit representation of the future."[1]

In contextual studies, the interpreter should study first the immediate context or that which precedes and follows a given text. Then, he may need to search the more remote contexts of the passage. This involves the examination of parallel passages in the same book, in another book by the same author, in texts from the same time period, and even of the Bible as a whole.

One of the most difficult tasks for prophetic interpreters is setting up a harmony of the prophetic writings. This is many times more difficult than the harmony of the Gospels. Nevertheless, the task must be done. The interpreter may proceed with confidence in the necessary first step of harmonizing the prophetic Word with the help of contextual studies.

B. Some Pertinent Illustrations

To illustrate the pertinence of context in the interpretation of prophecy, let us look at Luke 20:35-36, where Christ is speaking:

> But they who shall be accounted worthy to obtain that world, and the resurrection from the dead, neither marry, nor are given in marriage. Neither can they die any more; for they are equal unto the angels, . . . being the children of the resurrection.

This passage (read cursorily and without much regard to its context) indicates that when Jesus comes again there will be no family life, for everyone then existing will become like angels. The rest of the Scriptures, however, when literally and normally read, reveals that there will be a group of mortal

---

[1]Patrick Fairbairn, *The Interpretation of Prophecy* (reprint ed.; London: Banner of Truth Trust, 1964), p. 182.

people who will enter the millennial kingdom in their non-resurrected bodies and will live normal, happy family lives as millennial inhabitants.

This seeming contradiction has prompted non-literal interpreters to ask rhetorically: "Which is to be our standard? Literal interpretation of Old Testament prophecy, or acceptance of the eschatological teaching of Christ?"[1]

The fuss over Luke 20 would probably not have assumed such proportions had the fact been recognized that Jesus qualifies His words with the phrase "and the resurrection from the dead" and even adds the modifier "being the children of the resurrection." The former phrase is actually found in the same sentence of the text under study.

The Sadduces had asked Jesus the question, "In the resurrection whose wife of them is she?" (v. 33). Jesus' reply would then deal with *resurrection* conditions in "that world." Jesus explains that those who attain unto the other world (of the kingdom) and are resurrected, will not marry and have children but will be like unto the angels (vs. 34-36). The whole context of Luke 20 deals with the condition of the resurrected. Nothing is said about non-resurrected inhabitants of that world. The revelation of family life in the millennial kingdom is made elsewhere in Scripture. The fact that Christ adds the qualifiers ("and the resurrection from the dead . . . being the children of the resurrection") implies the existence of people who will *not* be resurrected and be like the angels but who will, just the same, attain unto the kingdom age.[2]

---

[1] Floyd E. Hamilton, *The Basis of Millennial Faith* (Grand Rapids, Mich.: Wm. B. Eerdmans Pub. Co., 1942), p. 136. Hamilton repeatedly points to this "contradiction," mentioning it in pages 46-50, 126-27, 134-35, 143, etc. of his book.

[2] If καί in the phrase "*and* the resurrection from the dead" (Luke 20:35) means "even," the idea is even stronger.

Another illustration of the importance of contextual studies is Matthew 24:29-30, where Jesus gives the chronology of the Great Tribulation in relation to His second coming. The text reads:

> Immediately after the tribulation of those days shall the sun be darkened, and the moon shall not give its light. . . . And *then* shall appear the sign of the Son of Man in heaven . . . . And they shall see the Son of Man coming in the clouds of heaven with power and great glory. [Matt. 24:29-30 Italics added]

This text, when read as is may prove posttribulationism. It says that Christ will come for the saints "immediately after" the tribulation. However, a text apart from its context is only a pretext. The proper context of the passage under consideration is the Olivet Discourse of Christ (Matthew 24). The discourse is given during our Lord's lament over Jerusalem and the nation Israel which had rejected Him. The entire cast and context of the discourse is therefore with reference to the nation Israel; the church is nowhere referred to. The harmony of passages elsewhere in Scripture combines to teach that Christ will come for the church before the tribulation, while this passage and its context do teach that *for the nation Israel* the second coming of Christ will be after the tribulation.

V. Interpret by the Analogy of Faith

The principle of the "analogy of faith" was first brought to the attention of Christians by the Protestants reformers. The principle is based on the observation that there is no better interpreter of Scripture than the Scripture itself. As the apostle Paul puts it, "Compare spiritual things with spiritual" (I Cor. 2:13; see Romans 12:6). The justification for comparing

Scripture with Scripture lies in the fact that the Scriptures do not contradict each other.

When applied to interpretation, the principle of analogy of faith demands that every interpretation be in harmony with the uniform teaching of Scripture. No interpretation is allowable which does not harmonize with the uniform teaching of the Bible on that given subject. Passages are to be explained, not on the basis of individual texts, but by the whole tenor of Scripture.

As James L. Boyer warns: "The prophetic Scriptures are not to be taken alone and interpreted without regard for the rest of Scripture. Always we must safeguard our interpretation of prophecy by comparing it with the full teaching of the whole Bible. God doesn't contradict himself."[1]   And Arthur Pink adds: "This requires from the expositor . . . that he take the trouble to collect and compare all the passages which treat of or have a definite bearing upon the immediate point before him, so that he may obtain the *full* mind of the Spirit thereon."[2]

The analogy of faith is a foundational principle and a basic presupposition in Scriptural interpretation. Without it as a basic assumption, the interpreter will find himself either evolving mutually contradictory Biblical systems of theology or else giving in to utter frustration. With this principle in mind, the interpreter confidently sees a scheme of future events and expects the harmony of its interrelated parts.

John F. Walvoord says regarding the analogy of prophetic truths: "The whole doctrine of prophecy should be allowed to

---

[1] James L. Boyer, *Prophecy: Things to Come* (Winona Lake, Ind.: Brethren Missionary Herald Company, 1950), p. 6.

[2] Arthur W. Pink, *Interpretation of the Scriptures* (Grand Rapids, Mich.: Baker Book House, 1972), p. 32.

be the guide for the interpretation of details. The main elements of prophecy are far more clear than some of the details. Difficult passages are often solved by a study of related Scriptures."[1]

An illustration of the analogy of faith principle in action is the prophecies concerning the future return of Christ. Without the analogy of prophecy, it is impossible (apart from spiritualization) to harmonize predictions in Scripture which report that when Christ returns, the unrighteous will be consumed in judgment (cf. Matt. 13:30; II Thess. 2:8-12; Rev. 19:15), the saints will be "changed" (cf. I Cor. 15:51), and no glorified person will propagate children (cf. Matt. 22:30), with prophecies which describe family life, children, and old persons at the millennium, including a Satan-led rebellion at the end of the thousand years (cf. Rev. 20:8). A period of time—the seven year tribulation periöd—for mortals to be born or saved after the rapture of the church will be necessary to produce a group that will enter the millennium in their mortal bodies.

VI.   RECOGNIZE THE PROGRESS OF REVELATION

A. The Doctrine Defined

The doctrine of progressive revelation teaches that the complete revelation of God was unfolded to man progressively and gradually, not all at once in complete, final form. God revealed Himself to man in progressive stages and periods. Even during New Testament times, Christ was still telling His disciples, "I have yet many things to say unto you, but ye cannot bear them now" (John 16:12). It was only after the

---

[1] John F. Walvoord, *The Millennial Kingdom* (Findlay, Ohio: Dunham Pub. Co., 1959), p. 132.

writing of the last New Testament book, the Apocalypse, that formal revelation was finally closed with this clear warning— "If any man shall add unto these things, God shall add unto him the plagues that are written in this book" (Rev. 22:18).

B. The Doctrine Clarified

1. *Revelations that are antecedent.*—Some interpreters believe that in the revelatory process, revelations given earlier have been absorbed into and supplanted by those given more recently. They say that Old Testament revelations, being prior to the New, have been mostly supplanted and should be interpreted in light of the New Testament.

Although God reveals Himself and His plan of the ages progressively and everything is not unfolded all at once, this does not mean that revelations anteriorly given have been replaced or contradicted. Progressive revelation is like a landscape that is progressively lit up as the rays of the sun advance over it at dawn. With the advance of the sun's rays, certain portions of the landscape are revealed earlier than others. And just because a given portion of a total landscape is illuminated earlier than another does not mean that a portion of the landscape has been supplanted.

Perhaps divine revelation may be seen also under the illustration of a three-act play:

ACT I:
  Setting: The Old Testament
  Substance: Hopes are born. Characters are introduced. Backgrounds are provided.

ACT II:
  Setting: The New Testament
  Substance: The Hero arrives. Some fulfillment of prophecy seen; other prophecies further

clarified or supplemented; still others superseded (not supplanted[1]). Final outcome of the future becomes more certain.

ACT III:
Setting: The Kingdom and the Eternal State
Substance: All remaining prophecies are fulfilled.

The observation of Charles Lee Feinberg is appropriate: "The spirit of God can be depended upon to give us a revelation in orderly fashion from incompleteness to completeness, without the fear that the latter portion will contradict the former. We maintain and insist that the Bible can be read in order and interpreted according to proper literal principles without misgivings that the New Testament will invalidate what is revealed in the Old Testament."[2]

2. *Revelations that are not repeated.*—In the unfolding of divine revelation, there are times when a revelation given previously is not repeated: the more recent revelation has left it out. This does not mean that the former revelation, being unrepeated, has been contradicted or supplanted. God's Word is forever settled in heaven. To demand that in order for a revelation to remain valid it must be stated again, is to disparage the veracity and harmony of Scripture.

"We can assume that God intended His people to believe what was already available in the Holy Scriptures," comments William K. Harrison. "Therefore there would be no need to repeat facts already clearly declared in the Old Testament.

---

[1] See below, *Revelations that are Provisional,* pp. 114-115.
[2] Charles Lee Feinberg, *Premillennialism or Amillennialism?* (Wheaton, Ill.: Van Kampen Press, 1954), p. 212.

Consequently no one has a right to demand such repetition."[1]

Thus, the future earthly kingdom prophesied in the Old Testament need not be fully reiterated in the New for the concept to remain in order. The New Testament gives additional details concerning the prophesied kingdom (such as its duration), but the New Testament should not be asked to repeat all the elements that have already been revealed in the Old.

An able playwright would develop the plot of his story in gradual, progressive fashion, building the more recent developments upon elements that have already been described. Only what is necessary to the plot is repeated. Past elements already described are assumed valid unless otherwise stated. The revelations contained in the Old and New Testament follow this development.

3. *Revelations that are provisional.*— In the Old Testament, there are of course a number of things which are provisional (e.g. the sacrifices), typical (e.g. the tabernacle), and elementary. These elements have been superseded at the first advent of Christ. However, they should not be thought of as having been contradicted or supplanted.

That everything in the Old Testament is elementary, provisional, and typical is the common belief of modernistic theologians who consider the Old Testament revelation to be "the lower steps of man's painful climb and a level of religion largely superseded."[2]   Many non-literal prophetic interpreters who are conservatives also say the same thing: "The Old and the New Testament are related to each other not

---

[1] William K. Harrison, *Hope Triumphant* (Chicago, Ill.: Moody Press, 1966), pp. 114-15.

[2] John Bright, *The Kingdom of God* (New York, N.Y.: Abingdon-Cokesbury Press, 1953), p. 288.

merely as type and antitype, but also . . . as a primitive and a more perfect revelation."[1]

It is also a mistake to think that everything in the New Testament is determinative and climactic. Revelations concerning the Antichrist, the Tribulation, and the future Kingdom are often more fully detailed in the Old than in the New Testament. And even within the confines of the New Testament, the Pauline epistles have more to say about salvation by grace than the Book of James.

For any given facet of prophecy, therefore, the interpreter should not limit his search to only one part of the Scripture. He should consider all portions of God's Word as pertinent to the study of prophecy.

C. Progressive Illumination

In a discussion on the progress of revelation, the doctrine of the progress of *illumination* must also be considered. God's revelation to man ended with the close of the New Testament canon. No new revelation has since been granted. James L. Boyer says: "There are no revealers of new divine truths today. God has said all He has to say in this book. This book is all the prophet and all the prophecy there is today. There are those who edify the church by expounding the prophecies of this book, but they are not prophets."[2]   With the completion of divine revelation, the Holy Spirit works in illuminating the church regarding the completed canon of Scripture.

Just as the giving of revelation was progressive, the illumination of the Holy Spirit is progressive—both in each

---

[1] Louis Berkhof, *Principles of Biblical Interpretation* (Grand Rapids, Mich.: Baker Book House, 1966), p. 136.

[2] James L. Boyer, "The Office of the Prophet in New Testament Times," *Grace Journal*, I, No. 1 (Spring, 1960), 20.

believer's life and in the history of the church. When Christ promises concerning the Holy Spirit that "He will guide you into all truth . . . and show you things to come" (John 16:13), He certainly does not mean that the Holy Spirit will illuminate all things to all believers *all at once*, for He immediately adds this explanation, "He shall glorify me; for he shall receive of mine and shall show it unto you" (v. 14). In other words, the illumination of God's written revelation will proceed in a manner which will most glorify Jesus Christ.

Down the Christian centuries, as the Holy Spirit illumines the Word, doctrines are thought through and refined, orthodoxy is preserved, and Christ is glorified. John F. Walvoord traces this process of illumination, saying: "There is some evidence that the church has been progressing throughout the centuries of its history through the major areas of doctrine beginning with *bibliology* and *theology proper* as in the early centuries of the church, advancing to such subjects as *anthropology* and *hamartiology* in the fourth and succeeding centuries, and dealing with *soteriology* and *ecclesiology* in the Protestant Reformation. It has been mostly in the last century that *eschatology* has really come to the fore as an area for scholarly study and debate."[1]

Moreover, since Christ promises that the Holy Spirit's work of illumination will concern even "things to come" (John 16:13), we may expect that as the church age draws to a close, and more prophetic events are about to transpire, the Holy Spirit will grant more illumination relative to the refinements of prophecy. It seems as if God has allowed other doctrinal issues to be threshed out in church history before fully opening up the study of prophecy to the church at the end age. The

---

[1] John F. Walvoord, *The Church in Prophecy* (Grand Rapids, Mich.: Zondervan Pub. House, 1964), p. 127. [Italics added]

phenomenal growth of interest in the study of prophecy within the last century or so is significant. This may partially explain why the doctrine of the pretribulational rapture—the logical capstone of the entire eschatological structure [1] — is now being emphasized by a significant portion of the church.

It is now appropriate to explain why pretribulationism as a distinct doctrine did not emerge until in relatively recent history. As we have already noted, the early church was over-whelmingly premillennial. But premillennialism must be refined and further systematized before the doctrine of the pretribulational rapture could be recognized. The early church never got the chance. The refinement and systematizing of prophecy did not get started before the Alexandrians arose and toppled the church off premillennialism. From then on and through the Middle Ages, the church's very relationship to the millennium came under attack and ridicule, and the development of pretribulationism was of course stunted.

Then came the Reformation. While the Protestant reformers dealt a severe blow to the allegorization then on a rampage and brought about a revival of premillennialism in *post*-Reformation times, they had neither time nor inclination for prophetic studies—much less its refinements. Martin Luther avoided the teachings of prophecy for years. And John Calvin refused to write a commentary on the Book of Revelation, saying, "The study of prophecy either finds a man crazy, or it leaves him so." [2]

---

[1] Once the truth of pretribulationism is seen, the entire prophetic Word seems to fall into place, and a harmonious picture of God's dealing with His church in redemptive grace is completed. Pretribulationism is based not so much on single texts or arguments but on the accumulation of evidences and texts, being a systematic refinement of premillennialism.

[2] Cited by Augustus Hopkins Strong, *Systematic Theology* (Phila., Pa.: The Judson Press, 1907), p. 140.

This disinclination of the reformers is understandable, for vital issues such as justification by faith and the refinements of ecclesiology were demanding the reformers' full attention. Since eschatology was not a major issue and the subject was actually shunned by the reformers, the Protestant churches continued to embrace Roman Catholic amillennialism almost *in toto*. And as amillennialism remained in vogue, pretribulationism was never seriously discussed. It was not until after the ascendancy of premillennialism in post-Reformation times (by virtue of the literal method) that the Lord's return was again viewed by a significant portion of the church as before the tribulation.

Thus, the doctrine of progressive illumination accepts the fact that certain revelations of Scripture will be better understood during different periods of church history. It is not true that a doctrine is necessarily wrong just because it has been refined and systematized, or has re-emerged, in later history.

Clarence Mason illustrates progressive illumination in the case for modern missions: "The emphasis on missions, so evident in the Early Church, was lost in the Dark Ages under Rome . . . . The Reformers did little or nothing to revive missionary activity and some spoke against the idea. Today, everyone recognizes William Carey as the Father of the Modern Missionary Era (1790) . . . . Is the missionary truth and emphasis, so recently developed, to be urged as dangerous and automatically untrue because of that fact?"[1]

VII. GRANT ONE INTERPRETATION TO EACH PASSAGE

We have already noted that God desires His revelation to be comprehended. The basic prerequisite of comprehension is

---

[1] Clarence E. Mason, Jr., "Eschatology" (Class notes, Philadelphia College of Bible, Philadelphia, 1970), p. 23.

the assumption that the linguistically displayed sense of the speaker or writer is his originally intended sense. Otherwise, ambiguity creeps in and normal communication is destroyed. Applied to Holy Scripture, the rule of comprehension demands that each passage of Scripture has but one basic meaning displayed linguistically. A multiplicity of senses and meanings makes comprehension difficult, if not impossible. The interpreter must give each passage of Scripture one interpretation.

A. Single Exegesis

The original readers and hearers of Scripture knew that God's Word had a message for them. The study of this basic, original meaning of Scripture is known as *exegesis*. One exegesis exists for each passage of Scripture.

The Westminister Confession of Faith affirms the principle of the single sense of Scripture: "The infallible rule of interpretation of Scripture is the Scripture itself, and therefore, when there is a question about the true and full sense of any Scripture (which is not manifold, but one), it must be searched and known by other places that speak more clearly."

B. Manifold Expositions

After exegesis of a given text, the interpreter should make practical and spiritual applications based on the interpretation. This is known as *exposition*.[1] Exposition is the deduction of spiritual truths, principles, and concepts from that which has been literally interpreted. While there is but

---

[1] Some interpreters call the process of interpretation and application "primary and secondary application."

one exegesis or interpretation to a passage, a number of applications or expositions of that interpretation may be made.

Thus, the proper interpretation of Psalm 122:6 ("Pray for the peace of Jerusalem, they shall prosper who love thee") is to see the prayer of the Jewish exiles for their beloved city Jerusalem. Applications may then be made in the Christian life.

Or, when God promises Abraham in Genesis 12:3 that "I will bless them that bless thee, and curse him that curseth thee," the prophecy is intended primarily for Abraham and the nations of his sojournment. Nevertheless, the age-old principle that God does bless those who are good to His chosen people (the Jews) should not be neglected in the application.

When the apostle Paul says, "Now all these things happened unto them for ensamples, and they are written for our admonition, upon whom the ends of the world are come ' (I Cor. 10:11), he was talking about applications.

The popular chorus *Every Promise in the Book is Mine* would certainly be more meaningful if it does not slight the distinction between what is "mine" by interpretation and "mine" by application. To appropriate all Scripture promises without regard to their proper intentions is the method of many non-literal interpreters.[1]

---

[1] Interpreter J. Barton Payne sings the praise of this method when he writes: "Classical post-tribulationism . . . takes seriously the old hymn entitled, 'Every promise in the Book is mine!' Revelation, not just chapters 2, 3 and 19:6-9, but the whole book is appreciated as applying to all. . . ." (*The Imminent Appearing of Christ* [Grand Rapids, Mich.: Wm. B. Eerdmans Pub. Co., 1962], p. 163).

But Payne is a covenant premillennialist, and surely he would not take *every* promise in the Old Testament as directly applicable—otherwise he would end up an amillennialist.

C. Illustration: The Sermon on the Mount

Perhaps the principle of "single interpretation, manifold applications" faces its most crucial test case with respect to the Sermon on the Mount (Matt. 5-7).

Many interpreters see the Sermon on the Mount as directly and primarily applicable to Christians today. To do this, interpreters depend heavily on the method of spiritualization, for it is apparent that the laws and regulations found in the Sermon cannot be *directly* applied today without producing insurmountable problems and repercussions.

The requirements of turning the other cheek and not asking for that which had been borrowed, although applicable under some conditions, would be difficult to apply under *all* circumstances. As Charles Ryrie observes: "But if the laws of the Sermon are to be obeyed today they could not be taken literally, for as [George Eldon] Ladd points out, every businessman would go bankrupt giving to those who ask of him. This is the dilemma every interpreter faces. If literal, it cannot be for today; if for today, it cannot be literal."[1]

Moreover, a casual reading of the Sermon reveals that it contains an embarrassing absence of church truths. Nothing is said regarding Christ's sacrifice for sin (found as early as John 3), the faith which brings salvation, prayer in the name of Christ, the Holy Spirit, and even the church itself. These are all foundational truths taught by Christ during His early ministry (cf. John 14:13, 26; Matt. 16:18-19; etc.).

If this most lengthy and didactic of Christ's teachings were truly intended to be primarily related to the Christian church, its omission of basic church truths would be highly irregular.

---

[1] Charles Caldwell Ryrie, *Dispensationalism Today* (Chicago, Ill.: Moody Press, 1965), pp. 106-7.

There are, of course, parallels between precepts in the Sermon and those found in the Epistles, but this does not mean that one equals the other. The ten commandments are all reiterated in the New Testament except one, but this does not mean that the Ten Commandments and the New Testament precepts are one and the same.

Even non-dispensationalist George Eldon Ladd admits that the words of the Sermon, when taken normally, must describe conditions that are yet future: "In the sermon on the Mount, the kingdom is repeatedly viewed as something in the future which is yet to come. Six of the beatitudes are cast in a futuristic setting (Matt. 5:4-9). . . . The situation reflected in these promises of future blessing is that of a future and final world order . . . ."[1]

In view of these considerations, the proper conclusion with regards to the Sermon on the Mount is that the *full* and *non-modified* fulfillment of this portion of Matthew is possible only in relationship to the future institution of the Messianic Kingdom. It is applicable primarily to the nation Israel as she anticipates the institution of the kingdom at the millennium.[2] It has no primary application in the church and should not be so taken.

---

[1] George Eldon Ladd, *Crucial Questions about the Kingdom of God* (Grand Rapids, Mich.: Wm. B. Eerdmans Pub. Co., 1952), p. 67.

[2] The Sermon does not relate to the period of the millennium itself, for the prayer "Thy kingdom come," the record of people being persecuted for righteousness' sake and in hunger, as well as the presence of evil and evil men are certainly contrary to the revealed character and nature of Christ's future kingdom on earth.

Since the Sermon on the Mount was spoken before Christ was rejected by the Jews and during His offer of the kingdom, the Sermon will again be directly applicable in relationship to that same kingdom (the millennial kingdom) just before its institution.

That the Sermon is fully and directly applicable during the institution of the kingdom is not to imply that the Sermon has no relevance or spiritual application for Christians today. The Sermon on the Mount is an excellent practical and spiritual guide and has multiplied applications for the Christian. "It should be plain to any spiritual mind," observes Ironside, "that the principles of the kingdom which He sets forth are the same principles that should hold authority over the heart of all who acknowledge the lordship of Christ."[1] Principles and truths drawn from the Golden Rule and the Beautitudes, for instance, are easily and beautifully applicable in the Christian life.

Moreover, there are many moral and ethical teachings of Jesus in the Sermon which remain true for every age. These teachings certainly would transcend the limits of the ages and dispensations. It is always true that those hungering for righteousness are filled, that the poor in spirit (and not the proud) are blessed in God's sight, and that the pure in heart does see God.

Christ's Sermon on the Mount in Matthew 5-7 is a good illustration of the fact that while a given passage of Scripture should have but one primary interpretation, a variety of practical and spiritual applications could and should be made.

VIII. CHOOSE THE SIMPLEST ALTERNATIVE

A. Rule of the Simplest Alternative

During the interpretation of Scripture, when alternative interpretations seem equally plausible and contain equally good sense, the general rule of thumb is to choose the one

---

[1] Harry A. Ironside, *Wrongly Dividing the Word of Truth* (Neptune, N.J.: Loizeaux Bros., Inc., n.d.), p. 14.

interpretation which imposes the least strain on credulity. As Milton Terry affirms: "That meaning which most readily suggests itself to a reader or hearer is, in general, to be required as the meaning and that alone."[1]

In the interpretation of the rash vow of Jephthah in Judges 11, interpreters marshall equally good reasons for seeing Jephthah's daughter offered up as a burnt offering or given up as a perpetual virgin in the sanctuary of Shiloh. The alternate views are so compelling that the result is pretty much a draw. In this case, the rule of the simplest alternate should be applied. Jephthah's daughter was offered up.

It must be noted that the choice of simpler alternatives presupposes the existence of *valid* alternates. The interpreter must not choose simple alternatives for simplicity's sake. One should investigate diligently the entire aspect of the case, consider the logical and natural harmony of God's Word, and, after the consideration of the harmonized facts, embrace that which is easy of acceptance.

B. Simplicity and the Eschatological Systems

One reason why interpreters have chosen the non-literal eschatological systems is that these systems seem easier to grasp.

1. *The postmillennial system.*—Loraine Boettner, a postmillennial interpreter, admits his preference for the simpler scheme of postmillennialism, saying: "Frankly, we have no desire for such a state as Premillennialism sets forth, but prefer at death to enter directly into the heavenly Kingdom."[2]

---

[1] Milton S. Terry, *Biblical Hermeneutics* (New York, N.Y.: Eaton and Mains, 1911), p. 103.

[2] Loraine Boettner, *The Millennium* (Phila., Pa.: The Presbyterian and Reformed Pub. Co., 1964), p. 80.

And postmillennialism is most certainly the simplest of all major eschatological systems. The postmillennial system affirms that the world is going to get better and better as Christianity continues to spread world-wide. And as an increasingly large percentage of the world is Christianized, the *millennium* is said to have arrived. "Christ will return to a truly Christianized world,"[1] says Boettner.

Conservative postmillennialists believe that the kingdom will be brought in through Gospel preaching and influence. Liberal postmillennialists however think that education, social reform, legislation, and human endeavor will bring in the kingdom. "Are the ills of society to be righted by an early and sudden destruction of the present world, or is permanent relief to be secured only by a gradual process of strenuous endeavor covering a long period of years?"[2] asks a liberal postmillennialist. Despite the difference in approach among postmillennialists, there is nevertheless a key word in their system. It is *progress*. That is, things will progressively turn better; the world will not end in a sudden catastrophic event at Christ's coming.

But the tenets of postmillennialism stand condemned in light of passages of Scriptures, such as Matthew 22:14 and Luke 18:8. Contemporary world events also have sent this view into a tailspin. Instead of getting better and better, the world seems to be getting progressively worse. Not surprisingly, therefore, postmillennialism lost its viable force in evangelical theology after the Second World War.

2. *The amillennial system.*— Floyd Hamilton, a leading amillennialist, describes the eschatology of his system saying, "When Christ comes, the dead are all raised, the

[1] *Ibid.*, p. 14.
[2] Shirley Jackson Case, *The Millennial Hope* (Chicago, Ill.: University of Chicago Press, 1918), p. v.

righteous raptured, the wicked destroyed by fire, the great judgment occurs, and the new heavens and new earth follow immediately."[1]   Such a greatly simplified scheme of the future is possible only through spiritualization.

Hamilton in the final page of his book *The Basis of Millennial Faith* tells how this is done: "By eliminating the alleged millennium, putting the two resurrections into one, the different judgments into one, and *declaring* [Italics added] that when Christ comes, He comes to end this age and judge the world, we get rid of all the difficulties that beset both premillennialism and postmillennialism."[2]

This method of head-in-the-sand spiritualization in order to avoid involved time schemes and prophetic details is certainly unworthy of the interpreter of prophecy. Prophecy appears relatively simple and comprehensible (albeit comprehensive) when read normally. It should not be simplified through spiritualization. John F. Walvoord is prompted to observe regarding the amillennialists: "Amillennarians do not need to hold prophetic conferences and preach often on prophetic themes. It is comparatively easy to grasp a simple formula of final resurrection, final judgment, and eternal state."[3]

3. *The posttribulational system.*—When one compares the tenets of posttribulationism with pretribulationism, the former is found to be simpler. George Ladd, who supports posttribulationism, reaffirms this principle of simpler alternative: "The author takes it as a basic hermeneutical principle that in disputed questions of interpretation, the simpler view is to be preferred; the burden of proof rests upon the more elaborate explanation."[4]

---

[1] Hamilton, *Basis of Millennial Faith*, p. 110.
[2] *Ibid.*, p. 144.
[3] Walvoord, *Millennial Kingdom*, p. 61.
[4] George Eldon Ladd, *The Blessed Hope* (Grand Rapids, Mich.: Wm. B. Eerdmans Pub. Co., 1956), p. 165.

It is true that when one accepts the literality of the tribulational passages (especially in the Book of Revelation), one immediately assumes the responsibility of harmonizing hundreds of prophetic details relative to the scheme of eschatology, and foregoes the luxury of spiritualizing away many of these details.

But this is a necessary responsibility in prophetic interpretation. The details of prophecy are really easier to explain and accept when taken literally than when spiritualized. In Revelation 16:12, the River Euphrates is prophesied as drying up for the crossing of the kings of the east. It is simpler to accept a temporary, miraculous draining of the Euphrates[1] and to harmonize this event with end-time developments, than to spiritualize it as the "failure of the support which mystical Babylon was to derive from the nations and kingdoms of the earth."[2]

The choice between pretribulationism and posttribulationism is really not between simpler and more complex alternatives. It is basically a choice between willingness and unwillingness to accept the details of prophetic Scripture as harmonized.

Notice how Jesus describes the tribulation: ". . .great tribulation, such as was not since the beginning of the world to this time, no, nor ever shall be" (Matt. 24:21). Passages from the Old Testament prophets, the synoptic Gospels, and Revelation 6-19 reinforce the fact of the unprecedented awfulness of the tribulation. The human sufferings and divine judgments to be poured out during this period will be unparalleled. This

---

[1] The draining of the Euphrates happened at least once before in history. The Persians under Cyrus were able to capture the impregnable city of Babylon by diverting the waters of the Euphrates whose channel ran directly under that ancient capital city (cf. Daniel 5:30-31).

[2] Fairbairn, *Interpretation of Prophecy*, p. 524, App. M.

is the picture of the tribulation which the harmonized facts of revelation afford.

Posttribulationists try to tone down the severity of the Great Tribulation and reason that since every generation of Christians has had to go through some sort of suffering and tribulation, why should the last generation of Christians be allowed to escape the tribulation at the rapture?

The logical reasoning however should be, Why should the last generation of Christians be subjected to an unprecedented period of the tribulation? Will it not be said that believers already dead are more favored than those living when the Great Tribulation strikes? If posttribulationism is divinely ordained, the final generation of Christians would, with justice, covet an early grave and welcome the undertaker.

C. Simplicity—Whose Criterion?

It is imperative to note that, although the choice of alternate interpretations will in many cases be made by the interpreter himself, in a large number of cases, the choice should be based not on the views of the modern interpreter but on that of the *original* recipients of Scriptures (if a difference exists). When alternatives are available to the interpreter, he should ask how the original readers would have understood it.

For instance, in Acts 15, the apostle James at the Jerusalem Council refers to Amos' prophecy. To interpret this prophecy, one must inquire, What did the council members take James' quotation of Amos to mean?

The Jerusalem Council was convened to decide the question of whether Gentile Christians should or should not be circumcized as Jewish proselytes. The council members were all Jewish believers who, with their unique Jewish backgrounds, would be fully conversant with the features of the kingdom promised by their prophets. As leader of the Jerusalem church, the apostle James certainly assumes this as he stands up to address the council members, saying:

Symeon hath declared how God . . . [takes] out of them a people for his name. And to this agree the words of the prophets, as it is written: After this I will return and will build again the tabernacle of David . . . that the residue of men might seek the Lord, and all the Gentiles upon whom my name is called. . . . Known unto God are all his works from the beginning of the world. [Acts 15:14-18]

James first emphasizes what Symeon (Peter) has said concerning "no difference" (v. 9) between Jews and Gentiles in the church. To further stress this New Testament teaching before the council, James points out that this was *in harmony with* that which will happen during the kingdom age (as predicted by the prophet Amos) when there will be both Jewish believers and Gentiles believers (cf. vs. 16-17). The fact that James uses the words "To this agree the words of the prophets"—an introductory formula *never* used in the Bible to introduce an actual fulfillment—is an evidence that he did not mean to quote Amos' prophecy as an actual fulfillment.

The prophecy of Amos is cited by James to unfold the sequence of God's future program. The argument of James is that, since even in the kingdom age there will be the categories of Gentile and Jewish believers, there is no reason why Gentiles should now be required to become Jewish proselytes.

As Charles Zimmerman explains: "James was not quoting the prophecy as being directly relevant to the present. He was outlining the course of events as they were developing and would continue to develop . . . . Peter had declared one thing. He put 'no difference between' them (Acts 15:9). This was not out of harmony with those things which would follow according to Amos."[1]

To modern day interpreters, this explanation of Acts 15 may not be representative of the simplest alternative. Nevertheless, the choice of simplicity lies in what the early recipients of Scripture would most readily take a text to mean, rather than how a modern interpreter would view things. We return to the basic hermeneutical premise that the interpreter of the Bible should think the thoughts of Bible characters and live their lives.

---

[1]Charles Zimmerman, "To This Agree the Words of the Prophets," *Grace Journal*, IV, No. 3 (Fall, 1963), 37.

VI

LANGUAGE OF PROPHECY

Language is the uniformly accepted conveyance of thought. When a person wishes to express his mind, he uses the normal medium of language. When God wants to reveal future things, He chooses regular human language instead of an ethereal, heavenly one. The interpreter therefore need not devise some sort of code to decipher God's revelation to man, for in God's use of regular earthly language, the task of interpreters is made that much easier.

God's future program is expressed in written language. No interpreter may therefore hope to succeed in knowing the future without some mastery of the language of prophecy.[1]

It is not unusual for non-literal interpreters to affirm that the language of prophecy is "nearly always" figurative. Girdlestone commits this mistake by saying, "That which makes the language of prophecy so vivid and yet so difficult is that it is always more or less figurative."[2]

This view of the language of prophecy is hoary with age. During the days of the prophets, there were skeptics already who tried to evade the import of the prophets' messages by saying that prophecy is too figurative to be taken literally.

---

[1] By "language," we mean its linguistic expression.
[2] Robert Baker Girdlestone, *The Grammar of Prophecy* (Grand Rapids, Mich.: Kregel Pubs., 1955), p. 48.

Ezekiel once complained to God in exasperation: "Oh, Lord God! They say of me, 'Doth he not speak parables?'" (Ezek. 20:49).

The proper approach to prophetic language is to refrain from generalizing regarding its figurative status and to be willing to assign it a nonfigurative character as a basic starting point.

I. Plain, Actual Language

A. Rule of Nonfigurativeness

Bible prophecy is given to show and to reveal—not to puzzle and to veil. When the apostle Peter describes prophecy as "a more sure word . . . a light that shineth in a dark place" (II Pet. 1:19), he decisively removes prophecy from the dark, the mysterious, and the uncertain. Therefore, in the interpretation of prophecy, the supposition should predominate that the language of prophecy is largely nonfigurative.

Normal human communication demands the fundamental principle that what is being spoken or written be predominantly nonfigurative. A.B. Davidson is happily correct when he says: "This I consider the first principle in prophetic interpretation—to read the prophet literally—to assume that the literal meaning is *his* meaning—that he is moving among realities, not symbols, among concrete things like peoples, not among abstractions like *our* Church, world, etc."[1]

A necessary qualification of the interpreter of prophecy therefore is that he feel at home in the *written* record of the

---

[1] A.B. Davidson, *Old Testament Prophecy*, ed. by J.A. Paterson (Edinburgh: T. & T. Clark, 1903), p. 167. Nevertheless, Davidson goes on to note that while the prophets might have meant their prophecies literally, God had other things in mind (*Ibid.*, pp. 168-69).

prophetic Scripture and schedule no mental reservation against its factual revelation. He should immerse himself in the written words of prophecy, studying them "precept upon precept, line upon line, . . . here a little, and there a little" (Isa. 28:10).

Whenever the interpreter is studying prophecy, he should have the "six honest, serving men" of Rudyard Kipling at his finger tips:

I keep six honest, serving men
They taught me all I knew;
Their names are What and Why and When,
And Where and How and Who.

The interpreter should be interested enough in the written words of prophecy to ask prophecy's who's and what's. To slight the examination of the written details of prophetic revelation, since most of these are supposedly figurative anyway, is to exclude oneself from proper interpretation of prophecy. Interpreters overstate the case when they affirm that one cannot be too sure of the language of prophecy and its fulfillment "even though it seems to be expressed in the simplest and most literal words."[1] How much simpler should God express it before one would accept?

B. Interpretation of Revelation 20

A passage which shows how plain and actual the language of prophecy can be is Revelation 20:1-3a, which reads:

And I saw an angel come down from heaven, having the key of the bottomless pit and a great chain in his

---

[1]Roderick Campbell, *Israel and the New Covenant* (Phila., Pa.: The Presbyterian and Reformed Pub. Co., 1954), p. 199.

hand. And he laid hold of the dragon, that old
serpent, who is the Devil and Satan, and bound him
a thousand years, and cast him into the bottomless
pit.

Normal reading of this prophecy is not only possible, but,
in all fairness to customary language, should be done first. We
take it that the apostle John visually sees the angel bind Satan
with a *chain* and cast him into the pit for a thousand years.
The fact that this is seen under an anticipatory vision makes
no real difference. Visional subjects are anticipated actualities,
just as visional words are anticipated revelational words.

John of course does not actually *see* the purpose of Satan's
binding (which is, "that he should deceive the nations no
more") nor the length of his imprisonment (namely, "a thousand years"[1]). These are revelations given to him verbally.
They should not be regarded as figurative, for John never
dropped his readers any hints about their figurativeness.

Once the literality of Revelation 20 is accepted, difficulties
begin to be resolved. Consider the *chain* over which non-literal
interpreters habitually wring their hands, saying: "I suppose
that no one would insist that Satan is to be bound with a literal
chain of iron or some other metal, for Satan is a spirit and
material chains could not hold him captive for a moment."[2]
The text does not say that the *chain* that will bind Satan is to
be a chain of iron or steel or some other metal. The chain of
Revelation 20 is a spirit-chain of such a character and con-

---

[1] The Latin word for "one thousand" is the word from which we
get "millennium." The doctrine of the millennium has also been
called "chiliasm," which comes from the Greek "chilias" or "one
thousand."

[2] Floyd E. Hamilton, *The Basis of Millennial Faith* (Grand
Rapids, Mich.: Wm. B. Eerdmans Pub. Co., 1942), pp. 129-30.

sistency as would fetter and hold spirit-beings (cf. Jude 6).[1] Spirit-beings, such as Satan himself, are real beings, and only real chains can bind real beings. It is logical to see a spirit-being (angel) bind another spirit-being (Satan). That which cannot bind anyone are the figures, tropes, and shadows let out by interpreters who themselves are hopelessly entangled in them.

Some interpreters complain that "in Revelation 20 we do not understand John to write of a literal dragon or of a literal serpent."[2] It is surprising how any interpreter could miss the Johanine identification of these infernal creatures in the same verse as figurative of "the Devil and Satan" (v. 2).

As for the phrase "one thousand years," interpreters theorize that this "is clearly not to be understood as an exact measure of time"[3] but is to be considered "a long period, determined by the will and counsel of God."[4] But why not accept what God has stated six times in this text? A period of 1,000 years is surely not out of the bounds of God's counsel and will.

The evangelist D.L. Moody explains why the Book of Revelation is so often considered a figurative book: "Some one says it is the only book in the whole Bible that tells about the devil being chained; and as the devil knows that, he goes up and down Christendom, and says: 'It is no use, you reading the Revelation; you cannot understand the book; it's

---

[1] The horses in the celestial armies (Rev. 19) are also spirit-horses.

[2] Loraine Boettner, *The Millennium*, (Phila., Pa.: The Presbyterian and Reformed Pub. Co., 1964), p. 64.

[3] *Ibid.*

[4] Herman Hoeksema, *Reformed Dogmatics* (Grand Rapids, Mich.: Reformed Free Pub. Ass'n. 1966), p. 822.

too hard for you!' The fact is, he doesn't want you to understand about his own defeat."[1]

In determining the language of prophecy, if one must err, let him err in the natural process of taking God at His own word. God means what He says. Some interpreters may object by countering: "[God] means what He says, but does He fix a rigid literal limitation to His meaning? Or, in what God says, are His chosen literal objects intended to represent, to reveal and to direct to the spiritual? Therefore, is it not in this latter objective that we may discover what He means?"[2]

By the affirmation "God means what He says and says what He means," we are fully cognizant of the fact that at times what God says is signified under figures and symbols. Nevertheless, it is unsafe to make God signify more than what is proper under normal human communication. If God's sayings are to be comprehended, the interpreter must not make God indulge in an excess of signified sayings. The rule of safety and sanity is to accept the fact that God truly means what He actually says, and that He does not signify, unless factors such as context otherwise notify.

It is noteworthy that the prophecies of Daniel, although couched in visions, have had the most definite fulfillment in the history of the nations up to the present time. In the prophecies of Daniel at least, God certainly says what He means, and notifies the reader whenever figures and symbols are used.

II. FIGURATIVE LANGUAGE

Old Testament prophets, in writing prophecy, also use figurative language. Once when God commands Ezekiel to

---

[1] Cited by George N.H. Peters, *The Theocratic Kingdom* (3 vols.; Grand Rapids, Mich.: Kregel Pubs., 1952), I, 174.

[2] John Wilmot, *Inspired Principles of Prophetic Interpretation* (Swengel, Pa.: Reiner Pubs., 1967), pp. 7-8.

"put forth a riddle" (Ezek. 17:2), the command does not puzzle the prophet nor put him under a quandary. The Bible prophets couch their prophecies in figurative language whenever so commanded. Thus Hosea testifies that God has "also spoken by the prophets . . . and used similitudes" (Hosea 12:10).

A. Distinguishing Figures from Non-figures

The determination of what is figurative and what non-figurative in prophecy is a question centuries old. From Augustine's *De Doctrina Christiana* to the present, interpreters have attempted to give different rules and guidelines. A thorough understanding of the basic nature of figurative language is therefore necessary.

A *figure* is a legitimate grammatical device intended to convey more clearly an original, literal idea. It is a literal concept made more graphic.

When the Christians at Tyre urged the apostle Paul not to go to Jerusalem, their pleas were voiced plainly and non-figuratively (Acts 21:4). But when Paul arrives at Caesarea, the prophet Agabus makes the plea graphic by a figurative act:

> [Agabus] took Paul's girdle, and bound his own hands and feet, and said, "Thus saith the Holy Ghost, 'So shall the Jews at Jerusalem bind the man that owneth this girdle.' " [Acts 21:11]

In this instance, the prophet Agabus uses a figurative act to convey graphically and vividly the original idea spoken by the Christians at Tyre.

Aside from figurative acts, the Scripture also contains figurative words. In Revelation 22:15, the angel describes conditions outside the Eternal City, saying: "For outside are dogs, and sorcerers, and whoremongers, and murderers, and idolators." One must not suppose that actual, literal dogs, however loyal to man in life, will follow their evil masters to a godless eternity. The angel uses *dogs* as a figure to make more repelling and repulsive the character of evil men. Another case of the enumeration of a series of literal objects which passes over into the figurative is found in Ezekiel 39:18 ("princes of the earth, of rams, lambs, goats, bullocks, fatlings of Bashan"), where the animals cited are figurative of the various ranks of fallen men.

From the above illustrations, we may conclude that the key to determining the figurative from the nonfigurative lies in ascertaining whether a given word or act is at variance with the essential nature of the subject being discussed. If a word or act, taken in the literal sense, fails to harmonize with either the flow of thought in the text or context, or with the analogy of Scripture, it is to be understood as figurative. Otherwise, it is nonfigurative. To know the context and the flow of thought in the text under study, as well as in the totality of prophetic Scripture is to understand the distinction between what is figurative and what nonfigurative in prophecy.

B. Reasons for Figurative Language

As we have mentioned previously, figures of speech are charming ornaments of language which enliven writing and conversing. The literal sense intended by the writer or speaker is oftentimes made more vivid and graphic when conveyed through the drapery of figures.

Another reason exists for the presence of figures in prophecy. Prophecy tells of things to come. Apart from the use of some figures, the seers, under divine inspiration, would not be able to adequately convey unearthly objects and concepts without indulging in obscurity. The smiles "horses" heads *like* lions' heads" (Rev. 9:17) and "pure gold *like* clear glass" (Rev. 21:18; 21:21) are non-earthly objects made more understandable under inspiration by virtue of figures.

A third reason why prophecy must occasionally be figurative is that prophecy cannot be completely open without tempting evil men to tamper with the manner and time of prophetic fulfillment. Many Bible prophecies must be phrased in guarded and relatively cautious language. As George Peters observes: "If everything relating to the Kingdom would have been clearly revealed, in a systematic order, we are confident that such would have been *the hatred of earthly kingdoms* toward it, that no believer in it would have been safe . . . . [God withheld] a plainer statement of various particulars, lest it should *unnecessarily* excite unremitting persecution."[1]

This does not mean that prophecy is obscure and dark, for the illumination of the Holy Spirit in the heart of the consecrated interpreter will enable him to accept and understand the cautious language of prophecy—a condition which evil man can never hope to achieve. "An unsaved man simply doesn't have the capacity to understand prophecy," James Boyer points out, "the study of prophecy is impossible and meaningless to him. The Holy Spirit may use it to arouse his interest and lead him to Christ, but until he makes that response he cannot be expected to understand."[2]

Prophecy is given more primarily to reveal the future to believers than to veil it from unbelievers. For this reason, it is the obligation of believing interpreters to assign a largely non-figurative role to the prophetic Scripture.

---

[1] Peters, *Theocratic Kingdom*, I, 148.
[2] James L. Boyer, *Prophecy: Things to Come* (Winona Lake, Ind.: Brethren Missionary Herald Co., 1950), p. 7.

C. Classification of Figures of Speech

In general, there are twelve classes of figures in the Bible, as follows:

1. *Simile* — comparison of two unlike things using adverbs such as "like" and "as." Instances of similes in prophecy are:

"His eyes were as a flame of fire" (Rev. 1:14)

"The moon became as blood" (Rev. 6:12)

"Three unclean spirits like frogs" (Rev. 16:13)

2. *Metaphor* — similar to simile but without the adverb:

"Tell that fox" (Luke 13:32)

"Thou worm Israel" (Isa. 41:14)

"Jehovah is my rock and fortress" (Ps. 18:2)

"The moon shall be turned into blood" (Joel 2:31)

3. *Metonymy* — use of one name for another related name:

"If the house be worthy" (Matt. 10:13)

"Egypt where our Lord was crucified" (Rev. 11:8)

4. *Synecdoche* — similar to metonymy but physical resemblance is stressed:

"All the world should be taxed" (Luke 2:1)

"Behold the Lord maketh the earth [Israel] empty" (Isa. 24:1)[1]

5. *Personification* — citing of inanimate objects as if animate:

"The trees shall clap their hands" (Isa. 55:12)

"The earth mourneth and fadeth away" (Isa. 24:4)

---

[1] In the Bible, when the word *earth* is used in distinction from heaven, the natural and wide sense of *world* is meant; but when it is being distinguished from the Gentiles, it has the narrower meaning of *Israel*.

6. **Apostrophe**— addressing of an absent object:
"O Absalom! My son! My son!" (II Sam. 19:4)
"O death, where is thy sting?" (I Cor. 15:55)

7. **Hyperbole**— an exaggeration:
"Oh that mine head were waters!" (Jer. 9:1)
"The light of the sun shall be sevenfold" (Isa. 30:26)

8. **Irony**— the opposite is said:
"Cry aloud: for he is a god!" (I Kings 18:27)

9. **Allegory** — an extended metaphor:
"This Hagar is Mount Sinai in Arabia" (Gal. 4:24)[1]

10. **Parable**— an extended simile:
"Behold, a sower went forth to sow" (Matt. 13:3)
"The kingdom of heaven shall be likened unto ten virgins" (Matt. 25:1)

11. **Riddle** — statements designed to puzzle and hide. The Scripture contains a very restrained use of riddles. When a riddle is used, it is often indicated as such (Rev. 13:8 "Here is wisdom . . 666") or is immediately solved in the context (Samson's riddle).

12. **Fable**— animals or things in imaginary actions. There are only two fables in the Scripture. These are Jotham's fable in Judges 9 and Jehoash's fable in II Kings 14. Both of

---

[1] Here is the *only* case of an Old Testament event seen by the New Testament as an allegory. This method however is entirely different from the allegorical method of non-literal interpreters.

In Galatians 4, Paul assumes the literal existence of Hagar, Sarah, Mount, Sinai, Jerusalem, etc. He cites them as allegories *only* for the purpose of illustration. In fact, Paul himself mentions that he is about to depart from normal interpretation by adding the parenthetical statement, "which things are an allegory" (Gal. 4:24).

As Schmoeller rightly comments: "Paul to be sure allegorizes here, for he says so himself. But the very fact of his saying this

these are non-prophetic and are immediately explained in the context.

Symbols and *types* are strictly not figures of speech and have not been included in this discussion of the language of prophecy (linguistically considered). They will be discussed in the following chapter.

D. Interpreting Figurative Language

Figures are interpreted, not from the literal words making up the figures but from the original, literal sense conveyed in the use of the figure. The literal sense conveyed by the figure, and not what the figurative words literally convey, is the original sense intended by the Bible writer. Thus, once the interpreter has definitely pinpointed a figure, he must forthwith seek the original, literal intent of the writer behind the use of that figure. While appreciative of the charm of figures, the interpreter is never satisfied until the literal sense intended by the Bible writer is found.

Fortunately for the literal interpreter, the meaning intended behind the use of figures in Scripture is often given in the text or context. Careful study of the text, context, and parallel passages will almost always bring out the figures'

---

himself, the gravity of the hermeneutical difficulty disappears. He means therefore to give an allegory, not an exposition; he does not proceed as an exegete, and does not mean to say . . . that only what he now says is the true sense of the narrative" (cited by Milton S. Terry, *Biblical Hermeneutics* [New York, N.Y.: Eaton and Mains, 1911], p. 233).

The allegorical method is unknown to all the other New Testament writers and is never once sanctioned by Christ during His earthly ministry. Although it is proper to *interpret* an allegory (as we may interpret Galatians 4), it is wrong to allegorize a plain text of Scripture.

meaning. The identification and interpretation of Bible figures by the Bible itself is a rule and not an exception.

In the exclamation of John the Baptist, "Behold, the lamb of God" (John 1:29), the meaning intended by John's use of the figure *lamb* is to be found in the nature of Christ's life and death. Happily for the interpreter, the immediate context (v. 29 "that taketh away the sins of the world") clearly explains John's use of that figure.

It is significant to note that the presence of figures in the Bible never licenses so-called *figurative interpretation*. There is a world of difference between the interpretation of figures and figurative interpretation. The former is legitimate; the latter uncalled for.

In the interpretation of figures, prudence must be exercised in refusing to press the figure for meanings above and beyond its principal idea. "Behold I come as a thief" (Rev. 16:15) is not to be pressed too far!

For prolonged and extended figures which are based on analogies with parallel texts, the major point of a given figure's intended idea must be worked out first and its minor details reservedly interpreted. That is, the major scheme or outline of a given prophetic figure must be set up, with details added if and when given in the text. The eschatological "beast" is figured extensively in both Daniel and Revelation. The main outlines of the beast's end-time activities may be systematized right away. Other details should be guardedly worked out and filled in.

III. Prophecy and Poetic Speech

Poetry naturally contains an inordinate amount of figurative language. In fact, the most natural element in poetry is its figurative language. Is prophecy poetic speech and hence largely figurative?

A. View of Non-Literalists

Many non-literal prophetic interpreters readily categorize prophecy as poetry. Prophetic ecstasy is even described as poetical elevation. A.B. Davidson in *Hastings Bible Dictionary* (iv, 125) says that "Prophecy is poetical and figurative; its details are not to be pressed; they are only drapery, needed for the expression of the idea."[1]

When what is predictive is linked to what is poetic, what is predicted turns into an idealistic production of the mind. Prophecy becomes mere poetic descriptions of ideal conditions imagined by the prophets and given to help relieve some frustrations of the hour. As the liberal interpreter Shirley Jackson Case puts it, "At crucial moments in his experience the devout believer gave wings to his imagination and formulated a program of divine intervention phrased in language and imagery suited to his own immediate needs."[2] And Milton Terry adds that prophecy "was wont to soar above the evils which the prophet saw about him, and idealize a future golden age, in which all such wrongs should be abolished."[3]

On the supposition that prophecy is poetic speech, James Snowden is able to fault literal interpreters, saying, "Having laid down this [literal] principle, they then carry it out unflinchingly, turning the poetic pictures of the Hebrew prophets into literal descriptions of the coming Kingdom and accepting the absurdest consequences of such interpretation."[4]

---

[1] Cited by Augustus Hopkins Strong, *Systematic Theology* (Phila., Pa.: Judson Press, 1907), p. 136.

[2] Shirley Jackson Case, *The Millennial Hope* (Chicago, Ill.: University of Chicago Press, 1918), pp. 226-27.

[3] Terry, *Biblical Hermeneutics*, p. 336.

[4] James H. Snowden. *The Coming of the Lord* (New York, N.Y.: The Macmillan Co., 1919), pp. 196-97.

B. Nature of Hebrew Poetry

To determine whether prophecy is poetic, one should be acquainted with the nature and character of Hebrew poetry. Hebrew poetry differs radically from modern English poetry. The Hebrews were not concerned about rhythm and rhyme as we are today. They based their poetic rhythm on accented and tone syllables. Unfortunately, no person today knows what Hebrew poetry sounded like during Old Testament times, for the system of vowel pointings and accents in the Hebrew Bible was developed by scribes only in the Middle Ages.

However, we know that a great deal of elasticity is found in Hebrew poetry. Alliterations, assonances, refrains and parallelisms are used by the Hebrews in their poetry. The greatest single characteristic of Hebrew poetry is *parallelism*, in which an expression is repeated in a different way. Thus, in Psalm 15:1 ("Lord, who shall abide in thy tabernacle? Who shall dwell in they holy hill?"), the second question is a repetition of the idea, but stated differently. With this concept of Hebrew poetry in mind, let us discuss the relationship between the prophets and their use of poetry.

C. Prophets and Poetry

When writing prophecy, the prophets frequently construct their discourses following the structure of Hebrew poetry. But they introduce "only such peculiarities in rhythm and structure as could be employed as were compatible with the simple measure of Hebrew parallelism."[1]   Interpreter C. von Orelli notes that the discourses of the prophets "are expressed

---

[1] Patrick Fairbairn, *The Interpretaion of Prophecy* (reprint ed.; London: Banner of Truth Trust, 1964), p. 127.

in a rhythmically constructed rhetoric, which appears now in one and then in another form of melody, and often changes into prose."[1]

Moreover, the prophets frequently use legitimate figures of speech—sometimes quite extensively—in their prophecies. Since figures of speech (such as hyperboles, personifications, and metaphors) are very common in poetry, prophecy naturally appears to be poetic. When the prophet Isaiah writes that "then shall the moon be confounded and the sun ashamed when the Lord reigns in Mount Zion" (Isa. 24:23), he is using legitimate figures of speech.

It is true that the structure and style of prophecy often follow that of Hebrew poetry. But in no sense does this denote the capitulation of the prophet to poetical idealism or exaggeration. The Hebrew prophet is primarily a revelational preacher and peripherally an idealistic poet. To say that the prophets' imaginative minds paint extravagant scenes in prophecy is to cast aspersion on the integrity of God's servants, the prophets. God sees to it that the content of His revelation is preserved from any excessive or extravagant language. Merrill F. Unger notes: "As it was the primary aim of the Hebrew religious teachers to influence the heart and conscience, the poetical element, though never entirely suppressed, was held in restraint to further the ends of spiritual instruction."[2]

If the interpreter desires to stress the poetical in prophecy, let him therefore dwell on its structure and parallelism, not

---

[1]C. von Orelli, "Prophecy," *International Standard Bible Encyclopedia* (5 vols.; Grand Rapids, Mich.: Wm. B. Eerdmans Pub. Co., 1939, IV, 2463.

[2]Merrill F. Unger, *Unger's Bible Dictionary* (Chicago, Ill.: Moody Press, 1961), p. 893.

its revelational content. As Patrick Fairbairn aptly observes, prophecy "being a portion of the word which is all given by inspiration of God, and is as silver tried in a furnace, we must banish from our mind any idea of extravagance or conceit."[1]

IV. PROPHECY AND THE PARABLES

The prophets frequently design their prognostications in parabolic form. It is fair therefore that the prophetic parables receive this separate treatment, for they represent an unique type of prophetic material.

A. Description of Parables

A parable is an extended simile whose imageries always involve facts true to life. Unlike the fable, the parable makes no use of talking birds and beast, or of trees in council. The content of a parable is never fantastic or trivial.

Depending on how parables are classified, the Scriptures contain from 30 to 79 parables of all kinds. The Gospel of Luke has the most parables. Prophetic parables generally give information on the advance of the gospel in the world, the end of this age, the future of Jews and Gentiles, and the nature of the Millennial Kingdom.

One reason for the use of the parabolic method in Scripture is given by Richard Trench in his classic *Notes on the Parables of our Lord:* "Had our Lord spoken naked spiritual truth, how many of His words would have entirely passed away from the hearts and memories of His hearers. But being imparted to them in this form, under some lively image, or in some brief but interesting narrative, they awakened attention,

---

[1] Fairbairn, *Interpretation of Prophecy,* p. 116

and excited inquiry."[1]   Clothed in parabolic dress, a truth or moral lesson arouses attention and etches itself on the memory. The prophet Nathan prepares the heart of David for rebuke by telling him the parable of the Poor Man's Lamb (II Sam. 12:12-14).

Another reason for the use of parables is given by Christ. When the disciples ask Him, "Why speakest thou unto them in parables?" (Matt. 13:10), our Lord answers that it is a method for revealing truth to believers (v. 11) and hiding truth from unbelievers (vs. 13-15). The basic function of a parable is to reveal and conceal truth according to the receptivity of each individual's heart. It avoids the possibility of casting pearls before swine (cf. Matt. 7:6).

B. Interpreting Prophetic Parables

Since parables are legitimate figures of speech, the interpretation of parables should follow the procedure used in interpreting regular figures of speech. However, some special considerations are to be kept in mind when interpreting prophetic parables as follows:

1. *Do not make a parable walk on all fours.*—In every parable, many circumstances and details are introduced which are intended merely to complete the similitudes in the parable. The interpreter should not attempt to interpret all such details. A parable, like regular figures of speech, has but one central truth. Therefore, discover the central truth or theme which the parable is setting forth, and then explain the main circumstances of the parable in light of this truth, leaving out details incidental to its central idea.

When Christ interprets the Parable of the Tares (Matt. 13:36-43), He explains only the field, the good seed, the tares,

---

[1] Richard Chenevix Trench, *Notes on the Parables of Our Lord* (Grand Rapids, Mich.: Baker Book House, 1948), p. 1.

the enemy, the harvest, the reapers, and the final events of the harvest. He attaches no significance to the men who slept, the wheat's yielding fruit, the servants, and the question of the servants.

Unhappily, there is no determinative key as to what represents relevance in a parable and what incidental. "No special rule can be formed that will apply to every case, and show what parts of a parable are designed to be significant, and what parts are mere drapery and form. Sound sense and delicate discrimination are to be cultivated and matured by a protracted study of all the parables, and by careful collation and comparison."[1]

2. *Interpret by the context of the parable.*—Most frequently, the context of a parable contains ready-made interpretations and applications which make the explanation of a Bible parable easier. The interpreter should not therefore neglect the context of a parable.

The context of the Parable of the Good Samaritan (Luke 10:30-37) is disregarded in Origen's allegorization of this narrative: The man who fell among thieves is Adam. The robbers are the Devil and his minions. The priest stands for the Law; the Levite for the prophets. The Good Samaritan is Christ; the beast, Christ's body; the inn, the Church; the two pence, the Father and the Son; and the Samaritan's "When I come again," Christ's second coming.

3. *Interpret by proper time periods.*—There are three main time periods in parabolic prophecies: (1) the interadvent age, (2) the second coming of Christ, and (3) the millennial age. The prophetic parables are geared to these different time periods. The interpreter should not try to fit them arbitrarily into one general period, such as the present church age.

---

[1] Terry, *Biblical Hermeneutics*, p. 198.

The interadvent age, also known as the "mystery form of the kingdom," is the subject of most prophetic parables. For instance in Matthew 13, Christ uses a series of parables to describe how the kingdom program will develop during the time of the absence of the King from the earth. In these interadvent parables are seen the growth of evil within Christendom (Parable of the Leaven, vs. 31-33), the preciousness of the true church (the Hidden Treasures and Pearl, vs. 44-46), and the mixture of the true and apostate forms of Christianity (Tares among the Wheat, vs. 24-30; Dragnet, vs. 47-50). We see also the temporary rejection of Israel at the interadvent age in the parables of the Barren Fig Tree (Luke 13:6-9) and the Marriage of the King's Son (Matt. 22:2-14).

Certain other Bible parables portray the second coming of Christ. The most famous of these is probably the Parable of the Ten Virgins (Matt. 25). This parable climaxes the Olivet Discourse whose time period rightly ends at Christ's second coming. In this parable, the Bridegroom (Christ) comes to the marriage feast (millennial kingdom) and is accompanied by His bride (the church) who is unseen in the parable but understood to be present according to Jewish custom. The virgins in the parable represent living Israel who will pass through a judgment at the second advent of Christ to determine who will enter and who will be rejected from the kingdom.

A parable which portrays conditions during the millennium when the saints will be granted rulership with Christ is that of the Nobleman who goes to receive a kingdom and returns to reward his faithful servants (Luke 19:11-27).

4. *Do not prove doctrine with parable.*—Parables may be used to illustrate doctrines, but never to prove them. The Parable of the Ten Virgins does not prove either falling from grace (Arminianism) or the uselessness of empty profession

(Calvinism). The Parable of the Leaven, taken by itself, cannot prove optimism for the period of Christendom (post-millennialism).

VII

SYMBOLS AND TYPES IN PROPHECY

There are two species of prophecy which are so unique that they demand special consideration. These are symbolical and typical prophecies.

I. SYMBOLICAL PROPHECY

A. Description of Symbols

A symbol is a representative and graphic delineation of an actual event, truth, or object. The thing that is depicted is not the real thing but conveys a representative meaning. Thus, the lion in some prophecies symbolizes power and strength (cf. Rev. 5:5); the sword, the Word of God (cf. Rev. 19:15); and the sun-clad woman in Revelation 12, Israel in the tribulation.

Symbols are divided into symbols of *words* and symbols of *acts*. Symbolical *words* describe objects and things seen by the prophets in their visions. Objects such as trees, figs, candlesticks, beasts, horses and riders, and people appear as symbols in many prophetic visions. When it has been ascertained that these are truly symbols, their meanings will be found in other than that which the literal objects connote. It must be noted however that not every object seen in a vision is symbolic. Neither is it true that just because some objects in a vision are symbolic, everything else in that vision must be a symbol.

Proper names are sometimes also used as symbols in the prophetic Scripture. The context and the analogy of prophecy will generally bring these out. Utmost care must be exercised before a proper name is interpreted as a symbol. For example, while the names "David" (I Kings 12:16), "Babylon" (Rev. 17:5), and "Egypt" (Hosea 9:3) may well be symbolical, the name "Elijah" is not. [1]

Symbolical *acts* are actions performed symbolically by the prophet in order to convey specific messages to his contemporaries. Some interpreters think that symbolical acts are not performed outwardly by the prophet but are enacted only in the prophet's mind. As E.W. Hengstenberg observes: "For as the sphere of the prophets, as long as they were in an ecstatic state, was not the outward world, but the inward, *every* action performed by them in this state of ecstasy must have been an *inward* action also." [2] Interpreter Fairbairn thinks that symbolical acts performed outwardly are "exceptions." [3]

It is safer to assume that, as a rule, symbolical acts are enacted by the prophets under real life situations before spectators—not in in their heads where no one but themselves could see the performance and understand its meaning.

When Ezekiel is commanded by God to engrave the city of Jerusalem on a piece of brick, and place a pan between himself and the engraved city (Ezek. 4:1-3), this symbolical act is truly performed before spectators and not simply imagined by the prophet. Similarly, when Zechariah is described as making crowns of silver and gold for the head of Joshua the high priest

---

[1] See *Repeated Foreshadowings* for a discussion on "Elijah ", pp. 185-187.

[2] E.W. Hengstenberg, *Christology of the Old Testament* (4 vols.; Grand Rapids, Mich.: Kregel Pubs., 1956), IV, 394. [Italics added]

[3] Patrick Fairbairn, *The Interpretation of Prophecy* (reprint ed.; London: Banner of Truth Trust, 1964), p. 122.

(Zech. 6:9-15), although the act is intended by the prophet to be a symbol, he truly makes the crowns. The context will generally indicate when a symbolical act is *not* performed outwardly. Thus, the symbol of the Boiling Caldron in Ezekiel 24:3-12 is not actual, because its context definitely labels it a "parable."

B. Reasons for Symbols in Prophecy

There are at least two reasons why divine revelation must make use of symbols. *First*, future events must be brought forward to be perceived by the prophets. The prophets are not projected (as in a time machine) into eschatology, neither is the future advanced beforehand into reality. God uses *signs* to depict how the future will be worked out. As Revelation 1:1 reports, "God sent and signified it by his angel unto his servant John."

Second, prophecy sets forth the future, much of which relates to the rise and fall of nations, the outcome of wars and struggles, and the destinies of peoples and individuals. "Some of the events predicted are of such a nature, that the fate of nations depends upon them; and they are to be brought into existence by the instrumentality of men. If the prophecies had been delivered in plainer terms, some persons would have endeavoured to hasten their accomplishment, as others would have attempted to defeat it."[1]

Prophecy therefore must be in cautious language in order that only the faithful and the spiritually discerning might know. Symbols confuse unbelieving skeptics without necessarily frustrating believing Christians.

---

[1] Thomas Hartwell Horne, *An Introduction to the Critical Study and Knowledge of the Holy Scriptures* (4 vols.; Boston, Mass.: Littell and Gay, 1868), I, 378.

C. Sounding Out Symbols

Some interpreters see prophecy under a smoke-screen of pervasive symbolism. This is the mistake of Fairbairn who states: "A large proportion of the communications of prophecy came in the guise of symbolical actions."[1] Floyd Hamilton suggests that "difficulties" are resolved by interpreting prophecy "as teaching spiritual truths in symbolical language, under the religious symbolism of the age in which the prophecies were written."[2]

Literal interpreters of course admit that there are symbols in prophecy. But this is not saying that prophecy is predominantly or pervasively symbolical. Symbols are not hidden in every cranny and nook of the prophetic Scriptures, and the careful interpreter should refrain from searching for them with this assumption in mind. "Symbolic language is exceptional . . . . It is in no way characteristic of prophecy in general."[3] Even Louis Berkhof agrees by saying: *"Though the prophets often express themselves symbolically, it is erroneous to regard their language as symbolical throughout."*[4]

The best possible position to take in sounding out symbols is a two-fold one.

First, the interpreter should accept as symbols that which are so designated in the context or seen under the harmony of prophecy. King Nebuchadnezzar's four sectional image (Dan. 2), Daniel's four beasts from the sea (Dan. 7), and the women-

---

[1] Fairbairn, *Interpretation of Prophecy*, p. 128.

[2] Floyd E. Hamilton, *The Basis of Millennial Faith* (Grand Rapids, Mich.: Wm. B. Eerdmans Pub. Co., 1942), p. 144.

[3] William Kelly, *An Exposition of the Book of Isaiah* (London: C.A. Hammond, 1947), p. 46.

[4] Louis Berkhof, *Principles of Biblical Interpretation* (Grand Rapids, Mich.: Baker Book House, 1966), p. 150.

borne ephah (Zech. 5) are all symbols explainable from the context or the harmony of prophecy. "The Bible terminology is always the simplest of any literature," observes Lewis S. Chafer, "where symbolism is employed in the text, it will, almost without exception, be so indicated."[1]

Second, the interpreter should accept as symbols those elements which are truly impossible in the realm of reality, taking care to note that eschatological times are real times. The sun-clad woman (Rev. 12), the beast with seven heads and ten horns (Rev. 17), and the lifting of Ezekiel from Babylon to Jerusalem "by a lock of mine head" (Ezek. 8:3) would be impossible in actuality.

Once a prophecy is found to contain some symbols, inter-preters naturally succumb to the temptation of treating every-thing else in that prophecy as symbolic. This error is reflected in Fairbairn's statement: "The figurative character of the description, in its general features, not less than in the parti-cular images it employs, should be preserved *throughout* [Italics added] . . . . since we cannot suppose that the vision shifted from a symbolical or ideal description in one part to a plain matter-of-fact description in another."[2]

The recognition of symbols in a prophecy, however, does not carry with it the corollary that everything else in that prophecy is symbolical. The designation of symbols must be on an individual basis. Each symbol must be carefully exa-mined, weighed, and adequately supported by strong evi-dence, before a symbolical designation is made. Symbols are not cheaper by the dozen.

Thus, just because the "beast" in Revelation 19:19 is a symbol does not mean that the "kings of the earth and their

---

[1] Lewis Sperry Chafer, *Systematic Theology* (8 vols.; Dallas, Tex.: Dallas Seminary Press, 1948), IV, 259.

[2] Fairbairn, *Interpretation of Prophecy*, pp. 147-48.

armies" in the same verse are symbols. Just because the "sword" from Christ's mouth (Rev. 19:15) is a symbol does not mean that Christ and His saints in the same passage (Rev. 19:11-15) are symbols. Just because the Book of Revelation contains symbols does not mean that the millennium and the tribulational scenes described in the book are symbols.

D. When a Symbol is not a Symbol

Many interpreters err in seeing an inordinate amount of symbolism in Bible prophecy. For this reason, the interpreter should be conversant with the various situations under which symbols do not and cannot possibly exist. These situations are as follows:

1. *When the 'symbol' involves things possible.*—The prophetic Scriptures contain many descriptions of the future which are possible or plausible. In such instances, the interpreter should not assign these to the realm of symbolism. By accepting the literality of these descriptions, the interpreter gives the Scriptures the benefit of the doubt and honors God's written revelation. The locusts from the bottomless pit (Rev. 9) are not symbols of the Turks or Saracens. That these are actual locusts or locust-like creatures is a reasonable possibility.

Some prophecies appear impossible at first glance. But when these are given closer inspection, they will be found to contain plausible reasons for actual existence. An example of this phenomenon is the prophecy of Isaiah 65:25, which reads:

> The wolf and the lamb shall feed together, and the lion shall eat straw like the bullock, and dust shall be the serpent's meat. They shall not hurt nor destroy in all my holy mountain, saith the Lord.

Many interpreters reject the literality of this prophecy, commenting that for lions to eat straw like bullocks, and snakes to eat dust like angleworms, would require radical changes in their digestive systems. On the basis of this and related passages, skeptics are prompted to comment that "it was an awe-inspiring faith that dared to paint so gorgeous a picture . . . so far above all possibility of realization."[1]

Due to the alleged impossibility of anatomical changes in animals, interpreters have concluded that the prophecy is merely "a poetic description,"[2] or a figure of speech describing how "forces naturally antagonistic and at enmity with each other shall be gradually subdued"[3] in a progressively Christianized world. Saul of Tarsus, for example, "was a wolf ravening and destroying, but who was so transformed by the Gospel of Christ that he became a lamb."[4]

That this prophecy of Isaiah lies within the realm of the plausible is not hard to show. During the millennium, miraculous situations such as the longevity of man, the fruitfulness of the earth, and the elevation of the Dead Sea will occur. Moreover, since "there could have been no carnivorous beasts on earth before the Fall,"[5] and pre-Fall, Edenic

---

[1] Shirley Jackson Case, *The Millennial Hope* (Chicago, Ill.: University of Chicago Press, 1918), p. 78.

[2] Berkhof, *Principles of Biblical Interpretation*, p. 153.

[3] Loraine Boettner, *The Millennium* (Phila., Pa.: The Presbyterian and Reformed Pub. Co., 1964), p. 90.

[4] *Ibid.*

[5] John C. Whitcomb, Jr. and Henry M. Morris, *The Genesis Flood*, with a Foreword by John C. McCampbell (Grand Rapids, Mich.: Baker Book House, 1961), p. 461. For a detailed discussion of the vegetarian diet of animals before the Fall, see pages 461-64 in the same book.

conditions will be restored at the millennium, it is natural to expect the restoration of the vegetarian diet of animals on the millennial earth.

Even today, the giant Panda bear, which shares anatomical similarities with some of the most ferocious animals in existence, prefers a vegetarian diet, being more willing to munch on bamboo shoots than to stalk prey and feast on meat.

Another case of a *possibility* is found in the pearls of the New Jerusalem (Rev. 21:21). Some interpreters affirm that these pearls must be symbolical, for "it is out of all the order of nature to produce a pearl large enough to make a gate to such an immense city."[1] But the Sacred Record does not say that the gate-sized pearls will be produced by nature. The Divine Architect, who says that He will make "all things new" (Rev. 21:5), is able to create and form large pearls to beautify the Heavenly City.

Let us consider a group of prophecies which belong to the realm of the possible and are therefore not symbolical. When the millennial prophecies are normally and literally interpreted, the conclusion is unavoidable that non-resurrected inhabitants of the millennium and glorified saints and angels will mingle on the millennial earth. Many non-literal interpreters however object, saying that for mortals and immortals to mix on the earth is absurd and impossible and contrary to their concept of what millennial conditions should be.

Herman Hoeksema raises the objection: "[The literal method] involves itself in all kinds of absurdities. How can the glorified saints, in their resurrected bodies, which are spiritual

---

[1] Adam Clarke, *The New Testament with a Commentary and Critical Notes*, ed. by Daniel Curry, Vol. VI: *The Epistles and Revelation* (New York, N.Y.: Eaton and Mains, 1883), p. 630.

and heavenly, still exist and manifest themselves and operate in the old world? . . . And how can sinners and saints, the former in their old and sinful body, the latter in their glorified state, stand in the presence of Christ, the glorified Lord?"[1]

In reply, we pose a few questions: How could heavenly angels enter and presume to lodge within sinful Sodom? How could the resurrected Christ eat fish and mingle freely with His disciples after His resurrection? How could Paul and Stephen look at the glorified Christ when both of them were still mortals? How is God's Son able to take the form of "sinful flesh" (Rom. 8:3) and "dwell among men" (John 1:14), when glorified saints could presumably not mingle with earthly sinners?

On the basis of the Scripture and history, we conclude that the comingling during the millennium of mortals and immortals, the resurrected and the non-resurrected, and the earthly and the heavenly, is possible and not symbolical. What would really be an impossibility would be a prophecy such as this: One thousand human beings in mortal bodies are to occupy a room ten feet square with an eight foot ceiling.[2]

2. *When details superfluous to the 'symbol are given.*— When a 'symbol' is found, the interpreter must test his discovery by asking whether it contains details unnecessary and incidental to the intended symbolism. If so, its symbolism should be denied and its non-symbolical character affirmed.

The prophecy of the 144,000 in Revelation 7 contains so many incidental details, such as the genealogies, tribal names, and subdivided memberships of that group, that it cannot possibly be a symbol. The two witnesses of Revelation 11 must

---

[1] Herman Hoeksema, *Reformed Dogmatics* (Grand Rapids, Mich.: Reformed Free Pub. Ass'n, 1966), p. 819.

[2] Citing James Oliver Buswel, *A Systematic Theology of the Christian Religion* (2 vols.; Grand Rapids, Mich.: Zondervan Pub. House, 1963), II, 502.

be non-symbolic persons; otherwise the details given concerning their ministries, death, and resurrection, as well as the earthquake which killed 7,000 would be quite superfluous.

Perhaps the best illustration of the rule of "no superfluous details" is found in Ezekiel's prophecy of the Millennial Temple (Ezek. 40-48). Non-literal interpreters maintain that this prophecy is a symbol of the Christian church. However, this major prophecy in the Book of Ezekiel contains descriptions, specifications, and measurements of the millennial temple which are so exhaustive that one may actually make a sketch of it, just as one might of Solomon's historic temple. In fact, F. Gardiner in Ellicott's *Commentary on the Whole Bible* succeeds in sketching the layout of the millennial temple—all the while denying it is possible.[1]   This has prompted Alva J. McClain to comment that "if an uninspired commentator can make some sense out of the architectural plan, doubtless the future builders working under divine guidance should have no trouble putting up the building."[1]

The temple vision of Ezekiel is simply too extensive and contains too many details for the entire prophecy to be set aside as a symbol. If the entire vision were intended by God as a symbol of the church, what a strange and roundabout way for God to so express Himself!

3. When *the 'symbol' separates from itself.*—When handling symbols, the interpreter must accept no symbol which is found separated or apart from itself. Every symbol must behave as a composite unit and not be seen in action separated or apart from itself.

---

[1] F. Gardiner, "The Book of the Prophet Ezekiel," Vol. V of *Ellicott's Commentary on the Whole Bible*, ed. by Charles John Ellicott (8 vols.; Grand Rapids, Mich.: Zondervan Pub. House, n.d.), V, 314-32.

[2] Alva J. McClain, *The Greatness of the Kingdom* (Grand Rapids, Mich.: Zondervan Pub. House, 1959), p. 249.

Thus, the 24 elders of Revelation 7 cannot be symbolical, because one of the elders is described as coming forward to talk with John (v. 13). If the 24 elders were a symbol, it would mean that one-twenty-fourth part of a symbol came apart to talk with John!

Another popularly alleged "symbol" which is found separated from itself is the Millennial Temple of Ezekiel. In that prophecy, the temple and the city (Ezek. 48:8, 15) are definitely differentiated and distinguished. If both the temple and the city in Ezekiel 40-48 were a symbol of the Christian church, this would mean that the church becomes separated from herself.

E. Interpreting Symbols

In the interpretation of prophetic symbols, the interpreter must have the patience of Job. He must collect, sift through, and collate a large amount of prophetic data to set up a working "harmony" of prophetic symbols. Thomas Hartwell Horne calls the interpretation of symbols "almost a science in itself."[1]

1. *The immediate context.*—*The best possible material* for the interpretation of symbols is the immediate context in which given symbols are found. Under the guidance of contextual studies, the guesswork is taken out of many Bible symbols.

Interpreters of prophetic symbols generally agree that the two most symbolical books of the Bible—Daniel and Revelation— contextually explain their own symbols. Regarding the Book of Daniel, Milton S. Terry testifies: "The

---

[1] Thomas Hartwell Horne, *An Introduction to the Critical Study and Knowledge of the Holy Scriptures* (4 vols.; Boston, Mass.: Littell and Gay, 1868), II, 657.

symbols employed in the Book of Daniel are, happily, so fully explained that there need be no serious doubt as to the import of most of them..[1] And with regards to the Book of Revelation, Gerald B. Stanton witnesses: "When a symbol or sign does appear in the Revelation, it is often plainly designated as such in the immediate context, together with what the symbol represents."[2]

The four ferocious beasts of Daniel 7 are explained as four earthly kingdoms in Daniel 2. "The dragon, that old serpent" in Revelation 20:2 is immediately identified as "the Devil and Satan." "Sodom and Egypt" in Revelation 11:8 is identified at once as the city "where also our Lord was crucified" (Jerusalem). And the star which fell from heaven (Rev. 9:1) is identified as symbolic of a personal being (v. 2 "*he* opened the bottomless pit").

2. *The remote context.*—When the immediate context does not give a clear meaning to a symbol, the interpreter should examine similar or analogous symbols used elsewhere in prophecy. Thus, the "sword" which goes out of the mouth of Christ at His second coming must be interpreted in light of Hebrews 4:12 ("the Word of God"); the "time and times and half a time" (Dan. 7:25; 12:7; Rev. 12:14) must be compared with "forty and two months" (Rev. 11:2; 13:5) and "a thousand two hundred and three score days" (Rev. 12:6), as well as with Daniel's prophecy of the 70th week (Dan. 9:26-27).

Though such situations are rare, sometimes the meaning of a given symbol may not be readily understood from its near or far context. The common mistake of interpreters is to devise a

---

[1] Milton S. Terry, *Biblical Hermeneutics* (New York, N.Y.: Eaton and Mains, 1911), p. 262.

[2] Gerald B. Stanton, *Kept from the Hour* (London: Marshall, Morgan and Scott, 1964), p. 311.

symbolical interpretation for it. This does not settle the case, for it never touches on the literal meaning that is behind the use of the symbol. Charles Ryrie cautions: "If a symbol does not represent an actual or literal truth, then it must be a symbol of another symbol, and the process goes on and on and becomes completely meaningless. Somewhere along the line, a symbol *must* represent something *literal* in order that it may have meaning."[1]   As Nathaniel West puts it, "We are not to explain the symbol symbolically."[2]   In instances where the meaning of a symbol is not readily understood, one must withhold decision on the case until contexts, parallel passages, and the harmony of prophetic symbolism have been consulted.

3. *Some clarifications.*— It must be noted that not every word-picture in prophecy is a symbol. Many of these are plain, everyday figures of speech. When the angel in Revelation 19 invites the fowls to "the supper of the great God," figurative language is used. When Isaiah exclaims that "in the last days, the mountain of the Lord's house shall be established in the top of the mountains . . . and all nations shall flow unto it" (Isa. 2:2-3), the prophecy is not a symbol of the Christian church and world evangelization. The prophet Isaiah is using figurative language to describe the glory of the Jerusalem temple at the millennium.

It must also be clear that although an object or concept may not be a symbol, it can have symbolical *significance.* Thus, the 24 elders in Revelation 7 are certainly 24 glorified, actual persons, although they may well represent the saints in

---

[1] Charles Caldwell Ryrie, *The Bible and Tomorrow's News* (Wheaton, Ill.: Scripture Press Pubs., Inc., 1969), p. 22.
[2] Nathaniel West, *The Thousand Years in Both Testaments* (Chicago, Ill.: Fleming H. Revell, 1880), p. 96.

heaven. The "river of life" (Rev. 22:1) is a real and material river, although it corresponds to the abundance of spiritual life which will characterize those living in the Eternal State. The names of the apostles actually written on the walls of the New Jerusalem (Rev. 21:14) means that church saints are included in the eternal city.

Herman A. Hoyt comments regarding the New Jerusalem: "Every detail should be taken literally . . . . [But] everything in this city speaks of something about the glories and virtues of God, indicating that the materials serve a twofold purpose: (1) they are the substance of construction; and (2) they provide symbolism for contemplation."[1]

F. Symbolical Numbers

Non-literal interpreters often ascribe mystical significances or symbolical designations to numbers in prophecy. This is not justifiable. John J. Davis, after an extensive study of the symbolism of numbers in Scripture, states: "It is our conclusion that the mystical or symbolical interpretation of numbers has little place in a sound system of hermeneutics."[2]

Like prophetic words, prophetic numbers are to be accepted as actual and literal. Once, a revealing angel asks the prophet Zechariah what the latter is seeing. The prophet replies: "I see a flying roll; its length is twenty cubits, and its breadth ten cubits" (Zech. 5:1-4). When the angel then interprets the scroll to Zechariah, he ignores the numerical dimensions mentioned by the prophet. Apparently, the

---

[1] Herman A. Hoyt, *The Revelation of the Lord Jesus Christ* (Winona Lake, Ind.: Brethren Missionary Herald Co., 1966), pp. 104-5.

[2] John J. Davis, *Biblical Numerology* (Winona Lake, Ind.: BMH Books, 1968), p. 124.

"twenty by ten cubits" of the flying scroll are the actual, non-symbolical dimensions of the scroll.

When interpreters come to Revelation 9 and see an army of "two hundred thousand" (200 million), they are tempted to write it off as preposterous if literal. The entire world population at John's time did not approach this number. Never in the history of the human race until now has there been an army of this size. It is safe however to accept the size of this eschatological army, even though its number may be phenomenal.

There are times when numbers given in Scripture, while actual, also have symbolical significance. The number "7" is the most obvious example. Joshua's 7 priests blowing 7 trumpets around Jericho 7 days—and on the 7th day, 7 times around—has some significance. Or, the Book of Revelation being addressed to the 7 churches and unfolded through the 7 seals, 7 trumpet woes, and 7 bowls of wrath has symbolical significance in the repeated "7."

Nevertheless, it must be emphasized that although some prophetic numbers do contain symbolical significances, this does not negate the literality and actuality of the numbers. As Charles Lee Feinberg states: "Prophetic numbers are symbols just because and only because they are literal . . . . It is true that the seven lampstands of the first chapter of the Revelation are symbolical of completeness, but this does not imply that there are six or five lampstands. There are literally seven and the symbolic significance is derivable from the literalness of the number."[1]

II. TYPICAL PROPHECY

The subject of typology is a most difficult one. Affirmations on typology contain so many exceptions that soon

---

[1] Charles Lee Feinberg, *Premillennialism or Amillennialism?* (Wheaton, Ill.: Van Kampen Press, 1954), p. 21.

the exceptions begin to overrule the rules. Patrick Fairbairn exclaims in despair: "The landmarks that are set up today are again shifted tomorrow."[1] Oswald T. Allis says that typology is "very difficult; and it is easy to make mistakes, even serious mistakes, in dealing with it."[2] Special care is therefore necessary in the treatment of this kind of prophecy.

A. Description of Typology

The word τύπος (transliterated *type*) has the basic idea of an impression, a blow, or a stamp. New Testament writers use it to designate a pattern, a model, or an example.

The apostle Paul instructs young Timothy to be "an *example* to the believers" (II Tim. 4:12) and challenges the Thessalonians to be *"ensamples* to all that believe" (I Thess. 1:7). The word can also be used in a more technical sense: "Adam . . . who is the *figure* of him that was to come" (Rom. 5:14).

Since the word *type* is thus used quite loosely in the New Testament, an exact definition of a type based on the Scriptures is hard to make. Donald K. Campbell's definition however seems to be a successful one: "A type is an Old Testament institution, event, person, object, or ceremony which has reality and purpose in Biblical history, but which also by divine design foreshadows something yet to be revealed."[3]

There is a large group of things and events in the Old Testament which is uniquely related to elements in the New

---

[1] Patrick Fairbairn, *The Typology of Scripture* (Grand Rapids, Mich.: Zondervan Pub. House, n.d.), p. 1.

[2] Oswald T. Allis, *Prophecy and the Church* (Phila., Pa.: The Presbyterian and Reformed Pub. Co., 1964), p. 23.

[3] Donald K. Campbell, "The Interpretation of Types," *Bibliotheca Sacra*, CXII, No. 447 (July, 1955), 250.

Testament. These divinely intended resemblances beautifully depict the organic unity of the Word of God. As the *New Scofield Reference Bible* points out, typology "illustrates the principle that prophetic utterances often have a latent and deeper meaning than at first appears."[1]

The Messiah anticipated in the Old Testament becomes the New Testament's Christ (cf. Heb. 1), the Old Testament sacrificial system looks forward to the finality of the cross, and the requirement of faith as life-principle extends from the Old Testament to the New. It is these Scriptural similarities and resemblances which give birth to the subject of Bible typology.

There are of course certain things in the Old Testament which do not relate directly to those in the New Testament and should not be interpreted under type-antitype relationship. The different peoples of God (Israel and the Christian Church) are not identical concepts, and the kingdom prophesied in the Old Testament does not become the New Testament church.

As far as basic natures and characters are concerned, a type is no different from a prophecy. Prophecies and types both point to things future and are predictive in their natures. Types, however, are to be distinguished from prophecies in their respective forms. That is, a *type* prefigures coming reality; a *prophecy* verbally delineates the future. One is expressed in events, persons, and acts; the other is couched in words and statements. One is passive in form, the other active.

Some interpreters see an antithesis between typological interpretation and literal interpretation. They say that the interpretation of types automatically rules out literal inter-

---

[1] C.I. Scofield, ed., *The New Scofield Reference Bible*, new ed. edited by E. Schuyler English, *et al.* (New York, N.Y.: Oxford University Press, 1967), p. 994n.

pretation. They affirm that it is impossible to interpret typologically and literally at the same time. "It is difficult to understand how two such methods of interpretation as the *literal* and the *typological*—so completely opposite to one another as they appear to be—can not only be adopted by the same student of Scripture, but by that student pushed to their utmost limits!"[1] exclaims a non-literalist.

Typological interpretation however is not a different method of interpretation. In the interpretation of types, what is interpreted arises from the text, and is shown to have a higher application of the same sense of that text. The historical reality and existence of the type is never denied. Its typical prefigurement springs from a literal, historical base. When we say that the Passover lamb of the Jews is a type of Christ (I Cor. 5:7), we are not denying the historicity of Passover lambs vicariously slain in every Jewish home the night of the Exodus. We have projected a higher application of the Passover lambs to Christ, the Lamb of God.

Typological interpretation is therefore the unfolding of the literal base of the type, not the allegorization of that which is typified. Typological interpretation is the literal interpretation of types.

When an Old Testament element is said to be a type of an element in the New, this does not mean that one *equals* the other. One element may prefigure another, the resemblance between the two may be very close, but a type never equals its antitype. The Old Testament sacrificial lamb typifies—but does not equal—Christ. "It is one thing to say that Israel *typifies* the Church, as premillennialists rightly do; it is quite

---

[1]John Wick Bowman, "Dispensationalism," *Interpretation*, X, No. 2 (April, 1956), 184.

another thing to say that Israel *is* the Church, as amillennialists wrongly teach."[1]

B. Extent of Typology

No one has been able to compile a comprehensive list of persons, events, and features in the Old Testament which have typical significances. It is extremely difficult to define which Old Testament persons, objects and occurrences properly constitute a type.

Two extreme positions exist with regard to the extent of typology. The fanciful typologists see types lurking everywhere and anywhere in Scripture. Designation of types is by the imagination of the interpreter. This method of interpretation should not be tolerated. The other extreme declares that nothing in the Bible is a type unless the New Testament explicitly states it. That is, a type is not a type unless the New Testament specifically says so. "Whatever persons or things, therefore, recorded in the Old Testament, were *expressly declared by Christ or by His apostles* [Italics added] to have been designated as prefigurements of persons or things relating to the Old Testament," states Bishop Marsh, "such persons or things so recorded in the former are types of the persons of things with which they are compared in the latter."[2]

We must be careful that extreme positions do not influence us in deciding the extent of typology, for it is between these two extremes that the real extent of Biblical typology lies. It is safe to assume that a divinely designated type exists when

---

[1]Charles Caldwell Ryrie, *The Basis of Premillennial Faith* (New York, N.Y.: Loizeaux Bros., 1953), p. 43.

[2]Cited by Patrick Fairbairn, *The Typology of Scripture* (Grand Rapids, Mich.: Zondervan Pub. House, n.d.), p. 20.

(1) the Scripture expressly states it, (2) an interchange of name exists, and (3) there is an evident and manifest analogy. For instance, the Scripture indicates that Adam is a type of Christ (Rom. 5:14); the Passover is a type because Christ's name is interchanged with it (I Cor. 5:7 "Christ our passover"); and Joseph is typical of Christ because both lives are analogous in many respects.

Types must be based on either the explicit or the implicit teachings of Scripture. Imagination has no place in typology. A person's sanctity is not gauged by the number of types he can see in Scripture. Areas of the Bible where most typical materials might be found are the Old Testament tabernacle with its priesthood and offerings and the wilderness wanderings of the Israelites.

C. Interpretation of Types

A few do's and don'ts should be observed during typological interpretation as follows:

1. *Do use good sense.*—Types are like wild flowers; their beauty is spoiled by too much cultivation. The interpreter should refrain from poking into every nook and corner of the tabernacle or every facet of the patriarchs' lives in search of types. The interpreter must discipline himself severely in this regard.

2. *Do base the interpretation on clear analogy.*— The Scofield Bible Correspondence course cautions that "types are interpreted by their use in the New Testament and by their analogy with clearly revealed doctrines."[1]   There should be a clear resemblance, connection, and design between type and

---

[1]C.I. Scofield, *The Scofield Bible Correspondence School* (3 vols.; Los Angeles, Calif.: Bible Institute of Los Angeles, 1907) I, 46.

antitype. Jonah's experience inside the fish is a type of Christ in the tomb (Matt. 12:40), and the Passover lamb typifies the Saviour, Jesus Christ (I Cor. 5:7).

3. *Do not teach doctrines by types.*—It is legitimate for interpreters to illustrate doctrines by the use of types. Peter used the Noahic Flood to illustrate baptism (I Pet. 3:21) and Paul used the primeval creation of light to illustrate God's work of light in the heart (II Cor. 4:6). Modern interpreters may also do this. However, it is never right for modern interpreters to teach doctrines by types. Of course, the writer of Hebrews did use types to teach and prove doctrine, but Bible writers wrote under divine inspiration. We do not.

4. *Do not limit the antitype to an unreal fulfillment.*— Prefigurements of types are not necessarily always in terms of unreality, spirituality, and the heavenly. The madman Antiochus Epiphanes typifies the antichrist (Dan. 11) who will frolick in the tribulational scene in person. The unfolding of the type into the antitype can be from the literal to the literal— not necessarily from the literal to the non-literal. Louis Berkhof thus overstates the case when he says: "To pass from the type to the antitype is to ascend from that in which the carnal preponderates to that which is purely spiritual, from the external to the internal, from the present to the future, from the earthly to the heavenly."

5. *Do not exclude an expanded typology.*— As Bernard Ramm says, "Whenever we draw out an ethical principle, a spiritual rule, or a devotional from the Old Testament which is not a matter of its literal expression we have made a typological interpretation."[2]   Here we have left the area of typology proper and entered what we may call "applicational

---

[1] Berkhof, *Principles of Biblical Interpretation*, p. 262.

[2] Bernard Ramm, *Protestant Biblical Interpretation* (3rd rev. ed.; Grand Rapids, Mich.: Baker Book House, 1970), p. 262.

typology." Typology is given its widest possible definition and application, and enters the area of the non-technical.

D. Messianic Prophecy and Typology

The coming of the Messiah and the redemption He shall bring is the theme of a group of Bible prophecies known as the *Messianic prophecies*. A large percentage of these Messianic prophecies comes in the form of types.

Types of the Messiah are found not only in verbal prognostications but also in certain Old Testament offices and institutions, historical leaders, and individual happenings which prefigure Christ and His redemptive work. The Old Testament sacrifices, the Passover, the brazen serpent (John 3:14-15), the Jewish temple (John 2:19), the cities of refuge (Heb. 6:18), Jacob's ladder (John 1:45-51), aspects of the lives of Adam, Melchizedek, David, Solomon, and others, all have divinely intended typical prefigurements in Christ.

The first coming of the great Antitype Christ is an event so stupendous that many Old Testament saints actually lived life patterns which would prefigure His earthly experience centuries later. David and his devouring zeal for God's house (Ps. 69:9 "The zeal of thine house hath eaten me up") prefigures Christ's zeal for the house of God. Israel's history of sorrow and tears (Jer. 31:15) looks towards Herod's slaying of the infants following the birth of the Messiah (Matt. 2:17-28).

Many Messianic prophecies, especially in the Psalms and Proverbs, can be primarily applied only to Christ. Psalm 16:10 ("neither wilt thou suffer thine Holy One to see corruption") cannot fit the life of David whose body saw corruption.[1]   As Patrick Fairbairn observes, "The plain

---

[1] Other examples are Psalms 2 and 45.

import of the words seems to carry us directly to Christ, while it requires a certain strain to put upon them before they can properly apply to the case of David."[1]

On the other hand, one must not interpret the Messianic prophecies separate from their respective historical contexts. Herein lies the genius of typological interpretation. While allegorists see deeper and the *real* meanings under Old Testament events and lives, typologists rightly see both the historic and the Messianic blended under divine designation and unfolded according to set time factors.

---

[1] Fairbairn, *Typology of Scripture*, p. 135.

VIII

PROPHECY AND FULFILLMENT

I. KINDS OF PROPHETIC FULFILLMENT

The number of Bible prophecies which are already fulfilled is indeed large. That so many prophecies have been fulfilled proves that prophecy contains the element of fulfillment. Nevertheless, differences in the various fulfillments of prophecy exist.

A. Complete Fulfillment

Most prophecies, when designated as fulfilled, are fulfilled completely and once-for-all. When the assurance has been Scripturally given that what had been predicted has already taken place, it does not seem fair to expect more actual fulfillments of that prophecy.

The prophecies of the judgments on Babylon, Nineveh, and Tyre—long since fulfilled—await no further fulfillment. The prophecy of Bethlehem as the Messiah's birthplace (Micah 5:2) will not be fulfilled again. The prophecy of Isaiah 7:14 ("Behold, the virgin shall conceive and bear a son") allows for no successive fulfillment. None could be born of a virgin, and none could call it "his land" as Immanuel could.[1]

---

[1] The virgin's "son" could not genetically be the twelve-year-old Hezekiah born after Ahaz was enthroned, nor the children of Isaiah, nor some future unknown son of Ahaz.

175

The first coming of Jesus the Messiah is an event so exceptional and climactic that we would expect some Old Testament prophecies typical of Christ to enjoy a recurrence of fulfillment in the life of the great Antitype. And so, in a few instances, typical prophecies in the Old Testament relative to the life and work of Christ are *repeatedly* fulfilled throughout His lifetime.

Thus, after Jesus had healed Peter's mother-in-law, He healed a large number of people the next evening. Matthew 8:17 describes that evening of healing as the "fulfillment" of the prophecy of Isaiah 53:4a ("Surely he hath borne our griefs and carried our sorrows"). The fulfillment of Isaiah 63:4a is certainly not to be regarded as exhausted during that particular evening of miraculous healings. It must be seen repeatedly realized as Christ went about His ministry of healing while on earth.

B. Partial Fulfillment

Some other prophecies in Scripture have been partially fulfilled. What has been fulfilled does not exhaust the entire scope of what had been predicted. Fulfillment-wise, these prophecies continue to look forward to final and complete realization. It is unwarranted to suppose that unfulfilled portions of partially fulfilled prophecies should be spiritualized or allegorized.

Consider the words of the angel Gabriel to Mary, announcing the birth of Jesus:

> Behold, thou shalt conceive in thy womb, and bring forth a son, and shalt call his name JESUS. He shall be great and shall be called the Son of the Highest, and the Lord God shall give unto him the throne of

his father David, and he shall reign over the house of Jacob forever; and of his kingdom there shall be no end. [Luke 1:31-33]

The first portion of this prophecy has been literally fulfilled. Mary truly conceived a Son by the literal name JESUS, who was truly great and called the Son of the Highest. The remaining portion of the prophecy, *viz.*, He shall reign over the throne and house of David and of His kingdom there shall be no end, will certainly and literally be fulfilled at His second coming. The already fulfilled portion of this prophecy in the birth of Christ acts as a guarantee that the unfulfilled portion will also be literally fulfilled.

In II Samuel 7 and I Chronicles 17, God makes a promise to David which is definite and specific. The promise (also known as the Davidic Covenant) stipulates that (1) David's son will be his successor and will build the temple, (2) David's posterity will not lose the throne despite sin which will surely be punished, and (3) David's throne, house, and kingdom will be established forever. A portion of this prophecy has already been fulfilled. David's son (Solomon) truly became the successor to the throne and the kingdom was firmly established. Solomon truly built the temple and was later punished for disobedience in sin. We may therefore expect that in the person of David's greater Son, Jesus Christ, David's throne, house, and kingdom will be restored at the millennium according to prophecy.[1]

---

[1] Non-literalists, by making David's throne Christ's throne in heaven, David's house the household of faith, and the kingdom of David the Christian church, affirm that Christ is fulfilling this prophecy now with the glorified saints in heaven.

C. Double Reference

1. *Description of double reference.*—Many prophecies in the Bible contain both a near view and a far view. That is, these prophecies are given for two audiences separated in time. The fulfillment of such prophecies would relate both to nearer events as well as to more distant future events.

Edward Hartill explains this feature of Bible prophecy: "It is that peculiarity of the writings of the Holy Spirit, by which a passage applying primarily to a person or event near at hand, is used by Him at a later time as applying to the Person of Christ, or the affairs of His kingdom."[1] And J. Dwight Pentecost adds that "oftentimes in a prophecy there may be a near view and far view. Of these the near view may have been fulfilled and the far view awaits fulfillment, or both may be in the realm of fulfilled prophecy. Again there may have been a double reference to two events of similar character, both of which were in the distant future."[2]

There are many instances of double reference prophecies in the Scripture. Moses predicts concerning a prophet who would succeed him (in Deuteronomy 18) and, although Joshua fulfilled the prediction, Acts 3:22-23 applies it to the person of Jesus Christ. It is also customary for many premillennial interpreters to find Satan's career pictured in Isaiah 14 and Ezekiel 28 which describe the kings of Babylon and of Tyre respectively. Another illustration (which we shall later discuss) is the prophesied coming of Elijah which was fulfilled *typically* in the person of John the Baptist and will be fulfilled *actually* in the yet-future coming of Elijah the Tishbite.

---

[1] J. Edwin Hartill, *Biblical Hermeneutics* (Grand Rapids, Mich.: Zondervan Pub. House, 1947), p. 105.

[2] J. Dwight Pentecost, *Things to Come*, with an Introduction by John F. Walvoord (Findlay, Ohio: Dunham Pub. Co., 1958), p. 63.

Since double reference prophecies properly relate to the area of typology, the discernment of double reference in prophecy should follow the method used in the determination of types.

2. *On double fulfillment.*— Some literal interpreters use the term *double fulfillment* as a synonym for double reference. This usage however may cause some misunderstandings, for it connotes the erroneous impression that a prophecy may be fulfilled several times. Nevertheless, to say that some prophecies are capable of "double fulfillment" is far from saying that prophecy has the characteristic of manifold or successive fulfillment down history. The former properly acknowledges a message for both the immediate and the distant future; the later improperly sees the message being fulfilled repeatedly and successively.

It is true that because of the foreshortened view of the prophets, some prophecies contain a "near and far view," a "mountain peak view," or a "double reference" (even a "double fulfillment"). But this must not be stretched to mean manifold or progressive fulfillment.

For instance, Oswald T. Allis cites Zechariah 12:10 ("they shall look upon me upon they have pierced") as having a "progressive or germinant fulfillment down the Church age."[1] This prophecy however is a double reference prophecy, referring to Christ on the cross (cf. John 19:37) and to events at His second advent (cf. the context of Zech. 12). There might be an unlimited number of applications and fore-shadowments of this prophecy in believers' lives today, but applications are not fulfillments.

---

[1]Oswald T. Allis, *Prophecy and the Church* (Phila., Pa.: The Presbyterian and Reformed Pub. Co., 1964), p. 158.

3. *On manifold fulfillment.*—There are interpreters who see a lot of types, applications, tokens, and forerunners in the prophetic Scriptures. This is of course valid. The Scriptures do contain these delightfully practical and anticipative elements.

However, when interpreters start calling these elements actual *fulfillments*, the interpretation of prophecy comes to a standstill. When most everything is said to be "fulfilled," fulfillment becomes meaningless. Milton Terry, regrettably, champions this view, saying: "When a given passage is of such a character as to be susceptible of application to other circumstances or subjects than those to which it first applied, such *secondary application should not be denied the name of fulfillment* [Italics added]."[1]

It is possible of course to see present foreshadowings of certain yet-future prophecies and to make applications to the Christian church. But we are here in the area of "expanded typology." Premillennial interpreters may see a lot of types in Old Testament events and institutions, but they see them as applications and foreshadowments—not as actual fulfillments. Bernard Ramm therefore cannot be right when he observes that "multiple fulfillment is possible only if a much deeper and pervasive typical element is recognized in the Old Testament than typology proper."[2] Foreshadowments are not actual fulfillments, and expanded typology is not typology proper. Double reference or double fulfillment relates to interpretation, not to application.

Alva J. McClain pushes aside the idea of manifold fulfillment and illustrates his convictions from Isaiah 9:6-7

---

[1] Milton S. Terry, *Biblical Hermeneutics* (New York, N.Y.: Eaton and Mains, 1911), p. 402.

[2] Bernard Ramm, *Protestant Biblical Interpretation* (3rd rev. ed.; Grand Rapids, Mich.: Baker Book House, 1970), p. 263.

("For unto us a Child is born"). Normally and naturally read, this prophecy speaks of a Child to be born (in Bethlehem) whose kingdom will have no end. McClain goes on: "But now consider what happens if an unbroken mould of continuous time is clamped on the prophecy. Because the regal Child did not *immediately* take the literal throne of David, . . . the throne of David on earth is changed into the throne of God in heaven . . . . And Messiah's reign is reduced to the 'influence of the Gospel' or the rule of God in the 'hearts of men.' "[1] In other words, McClain rightly affirms that the theory of manifold fulfillment is a logical accessory to spiritualization.

4. *Double reference and double sense.*— The acceptance of double reference prophecies often conjures up the issue of double sense. That is, does double reference validate double sense? The subject of double sense will receive more extensive treatment under the chapter following. Suffice it to be said that double sense relates to the question of words while double reference relates to typology and fulfillment. If one accepts the validity of typology, one must necessarily accept the concept of double reference, but one need not accept double sense, for these are two different things.

Milton S. Terry, who rightly rejects double sense and accepts typology, says that "the types themselves are such because they prefigure things to come, and this fact must be kept distinct from the question of the sense of language."[2] Even Patrick Fairbairn, who allows a "wide and comprehensive import"[3] to Bible prophecy, wisely doubts the existence of prophecies which are "predictive of similar though

---

[1] Alva J. McClain, *The Greatness of the Kingdom* (Grand Rapids, Mich.: Zondervan Pub. House, 1959), p. 138.

[2] Terry, *Biblical Hermeneutics*, p. 494.

[3] Patrick Fairbairn, *The Typology of Scripture* (Grand Rapids, Mich.: Zondervan Pub. House, n.d.), p. 134.

disparate series of events, strictly applicable to each, and in each finding their fulfillment."[1]

D. Repeated Foreshadowing

1. *Description.*—Some prophecies in the Bible, while awaiting final fulfillment, may have repeated foreshadowings or prefigurements of that prophesied event.

The prophecy regarding the Antichrist or the Abomination of Desolation (Dan. 9:27) is foreshadowed in the inter-testamental Antiochus Epiphanes.[2]   Even at the fall of Jerusalem in A.D. 70, this prophecy is still not actually fulfilled. For the apostle John writes about the yet-future coming of the Antichrist and prefigurements of that abominable person, saying: "Children, it is the last hour, and just as ye have heard that Antichrist is coming, even now many antichrists have come into being, wherefore we know that it is the last hour" (I John 2:18). And thus, before the final arrival of the eschatological Antichrist, a number of prefigurements and foreshadowings of that person have preceded.

Again, when King Herod slays the Bethlehem infants at the birth of Christ, the wail of sorrow heard in the land is described in Matthew 2:17-18 as the fulfillment of Jeremiah 31:15 ("A voice was heard in Ramah, lamentations, and bitter weeping"). Under inspiration, Matthew sees that the actual fulfillment of Jeremiah comes at the birth of Christ, the great Antitype of prophecy, whereas Israel's long history of sorrow and grief portrays the truthfulness of Jeremiah's prophecy. It is hardly warranted to see actual repeated fulfillments of Jeremiah's prophecy down history. "Though a prophecy may be capable of successive fulfillments," states

---

[1] *Ibid.*

[2] Christ says that Daniel's prophecy regarding this man is still future (cf. Matt. 24:15).

Charles Zimmerman, "it does not seem likely that when a fulfillment is stated as such, it is intended to be accomplished in stages."[1]

2. *Prophecy of Joel.*—An illustration of foreshadowment, and one that is crucial to the interpretation of prophecy, is Peter's quotation of Joel 2:28-32 in Acts chapter 2—one of the longest quotations in the New Testament. It was made on the occasion of the descent of the Holy Spirit on the day of Pentecost. Peter's speech and the quotation from Joel follows:

> Ye men of Judea, and all ye that dwell at Jerusalem, . . . this is that which was spoken through the prophet Joel: And it shall come in the last days, saith God, I will pour out of my Spirit upon all flesh; . . . The sun shall be turned into darkness . . . . [Acts 2:14-21]

This prophecy of Joel is contextually scheduled for fulfillment just before the millennium. Why then did Peter quote it at Pentecost? Peter sees the coming of the Holy Spirit at Pentecost to be related to Joel's prophecy in a twofold way.

First, the apostle Peter recognizes the uniqueness of the day of Pentecost. This event had been predicted by Christ and expectantly awaited by the disciples (cf. John 14:16; 15:26; 16:7-15; Acts 1:8). The coming of the Holy Spirit launched a new order of things—the formation of the Body of Christ (I Cor. 12:13). Moreover, it ushered in the "end age"(I John 2:18) where the benefits of the millennial age would become more evident and might be anticipatively enjoyed by its future participants. Thus, although the millennial kingdom

---

[1] Charles Zimmerman, "To This Agree the Words of the Prophets," *Grace Journal*, IV, No. 3 (Fall, 1963), 33-34.

has not yet come, Christians are even now spiritual citizens of the kingdom.[1]

And so, the apostle Peter reminds the Jerusalem congregation that the blessings of the millennial kingdom, by virtue of Pentecost, are being applied and foreshadowed in those who already are citizens of the spiritual kingdom. Foreshadowings of the spirituality and blessings of the millennial kingdom are even now observable in the Christian church.

Second, Peter does not say that the entire prophecy of Joel was fulfilled that day at Pentecost. The customary formula of fulfillment ("that it might be fulfilled") is not used by Peter, but the introductory "this is that," a phrase not customarily used for actual, complete fulfillment of any prophecy. Peter desires to point out to the Jews that what is taking place among them is not something unheard of or induced under intoxication, but something actually conformed with their Old Testament Scriptures.

The Old Testament prophets (including Joel) had foretold an outpouring of the Spirit with supernatural signs just before the kingdom age. The apostle Peter wants to make it clear that if the Jews could accept the supernatural signs of the prophesied kingdom as Scriptural, so should they consider the church's Pentecostal signs. Peter therefore thinks it best to use Joel's prophecy by way of illustration and application. "Peter did not say that all the things Joel prophesied came to pass at

---

[1] The kingdom has both a future and a present form. The future form is the *Millennial Kingdom* spoken of so frequently in prophecy. The present form is the *Spiritual Kingdom* where God rules in the hearts of saved men today. Jesus has in mind this spiritual kingdom when He tells Nicodemus, "Except a man be born again, he cannot see the kingdom of God" (John 3:3; also Matt. 6:33, Gal. 5:21 and other passages). In addition, there is the *Eternal Kingdom* of God which comprehends the rule of God over all creation—saved and unsaved—down the ages.

Pentecost. Obviously they did not. Peter simply said that the Jews ought not to be surprised at the manifestation of the power of the Holy Spirit, since the Old Testament prophet predicted that the Spirit would come upon the nation Israel in a future time."[1]

3. *John the Baptist.*— Two prophecies in the Book of Malachi apparently indicate that Elijah the Tishbite will come again in some future time:

> Behold, I will send my messenger, and he shall prepare the way before me. [Mal. 3:1]

> Behold, I will send you Elijah the prophet before the coming of the great and terrible day of the Lord. [Mal. 4:5-6]

Many interpreters argue that these prophecies are fulfilled in the New Testament in the person of John the Baptist, and that since John was not the literal, personal Elijah, the prophecies of Malachi have therefore been *spiritually* fulfilled.

We believe however that the case of John the Baptist actually validates the literal interpretation of prophecy. We affirm that John's coming does not literally fulfill Malachi's prophecy but typifies and foreshadows the yet-future coming of Elijah the Tishbite. Here are some reasons.

First, during the birth of John the Baptist, the angel tells his parents that "he [John] shall go before him [Jesus] in the spirit and power of Elijah" (Luke 1:17). In other words, John would be an Elijah-like prophet and perform the Elijah-like ministry of turning the hearts of fathers to the children, the disobedient to the wisdom of the just, and the people to the Lord (Luke 1:11-17).

[1] Ernest Pickering, "Distinctive Teachings of Ultra-Dispensationalism," *The Discerner*, CXI, No. 11 (July-Sept., 1961), 14.

Second, when the Jews come to question John the Baptist, saying, "Art thou Elijah?" the answer John gives is clear-cut and straightforward: "I am not!" (John 1:21). On such a terse reply, John the Baptist categorically puts to rest any conjectures regarding proper identifications! If John himself denies that he was Elijah, who are we to insist that he is?[1] John did not fulfill Malachi's prophecy regarding the coming of Elijah the Tishbite; he is a type and prefigurement of the yet-future Elijah.

Third, Christ Himself, in His pronouncements on this subject, keeps the persons of Elijah and of John the Baptist separate and distinct. Christ always distinguishes between the future, personal Elijah (the Tishbite) and the present, typified "Elijah" (John the Baptist).

In Matthew 17:10-12, when answering the disciples' question that their rabbis believe in the personal coming of Elijah before the inauguration of the kingdom, Christ comes forward to emphasize two points: (1) that "Elijah truly *shall come* first and restore all things," and (2) that "Elijah *is come* already." Thus, Christ carefully divides the concept of "Elijah" into two distinct personages—one who "shall come" and one who "is come already." Christ points towards the personal Elijah the Tishbite who shall come in the future, but also accepts the typical John the Baptist, who, as the prefigured Elijah, has truly come.

Fourth, in His prescience and foreknowledge, God knows that the Jews would reject the Messiah, that the kingdom would be postponed, and that Elijah would become an anachronism if he were personally present during the first

---

[1] A non-literal interpreter says: "First, it may be that John did not know that he was the fulfiller of Malachi's prophecy" (Philip Mauro, *God's Present Kingdom* [New York, N.Y.: Fleming H. Revell Co., 1919], p. 67).

advent of Christ. If Elijah the Tishbite were resurrected in the person of John the Baptist, and the Jews had rejected the Messiah (as they did), John would have had to be un-Elijahed or remain an anamoly in God's program.

So, God sends a type or prefigurement of the prophet Elijah in the person of John the Baptist who ministers "in the Spirit and power of Elijah" (Luke 1:17). When Christ tells the Jews that "*if* ye will receive it, this is Elijah who was to come" (Matt. 11:14), He is noting the fact that John the Baptist would have been the personal, literal Elijah had the Jews accepted Christ and His offer of the kingdom.

The case of John the Baptist in relationship to Elijah the prophet is therefore a strong one for the literal interpretation of the prophetic Scripture.

II.   CONDITIONAL ELEMENT IN PROPHECY

A. The Conditional Element

That the Scripture contains conditional prophecies is apparent. In the Book of Deuteronomy, both blessings and curses prophesied could not possibly be fulfilled at the same time. Fulfillment either way would hinge on Israel's future actions. God makes this principle very clear in the Book of Jeremiah in relationship to the fulfillment of conditional prophecies as follows:

> At what instant I shall speak concerning a nation, and concerning a kingdom, to pluck up, and to pull down, and to destroy it, if that nation, against whom I have pronounced, turn from their evil, *I will repent of the evil* I thought to do unto them. [But] at what instance, I shall speak concerning a nation, . . . If they do evil in my sight, that it obey not my voice, then *I will repent of the good* with which I said I would benefit them. [Jer. 18:7-10 Italics added]

On the basis of this conditional element in prophecy, Girdlestone suggests that "It is probable that hundreds of prophecies, which look absolute as we read them, were not fulfilled in their completeness because the words of warning from the prophet produced some result . . . ."[1]

B. Bounds of Conditionality

Prophecy is not *all* conditional. Actually, it is best to affirm that by far the larger portion of Bible prophecy is unconditional. To hold otherwise is to make God's promise unreliable and His Word unsure. When prophecy is made to hinge on man's flippant ways and will, its fulfillment becomes totally unpredictable and uncertain. "When prophecy is made conditional," observes William Kelly, "its true character is annulled. In an exceptional instance, conditions may be either expressed or understood; but to take advantage of this fact, which no one disputes, in order to deny the general current of absolute prediction, is deplorably evil."[2]

We consider it a mistake for interpreters to see a widespread and pervasive element of conditionality in prophecy. This error is found in James Orr's representative statement that "Expressed or implied, this element is ever present, and ought not to be overlooked in the interpretation of prophecy."[3]   Olshausen even believes that the prophets "announced something for the very purpose that what is announced may not come to pass."[4]

---

[1] Robert Baker Girdlestone, *The Grammar of Prophecy* (Grand Rapids, Mich.: Kregel Pubs., 1955), p. 28.

[2] William Kelly, *An Exposition of the Book of Isaiah* (4th ed.; London: C.A. Hammond, 1947), p. 27.

[3] James Orr, *The Problem of the Old Testament* (New York, N.Y.: Charles Scribner's Sons, 1907), p. 463.

[4] Cited by Patrick Fairbairn, *The Interpretation of Prophecy* (reprinted.; London: Banner of Truth Trust, 1964), p. 60.

Since all prophecy does not contain the element of conditionality, what kind of prophecy does contain this element? In order for God to remain unchanged towards man, He must recognize and abide by changes in man's moral acts. Therefore, prophecies which are inherently dependent on human agency or related to man's moral actions contain the element of conditionality. The passage in Jeremiah 18:7-10 just cited illustrates this principle.

However, there are many other things concerning which "the Lord hath sworn and will not repent" (Ps. 110:4). As the apostle Paul puts it, "If we believe not, yet he abideth faithful; he cannot deny himself" (II Tim. 2:13). Even the prophet Balaam rightly witnesses to this fact, saying: "God is not a man, that he should lie, neither the Son of man, that he should repent. Hath he said, and shall he not do it? Or hath he spoken, and shall he not make it good?" (Num. 23:19).

The divine plan of the ages (including the plan of redemption), the covenants of God, the kingdom age, the final destinies of sinners and saints, are absolute predictions, contingent only upon God's ability to perform what He has promised. And the prophecies of the advents of the Messiah are certainly not dependent on the uncertain will and whims of human instrumentalities. Any prophecy therefore which depends on God or belongs to the ultimate counsels of His will should be considered unconditional.

In relationship to the program of God for the ages, an individual *per se* is exempt from necessary personal involvement and participation according to his own free will. Jesus warns Judas: "The Son of Man goeth as it is written of him, but woe unto that man by whom the Son of Man is betrayed" (Matt. 26:24). "The future things in themselves are not conditional," observes, Peters, "only our personal relationship to

the same."[1]   Although the individual's personal involvement
with Bible predictions may be said to be dependent on his own
free will, the foreknowledge of God also demands that the
person divinely designated, will, with the use of his liberty,
perform and experience that which has been predicted.

C. The Issue of the Bible Covenants

No discussion of conditionality in prophecy is conclusive
without a consideration of the Bible covenants and their
supposed conditional character. This is a significant area of
contention between literal and non-literal interpreters.

Throughout the Old Testament Scriptures, God makes
several important covenants with His people. He covenants
with Abraham (Gen. 12:1-3), with the nation Israel (Exod.
19:5-8), with David (II Sam. 7:12-16), and with future
Israel (Jer. 31:31-34). Non-literal interpreters see these
covenants (which promise a glorious future for Israel) as
conditional and contingent on Israel's obedience. As evidence,
they cite the case of the prophet Jonah whose predictions
against Nineveh supposedly hinged on the repentance of the
Ninevites. They also cite the promise which God made
with Eli's house and which was subsequently abrogated
(I Sam. 2:30).

Literal prophetic interpreters, on the other hand, affirm
that all Bible covenants (except the Mosaic) are unconditional
and absolute, being dependent solely on God for their fulfillment. The case of Jonah does not really relate to the issue of
the conditionality of covenants, for no covenant was ever made
with the people of Nineveh in Jonah's message. As for Eli, he
was living under the Mosaic economy, and that economy was
covered under a conditional covenant.

---

[1] George N.H. Peters, *The Theocratic Kingdom* (3 vols.;
Grand Rapids, Mich.: Kregel Pubs., 1952), I, 178.

The belief in the unconditionality of the Bible covenants comes from the literal and inductive study of Scripture, as shall be seen in the representative case of the Abrahamic Covenant

D. The Abrahamic Covenant

In Genesis chapters 12, 13, and 15, the covenant which God makes with Abraham promises that Abraham will have a posterity which will become a great nation, that the land of Palestine will be his descendants' everlasting possession, and that Gentile nations will participate in the promised blessing.

There are several reasons why literal interpreters regard this covenant with Abraham as unconditional. Some of the more significant reasons are as follows:

(1) The Abrahamic Covenant is expressly described as "eternal" in Genesis 17:13, 17, 19; I Chronicles 16:17; and Psalm 105:5, 10. In the New Testament, it is called "immutable" (Heb. 6:13-18).[1]

(2) The covenant is solemnized by a highly irregular and one-sided ritual. Just before the institution of the covenant, when Abraham asks the Lord regarding the land of Canaan, saying, "Lord God, whereby shall I know that I shall inherit it?" (Gen. 15:7), God tells him to take a heifer, a she-goat, a ram, a turtledove, and a young pigeon, then to divide each animal in halves (except the birds), and to set the pieces against each other for the covenantal sacrifice. But a strange thing happens. Let J. Dwight Pentecost tell it:

"When the sacrifice was prepared Abraham must have expected to walk with God through the divided animals, for

---

[1] The word "eternal" is used also of the other Bible covenants, thus: Palestinian Covenant (Jer. 32:36-44; Ezek. 11:16-21; 36:21-38), Davidic Covenant (II Sam. 23:5; Isa. 55:3; Ezek. 37:22-26); and New Covenant (Isa. 61:8; Jer. 32:40).

custom demanded that the two who entered into a blood
covenant should walk together between the parts of the
sacrifice . . . . However, when the covenant was to be entered
into, Abraham was put to sleep so that he could not be a parti-
cipant in the covenant, but could only be a recipient."[1]

(3) The covenant is repeated to Abraham even during his
several acts of disobedience (cf. Gen. 12:10-20; 16:1-16).
Why? Because God's promise to Abraham is not contingent
on human factors such as obedience, but on His own ability to
perform. When God covenants to give Abraham a posterity
and a land forever, He puts His own integrity to perform to the
test. The Abrahamic Covenant was never annulled because of
Abraham's disobedience.

"An unconditional covenant," explains Pentecost, "may
have blessings attached to that covenant that are conditioned
upon the response of the recipient of the covenant, which
blessings grow out of the original covenant, but these conditioned blessings do not change the unconditional character
of that covenant."[2]

(4) Even during New Testament times, the apostle Paul
continues to refer to the unbelieving Jews of his day as those
"to whom pertaineth the adoption, and the glory, and the
covenants" (Rom. 9:4). Later on, the apostle adds that
"concerning the gospel, they [the Jews] are enemies for your
sakes, but as touching the election, they are beloved for the
fathers' sakes" (Rom. 11:28).[3]

---

[1] Pentecost, *Things to Come*, p. 77.

[2] *Ibid.*, p. 68.

[3] Another covenant—the Davidic Covenant—is also reiterated
to Israel during her periods of apostasy and disobedience. See the
passages in Isaiah 9:6-7; Jeremiah 23:5-6; 30:8-9; 33:14-17;
Ezekiel 37:24-25; Daniel 7:13-14; Hosea 3:4-5; Amos 9:11;
Zechariah 14:4, 9; Psalm 89; Psalm 132; and many others. The
Davidic Covenant is further confirmed in the New Testament—

III. THE OLD TESTAMENT IN THE NEW TESTAMENT

There are about 600 quotations from the Old Testament in the New Testament. Roughly one-tenth of the New Testament is Old Testament material. New Testament writers apparently see the Old Testament as an excellent source from which hundreds of quotations, allusions, and applications could be made. The question is, Are these Old Testament quotations to be regarded as "fulfilled"by virtue of their being quoted?

A. An Overstated View

Many non-literal interpreters affirm that whenever the New Testament cites or mentions the Old Testament, it usually cites a fulfillment. "A foundational principle in seeking a true interpretation," affirms John Wilmot, "is the recognition that quotations from or reference to the Old Testament made in the New Testament *are not in a manner of application, but of forecast and fulfillment* [Italics added]."[1]

And thus, hundreds of Old Testament terms found in the New Testament—such as "heavenly Jerusalem" (Heb. 12:22), "royal priesthood" (I Pet. 2:9), "Christ our passover" (I Cor. 5:7), and "more perfect tabernacle" (Heb. 9:11)—are paraded as evidence that New Testament writers spiritualize the Old Testament. This is a totally inadequate, if not an outright deceitful, approach.

By giving such a broad definition to "fulfillment," non-literal interpreters clearly prejudice the case in their favor, for

---

during the birth of Jesus—by the angel Gabriel in Luke 1:32-33. An interesting provision in the Davidic Covenant is that sin in the line of David will not annul the covenant (cf. II Sam. 7:15).

[1] John Wilmot, *Inspired Principles of Prophetic Interpretation* (Swengel, Pa.: Reiner Pubs., 1967), p. 199.

such a definition assuredly points to spiritualized fulfillments. It is necessary that this technique be exposed, or attempts at refuting amillennial and postmillennial evidences will have to be on a book-for-book basis.

B. Real Use of the Old Testament

Literal prophetic interpreters believe that citations made by New Testament writers from the Old Testament Scriptures are made for purposes of illustrating and applying truths and principles as well as pointing out actual fulfillments. New Testament writers generally use the Old Testament in the following fourfold manner:

1. *Recognition of actual fulfillment.*— The New Testament cites many Old Testament prophecies showing actual fulfillments. Instances of actual fulfillment are usually introduced in the New Testament by the formula ἵνα πληρωθῇ ("that it might be fulfilled"). Although it is also true that "we find different formulas used by different writers to introduce one and the same passage; so that we cannot suppose that in all cases the formula used will direct us to the special purpose of the quotation."[1]

Instances of the New Testament citing the Old Testament to point out actual fulfillments are many. Old Testaments prophecies relating to the Messiah's birth, life, ministry, death, and resurrection are cited in detail by New Testament writers. In these cases, New Testament writers always approach Old Testament prophecy literally.

---

[1] Cited from Milton Terry by Homer A. Kent, Jr., "Matthew's Use of the Old Testament," *Bibliotheca Sacra*, Vol. 121, No. 481 (Jan.-Mar., 1964), 35.

2. *Choice of illustrative material.*—The subject of fulfillment is not the main reason for the New Testament use of the Old Testament. Actually, most New Testament quotations from the Old are made to explain or to illustrate some point.

The apostle Paul after saying that he determines not to preach Christ where He is known lest he should build on another man's foundation (Rom. 15:20), forthwith quotes Isaiah 52:15, "As it is written, To whom he was not spoken of, they shall see; and they that have not heard shall understand." By no stretch of the imagination is Paul's determination regarding his preaching methods to be considered an actual fulfillment of Isaiah's prophecy. Paul is simply using an Old Testament source to illustrate a personal principle.

The text "I am the God of Abraham" is cited by Christ Himself to prove that "God is not the God of the dead but of the living" (Matt. 22:32); the coming of the Deliverer "out of Zion" is cited from Isaiah 59:20 by Paul to explain how "all Israel shall be saved" (Rom. 11:26); and the "veil of Moses" in the Old Testament is used in II Corinthians 3:13-16 to illustrate the darkness of unsaved Israel.

A crucial instance of how the New Testament uses the Old Testament to illustrate a point is found in Hebrews 8, where the writer first talks about the Christian church and the "better" covenant mediated through Christ on the cross. Then he quotes Jeremiah 31 which describes the "new covenant" that God is going to make with Israel at the millennium. The passage reads:

> For if that first covenant had been faultless, then should no place have been sought for the second. For finding fault with them, he saith, Behold, the days come, saith the Lord, when I will make a new

covenant with the house of Israel . . . . and with the
house of Judah . . . . In that he saith, a new
covenant, he hath made the first old . . . . [Heb.
8:7-13]

By quoting Jeremiah 31, the writer to the Hebrews does
not imply that the "new covenant" of Jeremiah has been fulfilled in the Christian church. The context of Hebrews 8 does
not contain any statement affirming that Jeremiah 31 has
been (spiritually) fulfilled.[1]   If the new covenant of Jeremiah
31 were already in force and fulfilled in the church, the writer
to the Hebrews would have said so, as it would have quickly
ended the argument by those contending for the law of Moses.
However, no mention of the supposed present fulfillment of
Jeremiah 31 is made in Hebrews 8.

It is not true that every occurrence of the phrase "new
covenant" in the Book of Hebrews and elsewhere refers to
Jeremiah 31. For, while the phrase "new covenant" is repeatedly found in the Book of Hebrews and in the Gospels,
only here in Hebrews 8 is the phrase connected with Jeremiah
31—and Hebrews 8 does not teach actual fulfillment of the
new covenant.

The only New Testament passage which definitely teaches
the fulfillment of Jeremiah 31 is Romans 11:25-27. But the
trouble (for amillennialists) is, Romans 11 teaches that
Jeremiah 31 will be fulfilled not in the church now but during
Christ's second coming. Thus John F. Walvoord comments

---

[1] Although non-literalists would contend that "Christianity is
the fulfillment of the New Covenant spoken of by Jeremiah. This
fact is basic in the thinking of the New Testament writers. They *do
not tell us in so many words* [Italics added] . . . . but all the
evidence points to the fact. . . " (Roderick Campbell, *Israel and the
New Covenant* [Phila., Pa.: The Presbyterian and Reformed Pub.
Co., 1954], p. 53).

that Romans 11:27 "is a passage which amillennarians characteristically avoid as a plague."[1]

The quotation of Jeremiah 31 in Hebrews 8 is made to prove a point: that the new-found faith of the Hebrew Christians is superior ("a better covenant"), and that they should be dissuaded from further trust in the rituals and sacrifices of the Mosaic covenant which has been done away.

To prove this point, the writer to the Hebrews reasons that even in Old Testament times, the Mosaic covenant was already considered "old." For a "new" covenant had already been mentioned in Jeremiah 31. "In that he saith, a new covenant, he hath made the first old" (Heb. 8:13). Thus, the Book of Hebrews argues that the Mosaic covenant was never intended to be permanent and should now be superseded in lieu of the "better" covenant in Christ. By the illustrative use of Jeremiah 31, the writer to the Hebrews thus clinches the case for the Christian faith.

3. *Delineation of typical situations.*— New Testament writers use Old Testament typology in a twofold manner: (1) to point out specific typological fulfillments, and (2) to use them as examples and applications. The former may be found in the life of Christ who as the great Antitype fulfills the Old Testament Messianic prophecies. The latter is a broader use of typology and consists in the application of typical examples in the church and the Christian life.

The sacrifice of Christ outside the camp (typifying our fellowship in Christ's suffering—Heb. 13:13) and the calling of light out of darkness at the Creation (typifying sin and Gospel light—II Cor. 4:6) are examples of a broader use of typology.

---

[1]John F. Walvoord, *Israel in Prophecy* (Grand Rapids, Mich.: Zondervan Pub. House, 1962), p. 55.

4. *Appropriation of common concepts.*—Among any
group of people whose history is extensive, there arises in time
certain terms and concepts which, by constant usage and association, become *common property.* These concepts and terms
may be used with great effect by anyone addressing that
particular group of people, for these *common* concepts evoke
proper emotional and intelligible response.

When Christ tells Nathanael that ". . . ye shall see heaven
open, and the angels of God ascending and descending upon
the Son of Man" (John 1:51), He uses the common Jewish
acquaintance with the life-story of the patriarch Jacob. When
the writer of the Book of Hebrews mentions the "sacrifice of
praise" (Heb. 13:15), he is using a common religious concept.
And when the apostle Peter wants to show the early believers
(who were mostly Jews) their exalted position in Christ, he
uses descriptives taken from Jewish religious life, saying, "But
ye are a chosen generation, a royal priesthood, an holy nation,
a peculiar people . . . ." (I Pet. 2:9).

An important case of common property usage is found in
the phrase *Seed of Abraham.* New Testament writers see one
big household of God (Eph. 2:19; John 10:16) and several
groups within that household, each with distinct place and
responsibility. Since the various groups all relate to Abraham
either physically or spiritually (or both), New Testament
writers have properly chosen the common property phrase
Seed of Abraham to designate three groups under this common term: (1) the Israelites or physical descendants of
Abraham; (2) the faithful Israelites or the remnant within the
nation Israel—cf. Rom. 2:28-29; 9:6-13; and (3) Christians
because of their relationship to Christ who is "the Seed" (Gal.
3:16; see also Gal. 3:29; 3:3-9).

In handling common property terms during interpretation,
it is important that the original, basic usage of the term under

study be kept in mind. The terms *saints* and *the elect* do not designate New Testament believers alone. There is no basis for Hamilton's affirmation that "the term 'saints' is always applied to Christians in the New Testament."[1]   As Gerald Stanton instructs, "A few moments spent with a Bible concordance will reveal that Old Testament Jews are called 'saints.' "[2]   Like the term *elect*, *saints* is not a technical name for church members only, but may be used to identify any of God's people in all ages.

When one reads of the elect or the saints in the tribulational section of the Book of Revelation (i.e. chapters 6-18), it is a mistake to assume that these people are Christians going through the tribulation. Actually the term *saints* is used 12 different times in the Book of Revelation, but nowhere does the term *church* or *churches* appear after Revelation 3, except (obviously) Revelation 22:16. This is admitted even by posttribulationist George Ladd when he says, "God's people are seen in the Tribulation, but they are not called the Church but the elect or the saints."[3]

New Testament writers, by their use of these common religious concepts, show how practical and sensible they are in their choice of words. By no means should such usages imply that New Testament writers are spiritualizing the Old Testament.

It is an interesting fact that New Testament writers are very careful to retain the terms *Israel* and *Jews* in the proper, technical sense of Abraham's physical descendants, and not to

---

[1] Floyd E. Hamilton, *The Basis of Millennial Faith* (Grand Rapids, Mich.: Wm. B. Eerdmans Pub. Co., 1942), p. 134.

[2] Gerald B. Stanton, *Kept from the Hour* (London: Marshall, Morgan and Scott, 1964), p. 65.

[3] George Eldon Ladd, *The Blessed Hope* (Grand Rapids, Mich.: Wm. B. Eerdmans Pub. Co., 1956), p. 165.

obscure their technical meaning with common property usages.[1]   These two terms are never used in the Bible of Gentile Christians. Whether in the Old or the New Testament, Israel is always Israel and the Jews always the Jews. Under inspiration, New Testament writers have left these crucial words alone.

---

[1]The text in Galatians 6:15-16 ("Peace be on them . . . *and* upon the Israel of God") is not an exception. It is true that the word καί may mean "even" instead of "and." While amillennialists would affirm that the Greek word should here be translated "even," premillennialists say that "and" is correct.

According to the context of Galatians 6, Paul had strongly attacked the Jewish legalists, and therefore it is natural for him also to single out and remember with a special blessing those Jews who had forsaken this legalism to follow Christ, *viz.*, Jews who had become Christians. Context therefore demands that the present translation in the Authorized Version stand.

IX

HERMENEUTICAL ISSUES IN PROPHECY

Consciously or unconsciously, most interpreters approach prophecy burdened under a load of presuppositions and assumptions. This is not surprising, for it is virtually impossible to be completely neutral towards such a significant, albeit controversial, subject. Even the neglect of Bible prophecy itself represents one view of prophecy.

If one cannot hope to approach prophecy free of presuppositions, one should at least be willing to examine and evaluate these presuppositions in order that convictions might be based on studied knowledge. An attempt will be made under this chapter to set forth and discuss four common and popular assumptions relative to prophecy and its interpretation:

1. Prophecy as Prewritten History.
2. Prophecy with Alleged Double Sense.
3. Prophecy in Supposedly Colored Garb.
4. Comparative Value of the Testaments.

1. PROPHECY AS PREWRITTEN HISTORY

The concept of Bible prophecy as prewritten history is uniformly condemned by non-literal prophetic interpreters. Anton Mickelsen calls it "impossible"[1] and Milton Terry

---

[1] Anton Berkeley Mickelsen, *Interpreting the Bible* (Grand Rapids, Mich.: Wm. B. Eerdmans Pub. Co., 1963), p. 289.

brands it "the extreme literalistic error."[1] This controversial issue merits an in-depth study.

A. Issue of History Prewritten

Literal prophetic interpreters believe that prophecy is bound to history just like a calendar binds the past, the present, and the future according to regular time rules. Prophecy is not supra-historical or out of this world (so to speak), but is governed by and moves under proper historical time lines. Prophecy does not transcend regular history in the sense of its being time-less. God moves and ordains the future just as He does the past. History is "His story" and prophecy is "His story" told beforehand.

Non-literal interpreters, on the other hand, say that prophecy is *not* a record of future history, with its elements of time and progression. "Predictive prophecy is not history recorded before its occurrence,"[2] affirms Dana. "A time-centered, history-centered approach that . . . makes life revolve around events or persons and not about God . . . is either actual or incipient idolatry,"[3] warns Mickelsen.

One reason for the rejection of the concept of prewritten history lies in the fact that if the concept were accepted, then prophecy may be studied systematically and its literal fulfillment confidently expected. [4]

Although we believe that prophecy is future history prewritten, we certainly do not say that Bible prophecy is

---

[1] Milton S. Terry, *Biblical Hermeneutics* (New York, N.Y.: Eaton and Mains, 1911), pages 315 and 320.

[2] H.E. Dana, *Searching the Scriptures* (New Orleans, La.: Bible Institute Memorial Press, 1936), p. 228.

[3] Mickelsen, *Interpreting the Bible*, pp. 295-96.

[4] See Louis Berkhof, *Principles of Biblical Interpretation* (Grand Rapids, Mich.: Baker Book House, 1966), p. 148.

chronicled history with exact dates and details. Prophecy is not written in history book style. A cursory reading of the prophetic Scriptures makes this quite plain. What we mean by *history prewritten* is that the main outlines of future history—with a surprising number of details—have been revealed and will take place under regular time progression.

Bible prophecy introduces the future to us under the general schemes of ages, periods, movements, and progressions. And whenever details are additionally supplied—and these are surprisingly numerous—our knowledge of the future becomes that much more specific. As Nathaniel West says: "He who has learned to read the prophetic Dial may yet not see distinctly, nor tell precisely what o'clock it is in the kingdom of God, 'today' or 'tomorrow.' But he *can* know if it is midnight, or the cock crowing. He *can* tell if he is nearing sunrise, and 'the morning cometh!'"[1]

The phrase *prewritten history,* although capable of being misunderstood, should not be abandoned. By its emphasis on the continuity of history with prophecy, the certainty of prophetic fulfillment is upheld. The years and days of prophetic Scripture may be confidently taken at face value, and, being related to past and present history, a grand panorama of God's plan of the ages is seen. Thus, together with history past and history present, prophecy completes the story of God's program for the ages.

There are interpreters who prefer the phrase *anticipated history.* But this weakens the case for the literal interpretation of prophecy, for even non-literal interpreters anticipate some fulfillments of prophecy to be known at Christ's second coming:"We are told enough to make it clear that great and

---

[1]Nathaniel West, *The Thousand Years in Both Testaments* (Chicago, Ill.: Fleming H. Revell, 1880), p. 96.

glorious events lie ahead, but the manner in which those events are to be accomplished, and the details . . . are left largely unexplained."[1] Neither is the phrase *antedated history* suitable, for it erroneously implies specific dating.

It may be noted that when the bond between prophecy and history is toned down or severed, liberal interpreters and skeptics are emboldened to reject the possibility of any prophetic fulfillments. Down the centuries, skeptics have refused to acknowledge even prophecies that are already fulfilled, saying that these prophecies have been written clandestinely *after* the events had transpired. The rejection of the concept of prophecy as prewritten history lies behind such an erroneous supposition. Thus prophecy can easily be brushed aside once its miraculous connection with history is denied.

B. Real Purpose of Prophecy

The solution to the question of prophecy as history prewritten ultimately lies in discovering the purpose of God's gift of prophecy.

1. *View of non-literalists.*— Non-literal interpreters believe that the purpose of the gift of prophecy is "(a) Not to enable us to map out the details of the future; but rather (b) To give general assurance of God's power and foreseeing wisdom and of the certainty of his triumph . . . ."[2]

In other words, prophecy serves only to give us the general assurance that God knows all things. It is not to be used in mapping out the future. Prophetic students must not turn

---

[1] Loraine Boettner, *The Millennium* (Phila., Pa.: The Presbyterian and Reformed Pub. Co., 1964), pp. 103-4.

[2] Augustus Hopkins Strong, *Systematic Theology* (Phila., Pa.: Judson Press, 1907), p. 139.

prophets! And when fulfillment does come, a second purpose of prophecy is achieved, *viz.*, the accreditation of the prophet and the authentication of his message. "It is the historical fulfillment of a prophecy which proves that it came from God,"[1] states Allis.

Interpreters who view Bible prophecy under his light can never be sure how prophecy will turn, out, for they consider prophecy fully understandable only in the light of its fulfillment. "Prophecy is like the German sentence," A.H. Strong says, "it can be understood only when we have read its last word."[2]

Needless to say, the sight of prophetic charts being unrolled by interpreters greatly provokes non-literalists who issue taunting comments such as this: "[As we] study their complex diagrams and charts that sometimes look like intricate geometrical problems, we are reminded of the epicycles by which the old astronomers explained the movements of the heavenly bodies."[3]

2. *View of literalists.*— We agree with non-literal interpreters that God gives prophecy to prove His omniscience and to authenticate the prophets. But this by no means represent the "primary purpose"[4] of prophecy. To await an uncertain future affords neither confidence nor cheer in God's Word.

The primary purpose of God's gift of Bible prophecy is to guide, cheer, and edify His people *beforehand.* Prophecy does not look backward but forward. It does not authenticate and vindicate as much as it anticipates and prognosticates.

---

[1] Oswald T. Allis, *Prophecy and the Church* (Phila., Pa.: The Presbyterian and Reformed Pub. Co., 1964), p. 27.

[2] Strong, *Systematic Theology*, p. 140.

[3] James H. Snowden, *The Coming of the Lord* (New York, N.Y.: The Macmillan Co., 1919), p. 190.

[4] Boettner, *The Millennium*, p. 101.

"Behold, the former things are come to pass and new things do I declare: before they spring forth I tell you of them" (Isa. 42:9).

It is true that when we allow prophecy to exceed the limits of what present history can attest, we are affirming what is historically uncheckable. But this is where faith not sight comes in. The basic nature of prophecy elicits confidence in taking God at His Word. As William Kelly warns: "No maxim is more erroneous than the assumption that it is only the event which explains. This is to deny the proper value of prophecy, till, becoming history in effect, it ceases to be prophecy."[1]

C. Absolute Certainty of Prophecy

There are at least two reasons why we may confidently expect the fulfillment of the events of Bible prophecy. These are (1) the integrity of God, and (2) the precision of prophetic transmission.

1. *God stakes His integrity on fulfillment.*— In Isaiah 46:9-11, God goes on record to guarantee that what He has predicted He will perform: "I am God, and there is none like me, declaring the end from the beginning, and from ancient times the things that are not yet done . . . . I have spoken it, I will also bring it to pass; I have purposed it, I will also do it" (Isa. 46:9-11).

Once when Jesus was describing the future, He volunteered this surety: "If it were not so, I would have told you" (John 14:2). This parenthetical statement represents an iron-clad guarantee that, when dealing with the future, the Word of God provides an assured record. Of the 23 verses in

---

[1] William Kelly, *An Exposition of the Book of Isaiah* (4th ed.; London: C.A. Hammond, 1947), p. 27.

Zechariah 8 which describes the earthly Messianic kingdom, 15 repetitions of "Thus saith the Lord" and "Saith the Lord of hosts" can be found.

When God repeatedly signs His Name to prophecy, we may bank on His intent to perform and fulfill. When we interpret the prophecy of the Mount of Olives being split in two at the coming of Christ (Zech. 14:4), it is safe to possess what Hengstenberg scoffingly calls "a faith that would remove mountains."[1]

2. *Prophecy is given with precision.*— When transmitting the record of Bible prophecy, God takes pains to make certain that the prophets understand the visions being shown to them and that they write with precision the things being seen and heard.

The prophet Ezekiel is instructed on the necessity for precision: "Son of man, mark well, and behold with thine eyes, and hear with thine ears all that I say . . . and mark well the entering in of the house . . . ." (Ezek. 44:5). And in Zechariah 4 and 5, the revealing angel repeatedly intrudes into the prophet's vision to quiz him, "What seest thou?" "What is this?" "Knowest thou not what these are?"

Moreover, the prophets make certain that what is being revealed before them is accurately seen and heard even to the details. The prophets inquisitively question their revealing angels with freedom and insight. Daniel tells of a representative experience: "And I heard but I understood not. Then said I, 'O my Lord, what shall be the end of these things?'" (Dan. 12:8). As Edward J. Young observes, "The prophet, even though in the condition of receiving a vision, was never-

---

[1] E.W. Hengstenberg, *Christology of the Old Testament* (4 vols.; Grand Rapids, Mich.: Kregel Pubs., 1956), IV, 382.

theless capable of conversation and intelligent discourse."[1]
The fact that the prophets respond so perceptively with in-
cisive questions implies that they expect God to be revealing—
not hiding —things. It also implies that the prophets fully
expect the fulfillment of the events which they are seeing.

If prophecy is not intended to foretell real future events,
the painstaking effort and precision made by God and the
prophets as well as the large amount of details given during
the transmission and reception of prophecy would have been
totally irrelevant and meaningless. If God had intended to
merely convey general principles and statements of comfort,
cheer, and assurance, He need not have taken time and
trouble to communicate so many prophetic details and to
ensure that such details are precisely recorded. The fact that
God goes into so much effort in the prophetic Scriptures
proves that Bible prophecy should be accepted at face value,
for it contains trustworthy revelations of the future.

D. A Word of Caution

Since the concept of prewritten history does provide a
historical basis on which computations might be made, it has
been misused as a springboard for the setting of dates. But the
fault does not lie in the concept of prewritten history but
rather in its misapprehension and misapplication.

The interpreter who wishes to indulge in speculative date-
setting must remember that computative prophetic interpretation is forbidden by Scripture. Christ says in Matthew
24:23-24 that those who try to figure out the time of His
coming and to predict "Lo, here is Christ, or there" are
themselves false christs and false prophets. One thing com-

---

[1] Edward J. Young, *My Servants the Prophets* (Grand Rapids,
Mich.: Wm. B. Eerdmans Pub. Co., 1952), p. 188.

manded of all believers in this regard is to "Watch . . for ye know neither the day nor the hour in which the Son of man cometh" (Matt. 25:13).

It is true, in a sense, that the literal approach to prophecy facilitates the setting of dates. But it is also true that once date-setting starts, interpreters must spiritualize and allegorize prophecy in order that the rest of the prophetic Scriptures might fit into the date schemes thus evolved. Interpreters who set dates work under a hodge-podge of spiritualized prophecies enmeshed in a literalistic framework.

A classic example of date-setting and spiritualization is found in Seventh Day Adventism.[1] The beginning of troubles for the Adventists in this respect is their belief in post-tribulationism. Being posttribulational, it is easy for them to place the Roman papacy in the Great Tribulation, for they identify Sunday observance which allegedly started under the papacy as the "mark of the beast." Calculating the end of the tribulation period when the Lord is supposed to return, the Adventists decided and announced the year of Christ's return as 1844.

With the precise date of Christ's coming settled, the Adventists tried to fit their scheme of the tribulation into

---

[1] Date-setting also forces the Jehovah's Witnesses to spiritualize the advent of Christ by saying that Christ came in 1914, but that He went into the "spiritual temple" in heaven to start an invisible reign. This in turn forces the Witnesses to interpret Jesus' description of the separation of sheep and goats at His coming as a long drawn-out affair. Their theory states that from the year 1918 and on up to the Battle of Armageddon, people are being separated, based on their attitudes toward the Jehovah's Witnesses. The Battle of Armageddon begins when the Devil (represented in the nations) attacks the New World Society, and Christ and His angels return. Everyone outside the Society shall perish.

contemporary historical events, as follows: " . . . the great earthquake was the one that occurred on Nov. 1, 1755, which affected nearly 4,000,000 square miles and destroyed 60,000 persons in six minutes in the city of Lisbon; that the darkening of the sun took place on May 19, 1780, when New England and parts beyond . . . were plunged into darkness for at least fourteen hours, beginning about 10 A.M.; and the falling of the stars was seen on November 13, 1833, when the earth . . . experienced an amazing meteoric shower."[1]

When the 1840's came with no visible return of Christ, the Adventists then invented the theory of a heavenly sanctuary with two compartments. They explained that Christ did leave heaven, but that it was from the holy place of heaven to the other compartment (the Holy of Holies).

The doctrine of the "millennium" by Seventh Day Adventism is both strange and unique. Although it does not directly spring from date-setting, this doctrine employs abject spiritualization of prophecy. The Adventists believe that Christ will come before the millennium, and that He will reign with the saints in heaven, not on the earth. The earth, instead of being blissful during this "millennium," will become the prison-house of Satan and will be the scene of utter desolation.

At the end of this terrible "millennium," the wicked dead shall be resurrected so that they might be deceived by Satan, after which fire from heaven will extinguish Satan and his followers on the burning earth. Then will follow the actual happy "millennium" (or the Eternal State) when the earth will be cultivated, animals will be tamed, and so on.

Thus, Seventh Day Adventism contains elements from amillennialism, postmillennialism, and premillennialism. It

---

[1] Cited from Norman F. Douty, *Another Look at Seventh Day Adventism* (Grand Rapids, Mich.: Baker Book House, 1962), p. 131.

agrees with amillennialism in seeing no future for Israel and
no earthly reign of Christ on earth. It agrees with postmillennialism in accepting a heaven-located millennium when
Christ comes. And it agrees with premillennialism in saying
that Christ will come before the millennium.

II. PROPHECY WITH ALLEGED DOUBLE SENSE

The possibility of the prophetic Scriptures having a double
sense is an issue of long-standing among interpreters.
Patrick Fairbairn describes it as "a controversy on which
some of the greatest minds have expended their talents and
learning, and with such doubtful success on either side, that
the question is still perpetually brought up anew for
discussion."[1]   Despite this difficulty, one who wishes to
interpret prophecy must sooner or later settle the issue of
double sense.

A. Supposed Reasons for Double Sense

When an interpreter considers the written words of
prophecy to be shallow and superficial, and then seeks a
deeper level of meaning, import, or implication, he has accepted the concept of double sense. Interpreters who see
double sense in prophecy often base their position on the
supposition that since God knows all things, His word must be
full of hidden meanings and senses.

Roman Catholic theologians admit a *fuller* sense in
prophecy "precisely because the message is God's."[2]   Some

---

[1] Patrick Fairbairn, *The Typology of Scripture* (Grand
Rapids, Mich.: Zondervan Pub. House, n.d.), p. 107.
[2] Bruce Vawter, "Fuller Sense," *Catholic Biblical Quarterly*,
XXVI, No. 1 (Jan., 1964), 92.

Protestant interpreters similarly affirm: "As a rule, it is an unwarranted procedure to ascribe to an author thoughts or sentiments which he did not expressly utter. . . . But in the case of the Word of God, these restrictions do not apply. . . . In giving man His Word, He was not only perfectly aware of all that was said, but also of all that this implied. . . . Therefore *not only the express statements of Scripture, but its implications as well must be regarded as the Word of God."* [1]

Another reason why interpreters see double is that spiritual truths and realities cannot allegedly be expressed adequately in earth-bound language and must therefore be clothed in analogous or symbolical language. As *The Bible Handbook* puts it, "It is a necessity of the human intellect that facts connected with the mind, or with spiritual truth, must be clothed in language borrowed from material things" [2] Oswald T. Allis agrees: "God is a Spirit; the most precious teachings of the Bible are spiritual; and these spiritual and heavenly realities are often set forth under the form of earthly objects and human relationships." [3]

Yet another reason often cited is that the prophets mean one thing while God really has other things in mind. Gustav Oehler first affirms that "the prophets when beholding the future . . . mean just what they say," [4] but then goes on to explain that the thoughts of the prophets and the Holy Spirit had differed. A.B. Davidson is frank: "We may say quite

---

[1] Louis Berkhof, *Principles of Biblical Interpretation* (Grand Rapids, Mich.: Baker Book House, 1966), pp. 158-59.

[2] Joseph Angus, *The Bible Handbook* (2nd ed. rev.; New York, N.Y.: Nelson and Phillips, 1873), p. 215.

[3] Allis, *Prophecy and the Church*, p. 17.

[4] Gustav Friedrich Oehler, *Theology of the Old Testament*, rev. and trans. by George E. Day (New York, N.Y.: Funk and Wagnalls Pubs., 1883), p. 491.

fairly that the meaning or reference in the mind of the Spirit of Revelation was different from that of the Hebrew writer. To the one the whole was in view . . . while the view of the other was necessarily limited."[1]

While applauding the sincerity of the prophets, therefore, interpreters have excused the prophetic writings on the basis of the prophets' ignorance of the Divine meaning. The Divine and the instrumental writers of Scripture do not supposedly see eye to eye.

B. Some Replies to Double Sense

1. *On infinite mind and the written words.*— Concerning the reasoning that Infinite Mind should not be confined to mere words and thus a double sense should be sought, we state that God is not trying to reveal in Scripture all that He knows—only what He intends man to know. The prophet Moses is clear: "The secret things belong unto the Lord our God; but those things which are revealed belong unto us and to our children forever" (Deut. 29:29).

Of course, in the written revelation of Scripture, divine condescension is necessary, otherwise revelation would be in some incomprehensible, heavenly language. But this does not mean that God, in His choice of written, earthly language, is hampered in the expression of all that He wants man to know. The use of written language by God who created it in the first place means that He considers human language adequate in conveying divine revelation. Written language assuredly finite, does not mold God's revelation; it serves to convey it.

2. *On spiritual realities and the written words.*— The reasoning that spiritual reality can only be expressed

---

[1] A.B. Davidson, *Old Testament Prophecy*, ed. by J.A. Paterson (Edinburgh: T.& T. Clark, 1903), p. 327.

figuratively or as accomodated material objects springs from two unfounded presuppositions: (1) that spiritual realities should involve ethereal, abstract things, not material, earth-based objects; and (2) that material, earthly objects cannot be spiritual. Non-literal interpreters refuse to accept a material New Jerusalem, the earthly kingdom, and the millennial temple, because these are supposedly spiritual ideas forced to appear in material garbs.

But why must spiritual realities be restricted to the abstract and the ethereal? And cannot actual, earth-based objects be spiritual?[1]   "Simply because the kingdom is on the earth does not mean that it cannot be spiritual. If that were so, then no living Christian could be spiritual either, for he is very much a resident of the earth. Neither is it necessary to spiritualize the earthly kingdom in order to have a spiritual kingdom. If that were so, then again no Christian could be spiritual until he is spiritualized."[2]

---

[1] A number of Old Testament prophets predict a condition of millennial joy, peace, and gladness in the Spirit (cf. Isa. 35:10; 51:11; Ezek. 11:19; Joel 2:18-32; etc. If anything is apparent from the interpretation of these millennial prophecies, it is this, that the millennial kingdom—though earth-based—will be characterized by the highest ideals and standards of spirituality. The joys of Eden, the universal filling of the Spirit, faith giving way to sight, and hope springing up into realization, will be the heritage of all millennial participants.

Moreover, just because the worship centre of the world will be at Jerusalem does not mean that millennial inhabitants cannot also worship Him in their hearts. Critics, such as Hengstenberg, misunderstand this, saying: " . . . Zion is the only place of prayer for the whole earth, and therefore the only place where any one can have part in God Himself. These consequences of a literal interpretation ought to be well considered before anyone resolves to adopt it"(*Christology of the Old Testament*, IV, 389).

[2] Charles Caldwell Ryrie, *Dispensationalism Today* (Chicago, Ill.: Moody Press, 1965), p. 174.

It is interesting to note that liberals who attempt to get *truths* by spiritualizing the written words of Scripture never arrive at the spiritual truths they set out to secure.

3. *On God's and the prophets' intent.*— The prophetic Scriptures are of dual authorship: God the primary Author and the prophets as instrumental writers. The instrumental writers write under divine inspiration. While exercising their respective individualities and personalities, they write what God Himself would have written.

During God's communication of revelation, the prophets are expected to *understand* what is being revealed (cf. Dan. 10:11, 14). Between two persons, the most elementary principle of understanding is that both ascribe the same meaning to that which is being spoken or written. Surely, God would not load His Word with multiple senses, and then command the prophets to understand. This would be against the rules of fair play. God, in all fairness to the recipients of revelation, could not have intended one thing and then tell His instrumental writers to hear, see, and record other things. It is safe to suppose that God preserved the Scriptural writers from writing anything different from or contrary to what He had in mind to reveal.

C. A Conclusion

There is no sure way of determining the true sense of Scripture apart from the grammatically conveyed, customary sense of its written words. If the plain words of Scripture cannot be trusted, then all is lost.

Some would insist that, while they reject the literal sense in favor of a deeper sense, they are not looking for a double sense but the *real* sense. As Louis Berkhof explains, "certain parts of Scripture have a mystical sense which, in such cases, does not constitute a second, but the real sense of the Word of God."[1]

Nevertheless, regardless of what one calls it, the moment one leaves the plain, normal, and customary usage of the words of Scripture, and goes searching for the mystical, hidden, and super-added sense, that approach spells "double sense." Milton Terry's summation is certainly valid: "We may readily admit that the Scriptures are capable of manifold practical *applications*; otherwise they would not be so useful for doctrine, correction, instruction in righteousness . . . . But the moment we admit the principle that portions of Scripture contain an occult or double sense we introduce an element of uncertainty in the sacred volume, and unsettle all scientific interpretation."[2]

D. Typology and Double Sense

The existence of legitimate types in the Bible is often held up to justify double sense in the Bible. Since a type necessarily prefigures an antitype, interpreters have jumped to the conclusion that types justify double sense.

The issue of single versus double sense, however, concerns the question of the language of prophecy *per se*, while typology concerns the persons and events typified by the language of the type. Typology therefore does not represent an exception to the principle of single sense. Milton Terry says: "The types themselves are such because they prefigure things to come, and this fact must be kept distinct from the question of the sense of language."[3]

---

[1] Berkhof, *Principles of Biblical Interpretation*, p. 140.
[2] Terry, *Biblical Hermeneutics*, p. 383.
[3] *Ibid.*, p. 494.

III. Prophecy in Supposedly Colored Garb

It is almost standard among detractors of the literal method to explain prophecy in terms of "Jewish coloration," "historical and contemporary garb," "Israelitish form," and "Old Testament outer covering." By these slogans, interpreters mean that the words or form of prophecy are colored and influenced by the prophets' contemporary backgrounds, and should therefore not be interpreted literally.

A. Theory of Prophetic Coloration

"Prophetic coloration" is the theory that the record of prophecy comes to us encrusted in the historical experiences of the prophets and is colored by the thought forms of their life and times. *"The place, the time, the circumstances, and the prevailing view of the world and of life in general, will naturally color the writings that are produced under those conditions of time, place, and circumstances."*[1]   Roderick Campbell enumerates the factors influencing prophetic form, saying, "Much of the language of the Psalms and the Prophets is couched in the terminology of the Old Covenant, its history, its rulers, its symbolism, and its poetry."[2]

There are interpreters who theorize that the Old Testament prophets *purposely* choose familiar objects and concepts in order that their readers may better understand what they are saying, for, had they spoken in language and introduced scenery of the future, they would have been hopelessly unintelligible to their contemporaries.

---

[1] Berkhof, *Principles of Biblical Interpretation*, p. 114.
[2] Roderick Campbell, *Israel and the New Covenant* (Phila., Pa.: The Presbyterian and Reformed Pub. Co., 1954), p. 62.

Thus, Mickelsen believes that "the language of the prophet is colored by all his present and past surroundings . . . . When he refers to transportation, he talks about horses, chariots . . . ."[1]   Another insists that the visions in the Book of Revelation are taken from the writings of Isaiah, Ezekiel, Daniel, and Zechariah "which the Seer had no doubt studied enthusiastically either before or during his time of seclusion in Patmos."[2] Some interpreters even say that the prophets use the terminology of the Mosaic economy in describing the future "to prevent the Old Testament economy from sinking too much in the estimation of those who lived under it"![3]

There are interpreters also who explain that the prophets inadvertently used familiar and contemporary objects because God brings the revelation down to their levels. God allegedly manipulates things before the prophets so that spiritual, heavenly ideas appear in earthly, comprehensible garb.

James Orr supports this view: "It would have served no end, and is, under ordinary conditions, psychologically inconceivable, that the prophet should have been lifted out of all the forms of his existing consciousness, and transported into conditions utterly strange and inapprehensible by him."[4] Gustav F. Oehler agrees: "[Prophecy] is brought down as far as its form is concerned, to the plane of the beholder himself; hence prophecy is affected by the limits of the sphere of Old

---

[1] Mickelsen, *Interpreting the Bible*, p. 295.

[2] Robert Baker Girdlestone, *The Grammar of Prophecy* (Grand Rapids, Mich.: Kregel Pubs., 1955), p. 111.

[3] Thomas Hartwell Horne, *An Introduction to the Critical Study and Knowledge of the Holy Scriptures* (4 vols.; Boston, Mass.: Littell and Gay, I, 378-79.

[4] James Orr, *The Problem of the Old Testament* (New York, N.Y.: Charles Scribner's Sons, 1907), p. 462.

Testament life, the special relations of the age, and the individual peculiarity of the prophet." [1]

"And so," Charles Feinberg ruefully observes, "upon each
individual interpreter devolves the colossal task of determining what is essential in prophecy and what is connected
with the mere outward form of expression." [2]

B. Fulfillment of "Colored" Prophecies

Interpreters who see prophetic coloration are not sure
about the kind of fulfillment they should expect of prophecy.
In general, they posit two theories of fulfillment: (1)
Prophecies are fulfilled in greatly changed forms, and (2)
Prophecies are fulfilled in real, but non-actual, forms.

1. *In greatly altered form.*— Since the Old Testament
prophets allegedly borrow the thought-forms of their contemporaries to mold their prophecies, it is to be expected that the
fulfillment of these prophecies would differ greatly from the
written words or form of the prophecies. "A thousand things
may intervene to modify the expression of the idea in its
fulfillment. For the prophet spoke of the kingdom of God as it
was in his day . . . . He represented this as coming about in
the conditions of his own time, while these conditions have
quite disappeared . . . . Therefore it will come about in a way
very different from his conception of it." [3]

No more of prophecy should therefore be expected than a
realization of its essential, central idea! As James Orr says,
"The *idea* becomes the main thing; the particular *form* of the
idea—the clothing of imagery or detail it receives—is less
essential." [4]   Prophecy thus comes to a virtual standstill, for

[1] Oehler, *Theology of the Old Testament*, p. 491.
[2] Charles Lee Feinberg, *Premillennialism or Amillennialism?*
(Wheaton, Ill.: Van Kampen Press, 1954), p. 20.
[3] Davidson, *Old Testament Prophecy*, pp. 168-69.
[4] Orr, *Problem of the Old Testament*, p. 461.

its written form is suspect and its fulfillment need not be precisely demanded.

2. *In real versus actual forms.*— Other interpreters accept the fulfillment of prophecy, but on condition that objects and events described in prophecy be fulfilled in equivalent and not identical concepts, in real and not actual situations.

According to this principle of equivalents, predictions concerning future warfares (involving war implements such as bows, arrows, shields, horses, chariots, and riders) and those concerning the restoration of now-extinct nations (such as Moab, Elam, and Ammon) will be realized in their modern equivalents and counterparts. "Prophecies involving horses or chariots or camels are dealing with *transportation*; prophecies speaking of spears and shields are about *armaments*; and prophecies about surrounding nations are about God's *enemies*. A strict literalism would hardly be appropriate. . . ."[1]   Thus, Anton Mickelsen uses this equivalency rule in his covenantal position of "People of God=Jew and Gentile in Christ;"[2] and J. Barton Payne explains Micah 5:6 ("They shall waste the land of Assyria with a sword") by equating it to "a military operation in such a general location."[3]

At first glance, the principle of equivalents seems acceptable enough. It allows for real fulfillment of prophecy and avoids those "ancient" elements in prophecy. By its acceptance of prophetic fulfillment in real versus actual— instead of real versus ideal—situations, this theory is of course an improvement.

---

[1] Bernard Ramm, *Protestant Biblical Interpretation* (3rd rev. ed.; Grand Rapids, Mich.: Baker Book House, 1970), p. 244.

[2] Mickelsen, *Interpreting the Bible*, p. 297.

[3] J. Barton Payne, *The Theology of the Older Testament* (Grand Rapids, Mich.: Zondervan Pub. House, 1962), p. 492.

But the theory of equivalents has no real Scriptural pre-cedent. The larger number of Bible prophecies already fulfilled are found *not* fulfilled in equivalents. Charles Ryrie cites an example: "But suppose this principle of equivalents were applied to Micah 5:2. Then any small town in Palestine in which Christ would have been born would have satisfacto-rily fulfilled the prophecy."[1]

This theory, like Rabbi Hillel's "rule of equivalents," handily opens the floodgates to spiritualization. It can be used in so broad and wide-ranging a fashion that spiritualization of prophecy results.

C. Solution to Prophetic Form

It should be noted that there are many predictions in Scripture which concern events and persons in the prophets' days. The form and language of these prophecies, given under divine inspiration, would of course be divinely "slanted" to the thought forms of the prophets' contemporaries. And Mickelsen's observation that "the predictions of God's doings were given to a particular historical people to awaken and stir them"[2] would apply in such cases.

But this is only part of the story. Many prophecies in Scripture definitely concern the future and are given to enlighten future people. These prophecies do not arise from the needs of the hour or from contemporary events in the days of the prophets but from God's foreknowledge of the future. It is logical to assume that, in these instances, contemporary intelligibility would cease to exist as a factor in the mind of the Bible writer. The prophet faithfully transcribes the

---

[1] Ryrie, *Dispensationalism Today*, p. 89.
[2] Mickelsen, *Interpreting the Bible*, p. 287.

revelations, knowing that they would be suited for comprehension by a future audience.

Actually, there is a revelation made especially to the prophets that in their prophesying they need *not* know its "what" and "what manner of time," for they are not acting for themselves but for a coming age. The apostle Peter explains this revelation: "Unto them it was revealed that, not unto themselves but unto us they did minister . . ." (I Pet. 1:12). The prophets, even apart from the safeguard of inspiration, would therefore have had no reason and freedom to slant the forms of prophecy for the benefit of their contemporaries. "It is incredible that God should in the most important matters, affecting the interests and the happiness of man and nearly touching His own veracity, clothe them in words, which, *if not true* in their obvious and common sense, *would deceive* the pious and God-fearing of many ages."[1]

In the interpretation of prophecy, the acknowledgement of form and fulfillment as identical should be a basic principle. What is predicted will be literally fulfilled. No historical and contemporary adjustments—with obvious exceptions for figurative and symbolical languages—need be made on the language of prophecy. The interpreter should constantly ask himself, What if the descriptions were actual and true, how else would God have said it? One must trust the descriptions of the writers of Scripture. As W. A. Criswell reasons: "Is hell a place of fire and brimstone? Is heaven a place of gold and pearl and beautiful mansions? When I speak of these things, *I ought to use the language of God* [Italics added]. I have never been to heaven; I have never been to hell. I must trust God's revelation. . . . I must speak God's language and when I do, I

---

[1]George N.H. Peters, *The Theocratic Kingdom* (3 vols.; Grand Rapids, Mich.: Kregel Pubs., 1952), I, 315.

find that I am speaking in the power and unction of the Lord."[1]

It is interesting to note that whenever the prophets want to inform their readers that what they have written is couched in forms based on earthly analogies, they drop hints to this effect in the context. When Zechariah sees non-earthly creatures with wings similar to that of earthly birds, he notes the analogy ("their wings like bird's wings," Zech. 5:9). The seer John, hearing a voice similar to an earthly animal's, uses a comparison ("a loud voice, as a lion roareth," Rev. 10:3). It is safe to assume that when no hints are given or implied in the context regarding form changes, what the prophets report must be actual. When the apostle Paul is caught up to paradise and hears "unspeakable words, which is not lawful for a man to utter" (II Cor. 12:4), he clearly informs his readers regarding this fact.

D. The Case of Ancient Armaments

There are some prophecies which, in describing eschatological warfares, predict that the weapons to be used then will be bows and arrows, chariots and horses, spears and shields. Are these to be taken literally? If we adhere strictly to the proper view of prophetic form, we must consider these weapons the same as that which will be used in eschatology. They must not be equated with vastly different modern war devices, as the H-bomb or the supersonic jet fighter. Interestingly, these prophesied military instruments though centuries old have not yet been made obsolete. The horse, for instance, is still used in warfare on certain kinds of terrain.

It is significant to note that eschatological warfares will occur under conditions very different from what we now have.

---

[1] W.A. Criswell, *Why I Preach that the Bible is Literally True* (Nashville, Tenn.: Broadman Press, 1969), p. 91.

The eschatological warfare described in great detail in Ezekiel 38-39 is said to occur under peculiar circumstances (note the elements of stealth and secrecy in Ezekiel 38:11, and the defeat of the invaders by supernatural causes in Ezekiel 38:22). It is therefore not unthinkable that the war implements to be used in eschatological times should be of the unusual kind.

John F. Walvoord mentions one reason for the use of these relatively primitive weapons: "Modern missile warfare will have developed in that day to the point where missiles will seek out any considerable amount of metal. Under these circumstances, it would be necessary to abandon the large use of metal weapons and substitute wood such as is indicated in the primitive weapons."[1]

E. The Case of Now-Extinct Nations

Perhaps the most controversial issue on the form of prophecy is with regards to Israel's ancient neighboring nations. The prophetic Scripture contains predictions of Israel's ancient neighbors, mentioning them by name (e.g. Assyria, Philistine, Elam, Ethiopia, Moab, and Edom) and predicts that they will play a part in the eschatological scene.

Non-literal interpreters usually equate these names with Israel's present-day enemies in general, or spiritualize them as the "moral and spiritual conquests, to be wrought by the church over the nations."[2]   Non-literalists confidently dares

---

[1] John F. Walvoord, *The Nations in Prophecy* (London: Pickering and Ingles Ltd., 1967), p. 116. It should be clarified that Walvoord does not insist on the validity of the explanation.

[2] Joseph Addison Alexander, *Isaiah* (2 vols.; New York, N.Y.: John Wiley, 1852), II, 165.

the literalists to continue the literal approach in the case of these now-extinct nations, calling it "the insanity of literalism."[1]   "This one point alone," points out Boettner, "that the nations referred to have disappeared from the face of the earth and so could play no part in a future restoration of Israel, should be sufficient proof that the literalistic method of interpretation cannot be defended."[2]   Even Bernard Ramm observes that "the strict literalist would *ex hypothesi* have to call for not only the restitution of Israel, but all the nations which surround Israel."[3]

But when the literalist starts making some concessions to symbolism here, his opponents gleefully complete the encirclement: "If the symbolical description of the worship of the coming age and of the enemies of Israel be granted, what then becomes of the boasted literal interpretation of prophecy as a general principle?"[4]

The proper interpretation of prophecies concerning now-extinct nations, however, does not demand the revival of ancient nations, complete with ancient names. There are terms and phrases in the Scripture —such as titles and official designations —which would naturally and customarily change in form down the centuries. Literal interpretation, which accepts the customary meanings of words, takes these into consideration. Basic functions and compositions of persons and objects, remain, while official titles and customary designations may alter down the years.

Thus, prophecy speaks of *king, prince,* etc., which could well be fulfilled by persons with titles such as *president, premier,* and *chairman* (including *king* and *prince*) in escha-

---

[1] Davidson, *Old Testament Prophecy*, p. 476.
[2] Boettner, *The Millennium*, p. 88.
[3] Ramm, *Protestant Biblical Interpretation*, p. 247.
[4] Louis Berkhof, *The Kingdom of God* (Grand Rapids, Mich.: Wm. B. Eerdmans Pub. Co., 1951), p. 164.

tological times. The persons and objects prophesied remain
the same; their titles and designations may naturally and
customarily change.

Modern anthropologists have noted that the generic population of Israel's ancient neighboring nations are still trace-
able today. Amillennial interpreters admit as much, saying:
"What shall we say of the opinion, found among archaelogists,
that the lowest social class, today, in Palestine and the
surrounding countries, includes descendants of the ancient,
native Canaanites, and their neighbors? . . . Prophecy, thus
understood, might still be regarded as fulfilled."[1] If anthropologists are able to trace (sketchily perhaps) the
descendants of Israel's ancient neighbors, surely God can be
depended upon to know the ancestries and lineages of all
nations and peoples, in fulfilling His own prophecies regarding
the nations.

F. Summation

In conclusion, we affirm that prophecy is hermeneutically
neither colored nor garbed. If it appears so to be, it comes
from the existence of figures and symbols, which are almost
always so designated or implied in the context. All other cases
of prophetic coloration belong to the colored spectacles of
theological and philosophical presuppositions. Alva J. Mc-
Clain calls it "a set of colored spectacles through which Old
Testament prophecy is read, distorting some things and
filtering out completely other things."[2]

---

[1]Martin Jacob Wyngaarden, *The Future of the Kingdom in
Prophecy and Fulfillment* (Grand Rapids, Mich.: Baker Book
House, 1955), p. 186.
[2]Alva J. McClain, *The Greatness of the Kingdom* (Grand
Rapids, Mich.: Zondervan Pub. House, 1959), p. 260.

The proper view of prophecy with regard to its form is that whatever God ordains will speedily seem natural. "The day will surely come," says Gaebelein, "when all these events will come to pass. Much may be obscure at this time but God will see to the fulfillment in His own time."[1]

IV. COMPARATIVE VALUE OF THE TESTAMENTS

An issue of major importance in prophetic interpretation is whether revelations in the New Testament are superior to those in the Old, and whether the interpretation of prophecy should accordingly be adjusted. To this issue we now address ourselves.

A. View of Non-Literalists

Non-literal prophetic interpreters insist that Bible prophecy should be interpreted in light of New Testament truths and doctrines. In approaching prophecy, they affirm, the New Testament should be elevated above the Old Testament and made the sole guide and yardstick of interpretation. "In the first place the main guide to the interpretation of the Old Testament is certainly to be found in the New,"[2] states Berkhof. "I am convinced," says George Ladd, "that we must interpret the Old Testament by the New and not vice versa . . . ."[3]

The elevation of the New Testament over the Old Testament revelation during prophetic interpretation is a

---

[1] Arno C. Gaebelein, *The Prophet Ezekiel* (New York, N.Y.: By the Author, 1918), p. 266.

[2] Berkhof, *Kingdom of God*, p. 160.

[3] George Eldon Ladd, *Crucial Questions about the Kingdom of God* (Grand Rapids, Mich.: Wm. B. Eerdmans Pub. Co., 1952), p. 14.

method generally used to simplify eschatology and spiritualize prophecy. Note the reasoning of Berkhof: "It is very doubtful, however, whether Scripture warrants the expectation that Israel will finally be re-established as a nation and will as a nation turn to the Lord. *Some Old Testament prophecies seem to predict this, but these should be read in the light of the New Testament* [Italics added]."[1]

Under the excuse of giving greater honor to the New Testament, interpreters gain a semblance of respect and a following. "The more one studies the complexities and details of the [literal] theories, . . . the greater is one's relief when one turns to the simple teachings of the Word of God. If one follows the New Testament leadings . . . , the whole picture of the 'last things' as taught in the Word of God seems so simple and easy to understand . . . ."[2]

B. View of Literalists

Literal interpreters of prophecy of course readily admit that there is everything right in being guided by the New Testament. Because of Christ's advent, the New Testament certainly gives clearer light on many aspects of Scriptural revelation. And since the New Testament contains church truths which are more directly applicable to the Christian, it should rightly be valued for its precious teachings. But these are partial aspects of the total picture.

In the interpretation of the Scripture, we must deal with all areas of divine revelation. In areas such as soteriology, Christology, and ecclesiology, the Old Testament would not have as

---

[1] Louis Berkhof, *Systematic Theology* (4th ed. rev.; Grand Rapids, Mich.: Wm. B. Eerdmans Pub. Co., 1949), p. 699.
[2] Floyd E. Hamilton, *The Basis of Millennial Faith* (Grand Rapids, Mich.: Wm. B. Eerdmans Pub. Co., 1942), pp. 139-40.

VALUE OF THE TESTAMENTS 229

much to say as the New Testament. But in areas such as theology proper, angelology, anthropology, eschatology, and the ageless moral and ethical truths and precepts, the Old Testament is as revelational as the New.

It is true that the New Testament is the apex of divine revelation. But the whole revelational process leading up to this culmination is just as important. The doctrine of progressive revelation demands that newer revelations—given by God to complete, supplement, and (sometimes) supersede older revelations—must never supplant, annul, or superimpose on prior revelations.

When the Jews ask Jesus, "We heard from the Law that Christ abideth forever; and how sayest thou, The Son of Man must be lifted up?" (John 12:34), they ask the question of whether Old Testament revelation has been contradicted? The answer is that the Old and the New Testament are not mutually exclusive; both will be realized and fulfilled.

The interpreter who slights one portion of the Scripture in favor of another portion—when the revelation contained in the one is a continuation of or a repetition of the other—is himself splitting the Scriptures. To use the New Testament as a wedge to split the revelational process or as a magic wand to spiritualize away "older" revelations is to remove the basis from the entire revelational process.

The way of safety and respect is to take the entire Scriptures as one complete unit and not to exalt one portion of God's Word to be more credible over the other. "To make one portion of Scripture to be the sole and exclusive arbiter and interpreter of the Bible," says Peters, "is subversive of the light given in a general analogy and a continuous Divine plan."[1]   Charles Feinberg adds: "Any system that dif-

[1] George N.H. Peters, *The Theocratic Kingdom* (3 vols.; Grand Rapids, Mich.: Kregel Pubs., 1952), I, 64-65.

ferentiates as between later and former prophecies as to value, or between prophetic and didactic portions of Scriptures as to worth, stands self-condemned as false and inadequate."[1]

Here is perhaps one reason why destructive critics of the Bible have chosen to concentrate their attacks mainly on the Old Testament. They know full well that if the Old Testament falls, the New Testament topples. It is a phenomenon of the Scripture that any lowering of either one of its parts ultimately recoils on the other. To value one Testament above the other is to disparage both.

New Testament writers have a high estimate of the revelation contained in the Old Testament, and in writing the "new" revelation, they build on the validity of the "old." Christ tells the Jews to search the Old Testament Scriptures for the latter testify of Him (John 5:39). Abraham tells the rich man (Luke 16) that, "They have Moses and the prophets; let them hear them" (v. 29). The Bereans search the Old Testament to see if these things are so (Acts 17:11-12). And Paul affirms that he is preaching "no other things than those which the prophets and Moses did say should come" (Acts 26:22).

By their continued quotation from the Old Testament, constant reference to the covenanted promises and prophecies in the Old, and absolute respect for the prophets in the Old, Christ and the apostles indicate their high esteem of the Old Testament Scriptures. Should present-day interpreters do less?

C. "Calling the Bluff"

Suppose we do use the New Testament as sole guide in the interpretation of prophecy, what then?

---

[1] Feinberg, *Premillennialism or Amillennialism?*, p. 27.

First, a future earthly kingdom must be acknowledged. In Christ's teachings, He repeatedly deals with the physical, social, political, and religious aspects of the kingdom foretold in the Old Testament. The Olivet Discourse of Christ (Matt. 24) contains not only prophecies of His second coming but also of the coming kingdom. The apostle Peter in Acts 3 points to a "restitution of all things" (v. 21) occurring *after* the second coming of Christ, and identifies that period as that "which God hath spoken by the mouth of all his holy prophets since the world began" (v.21).[1]

Many interpreters are acquainted with the experience of Albert Schweitzer who shuts himself up with the Greek New Testament and comes out affirming that the New Testament teaches an earthly kingdom.[2]

Second, the future tribulation period must be recognized. In II Thessalonians (clearly a non-symbolical text), the apostle Paul introduces the Tribulation, the Man of Sin, and even the Tribulational Temple where the Man of Sin will sit as if he were God. Christ in Matthew 24 predicts an unprecedented and unique period of the "tribulation," saying: "For then shall be great tribulation, such as was not since the beginning of the world to this time, no, nor ever shall be" (v. 21).

There are interpreters who maintain that "the unparalleled tribulation spoken of in our Lord's prediction was visited upon the Jews when the Roman destruction took effect about 70 A.D."[3]   However it is debatable whether A.D. 70

---

[1] Amillennialist Oswald T. Allis admits that "This is a difficult passage" (*Prophecy and the Church*, p. 137).

[2] New Testament passages describing the kingdom on earth are Matt. 9:27; 21:9; 22:41-46; Luke 1:32-33; John 7:42; Acts 2:25-36; 13:22, 23, 34, 36, 38; 15:6; Rom. 1:3; II Tim. 2:8; Rev. 5:5; 22:16; etc.

[3] John Wilmot, *Inspired Principles of Prophetic Interpretation* (Swengel, Pa.: Reiner Pubs., 1967), p. 236.

in terms of suffering and judgment was more *unparalleled* than Hitler's Second World War. One thing is sure: according to Christ, there will be a period of tribulation on earth which will dwarf all others in the severity of its divine judgments and human suffering. This period is yet to come.

Third, the New Testament says that the nation Israel will be restored. In Romans 11, the apostle Paul decisively argues that Israel has *not* been cast away or superseded but temporarily set aside. Israel will again be restored. The "man without a country" will be vindicated as the person with an earthly country guaranteed him by the Owner of the Universe. A brief exegesis of Romans 11 is in order.

With the opening exclamation of Romans 11:1 ("Hath God cast away his people? God forbid!"), the apostle to the Gentiles argues that God is not through with His chosen people, the Jews. God still has a remnant in Israel according to the election of grace (v. 5), and the present blindness of Israel (vs. 8-10) will be removed at the second coming of Christ (v. 25).[1]

Then, Paul uses the illustration of the Olive Tree, which represents the place of privilege first occupied by Israel. Since Israel was disobedient, she was "broken off" from the Olive Tree (v. 17a), and another body (the church) has been grafted into the Olive to partake of its root and fatness (v. 17b). This newly grafted body, however, is not to boast of its new-found position, for the broken off branch (Israel) can and will be easily re-grafted (v. 23), and "so all Israel shall be saved" (v. 26). Then, the apostle adds an observation: "For the gifts and calling of God are without repentance" (v. 29).

---

[1] A Louis Harris survey in modern Israel recently reveals that only 13% of the Jews in Israel today would describe themselves as having even an interest in God.

The decisiveness of Romans 11 on the restoration of Israel has led many covenant theologians to admit something like this: "Whatever it is that Paul has in view, we can be sure of this: all the glorious things spoken of Israel and Zion will be fulfilled in a manner which is capable of embracing the whole of racial Israel."[1]

Frederick the Great once asks of his chaplain, "Give me in one word the proof of the divine origin of the Bible." The chaplain replies, "The Jews, your Majesty."

D. Revelation 20 and the Old Testament

An accusation often leveled against literal prophetic interpreters is that the connection between the kingdom prophesied in the Old Testament and the millennium described in the New Testament is man-made and artificial. Revelation 20, detractors point out, makes no mention of the Jews, Jerusalem, Palestine, or anything earthly. As postmillennialist John Wilmot observes, "The one millennial occurrence in the New Testament (and in the whole Bible) makes mention of none of the earthly characteristics so arbitrarily placed within that thousand years (Rev. 20)."[2]   And amillennialist Louis Berkhof charges that "The only Scriptural basis for this theory [of premillennialism] is Revelation 20:1-6, after an Old Testament context has been poured into it."[3]

The amillennial theologian Archibald Hughes once directed a lady to study the New Testament for information on the millennial kingdom. According to the report of Hughes, this is what transpired: "Many months later this lady come to me and said she had followed my advice but could not find a

---

[1] R. Campbell, *Israel and the New Covenant*, p. 205.
[2] Wilmot, *Prophetic Interpretation*, pp. 5-6.
[3] Berkhof, *Systematic Theology*, p. 715.

single reference to any millennium. I said, 'Well, you have learnt something.' She replied, 'I have learnt nothing!' I said, 'You have learnt something, for you know now that the New Testament has nothing to say about a millennium.' "[1]

Despite the intense pressure on literal interpreters to separate the Old Testament prophets from Revelation 20, the link between the prophets and the Book of Revelation must be maintained. Here are some reasons.

First, Revelation 20 is at the end of a long chain of revelations concerning the kingdom. To demand that Revelation 20 repeat the features of the kingdom already revealed by the prophets in the Old Testament is to be presumptuous. Would interpreters, for instance, reject the orthodox doctrine of the resurrection simply because I Corinthians 15 describes only the *kind* of resurrection bodies? The Book of Revelations has over 200 references to the Old Testament. It should therefore be understood in conjunction with and within the context of the Old Testament Scriptures. One must not attempt to interpret the Book of Revelation with the Old Testament shut.

Second the concept of the kingdom is actually a major element in New Testament eschatology. When Jesus was born, the angel Gabriel proclaims that He "shall reign over the house of Jacob forever, and of his kingdom there shall be no end" (Luke 1:33).[2]   Throughout Christ's earthly ministry,

---

[1] Archibald Hughes, *A New Heaven and a New Earth* (Phila., Pa.: The Presbyterian and Reformed Pub. Co., 1958), p. 209.

[2] Christ's kingdom is here said to be endless; the millennium is one thousand years. How do we reconcile the two? The Bible is clear that immediately after the thousand years, millennial conditions will give way to the Eternal State where God will still be on the throne. Therefore, the thousand-year· period should be conceived of as the first stage or phase of the Eternal Kingdom of God.

the subject of the Messianic kingdom on earth looms large and clear. Even up to the day of the Lord's ascension, the disciples are still asking, "Lord, wilt thou at this time restore again the kingdom to Israel?" (Acts 1:6). What the Old Testament first reveals regarding the kingdom, the New Testament supplements, and Revelation 20 now climaxes. The progress of revelation on the kingdom from Genesis to the Apocalypse is a natural one.

Third, in Revelation 20, "souls" are said to have "lived and reigned with Christ a thousand years" (v. 4). Since the souls *lived,* these can not be souls only but resurrected souls with resurrected bodies. This is emphasized in the contrast found in the next verse (v. 5) where the wicked dead "lived not." What would be the reason for the reunion of soul with body at the resurrection if there were no physical, material existence in the future? As interpreter J.A. Seiss correctly states, "a spiritualized earthiness is simply a white-washed sepulchre . . . . It has no substance, no reality for the soul to take hold on."[1]

Thus, while it is true that Revelation 20 makes no specific mention of things earthly and material, it implies as much in its description of the souls who *lived.* The immediate context of Revelation 20 —the preceding chapter—is full of descriptions regarding "earth," "nations," and "down out of heaven," as it records the coming of Christ. The revelation of the kingdom which the Holy Spirit gives in Scripture is wonderfully arranged without it being tiresomely repetitious.

Fourth, if we remove Old Testament kingdom prophecies from Revelation 20, we are left with no good reason why the thousand-year period should be inaugurated.

---

[1] J.A. Seiss, *The Apocalypse* (London: Marshall, Morgan and Scott, Ltd., n.d.), p. 494.

Without the continuity of Old Testament revelation, the millennium of Revelation 20 becomes an expendable appendage in the eschatological framework. "If there are no Old Testament prophecies which demand a literal, earthly fulfillment, then the purpose of the millennium becomes partially obscure,"[1] points out J. Ramsey Michaels of Gordon Divinity School.

Covenant premillennial interpreters generally accept the literality of the thousand-year period of Revelation 20 but refuse to tie this in with the Old Testament kingdom prophecies, affirming that the latter should be spiritualized, since the church has appropriated the promises. But if the church fulfills the Old Testament kingdom promises, and the kingdom is now on earth in the church, what then would be the rationale for another period of the kingdom at the millennium? In his effort to mediate," observes Michaels, "Ladd will be criticized on one side for making the millennium a mere appendix to his system, and on the other for retaining it at all! A satisfactory middle-of-the road position on this thorny and divisive question has not yet been found."[2]

For the literal prophetic interpreter, the doctrine of the kingdom is based on prophecies in the Old as well as the New Testament. By refusing the support of Old Testament prophecies which he generally assigns to the church, the covenant premillennialist knocks out the very basis of the kingdom he claims to await.

---

[1] J. Ramsey Michaels, review of *The Gospel of the Kingdom*, by George Eldon Ladd, in the *Westminster Theological Journal*, XXIII, No. 1, (Nov., 1960), p. 48.
[2] *Ibid.*

X

THEOLOGICAL DEBATES ON PROPHECY

Although the subject of Biblical hermeneutics is properly considered apart from theological discussions, it is not difficult to see how theological presuppositions and assumptions often determine and influence the choice of hermeneutics. Under this chapter, we shall discuss four significant theological issues which vitally influence and affect the hermeneutics chosen by many interpreters of prophecy. The issues are as follows:

1. The unifying principle of prophecy.
2. Israel and the Church.
3. Dispensationalism and Soteriology.
4. To be, or not to be, consistent.

I. THE UNIFYING PRINCIPLE OF PROPHECY

Conservative interpreters agree that God's revelation is not a hodge-podge of unrelated pictures, but comes under a unifying principle or theme which also reveals God's plan of the ages. The issue among theologians however is, What is the unifying principle of prophecy and how should prophetic interpretation be accordingly adjusted?

A. A Restrictive Viewpoint

A large number of interpreters, especially amillennialists and covenant premillennialists, believe that the sole unifying

principle of prophetic Scripture is the "principle of redemption." God's purpose and plan for the ages, they affirm,
is entirely redemptive. As Roderick Campbell says, "The
grand theme and purpose of prophecy is spiritual redemption
in history and time."[1] James Snowden adds: "One increasing
purpose runs through it [Scripture] from beginning to end,
the redemptive plan of God who so loved the world that he
gave his only begotten Son. . . . This golden thread is woven
into its entire web and texture and binds it into coherency and
harmony."[2]

This concept of the unifying theme of prophecy comes
from the teaching of *Covenant Theology*.[3] At the heart of
covenant theology is the belief that all relationships between
God and man from the beginning of time to its end are covered
under two covenants—Covenant of Works and of Grace.

The *Covenant of Works* is said to be made by God with
Adam before the Fall in the Garden of Eden, promising him
life or death in return for obedience or disobedience. Had
Adam not sinned during the course of this (unspecified) pro-
bationary period, he would have entered into immortality and
eternal life.

The *Covenant of Grace* is said to be made by God with the
elect sinner after the Fall, promising him salvation and eternal

---

[1] Roderick Campbell, *Israel and the New Covenant* (Phila.,
Pa.: The Presbyterian and Reformed Pub. Co., 1954), p. 57.

[2] James H. Snowden, *The Coming of the Lord* (New York,
N.Y.: The Macmillan Co., 1919), pp. 47-48.

[3] The designation *Covenant Theology* is misleading. It gives the
wrong impression that this theological system is based on the Bible
covenants (e.g. Noahic, and Davidic covenants), when in reality it
means belief in the theoretical covenants of *Works* and of *Grace*.

[4] Herman Hoeksema, *Reformed Dogmatics*, p. 220.

life through faith in Jesus Christ. This covenant is said to extend from the Fall to the end of time (i.e. the second coming of Christ). Since it comprehends virtually the whole period of the Scriptures, this covenant of grace is used by covenant interpreters to explain and to interpret the whole of Bible history and prophecy. [1]

Strangely enough, despite the overwhelming importance given to it, the covenant of grace is nowhere found in the Scripture. An agreement between God and man regarding salvation in the Garden of Eden could conceivable have been made, but its existence as a covenant proper is based on inference. Such an agreement is conceivable but it is not clearly revealed.

The covenant of grace concept demands that all prophecy be explained in terms of redemption and in light of the cross. "The great theme of the Bible is God and His redemptive dealings with mankind. . . . Whether the figurative or 'spiritual' interpretation of a given passage is justified or not depends solely upon whether it gives the true meaning [redemptive meaning]." [2]

Since Christ's redemption culminates at the cross, all post-cross prophecies are to be interpreted in terms of ideas, principles, and truths. As Campbell reasons: "The greatest of all predicted events has therefore already been fulfilled in the fact that Messiah *has already come.* Every other prediction (not

---

[1] Some covenant theologians have also posited a third covenant called the *Covenant of Redemption*, which is said to be an agreement between the Triune Godhead before man's creation, whereby the Father is to offer up the Son, the Son to give Himself as sacrifice for sin, and the Holy Spirit to apply the benefits of the Son's death to the elect. However, the validity of this covenant has been challenged even by covenant theologians themselves.

[2] Oswald T. Allis, *Prophecy and the Church* (Phila., Pa.: The Presbyterian and Reformed Pub. Co., 1964), pp. 17-18.

previously fulfilled) must be understood in the light of that one supreme fact."[1]

Notice how covenant interpreters use this principle of redemption to spiritualize the prophecy of the New Jerusalem in Revelation 21-22: "The vision depicts temporal, spiritual and redemptive reality and not eternal and ultimate glory. It depicts the glory of the grace of God in the redemption of man."[2] This principle of redemption is similarly used in the millennial temple vision of Ezekiel 40-48: "Not that we are to expect any of the details themselves given in Ezekiel to be literally fulfilled, but that the *truths* represented by those details will be realized in the new heaven and the new earth."[3]

Actually, the Scripture nowhere teaches that God has made only one covenant with man since the Fall, and that everything must be explained under this "covenant." The Scripture does teach that God makes several covenants with different people at different times. The covenants made by God and described in the Bible are the following:

1. Edenic Covenant—Genesis 1:26-28; 2:15-17.
2. Adamic Covenant—Genesis 3:14-19.
3. Noahic Covenant—Genesis 8:21-9:17, 24-27.
4. Abrahamic Covenant—Genesis 12:1-3.
5. Mosaic Covenant—Exodus 19:5-8.
6. Palestinian Covenant—Deuteronomy 28:63-68; 30:1-9.
7. Davidic Covenant—II Samuel 7:4-17; I Chronicles 17:3-15.
8. New Covenant—Jeremiah 31:31-34; Hebrews 8:6-13.

---

[1] R. Campbell, *Israel and the New Covenant*, p. 176.
[2] *Ibid.*, p. 57.
[3] Floyd E. Hamilton, *The Basis of Millennial Faith* (Grand Rapids, Mich.: Wm. B. Eerdmans Pub. Co., 1942), pp. 45-46.

The "covenants" of covenant theologians are apparently not the same as the above-mentioned Bible covenants. One is extra-Biblical, the other is Biblical; one is the product of man's theology, the other is from the Word of God. The terms *covenant theology* and *covenant theologians* are therefore misnomers, as the "covenants" of covenant theology are not the same as the covenants of the Bible. A better designation for this system is *Covenantism.*

Covenantism says that the advent of Christ and the institution of the church are crucial events in prophecy. This is true of course. But the cross of Christ and the church do not comprehend the entire tenor and theme of prophecy. Bible prophecy deals with God's programs for Israel, the Gentiles, the angels, as well as the church.

It is true that the benefits of Christ's redemption extend from Genesis to Revelation, that all men are saved wholly and only through the cross of Christ. But this is one aspect of God's program for the ages. To make one aspect of God's program (i.e. redemption) cover the entire plan of God for the ages is to commit the reductive error. There are many aspects of God and many phases of His program which cannot be comprehended under the soteriological theme of redemption. The revelation that "God is a consuming fire" (Heb. 12:29), and His dealings with Lucifer and the fallen angels, certainly do not relate properly to redemption. Even non-dispensationalist James Orr is willing to make this observation: "[Covenant theology's] most obvious defect was that, in using the idea of the Covenant as an exhaustive category, and attempting to force into it the whole material of theology, it created an artificial scheme which could only repel minds of simple and natural notions."[1]

---

[1] James Orr, *The Progress of Dogma* (London: Hodder and Stoughton, 1908), p. 303.

Contrary to the popular notion that covenantism originates with the church father Augustine,[1] the theory of the covenants was not developed until the 17th century (after the Reformation). None of the reformers knew anything about covenantism, although their writings are made to fit into the covenantal scheme.[2]

Clarence E. Mason aptly traces the origin of covenantism, and we quote him at length: "After Calvin's death in 1564. Holland gradually became the center of Calvinistic theological activity. . . . Theological tension was high in Holland following the Synod of Dort (1619) . . . particularly against the teaching of double predestination (the decrees of election and reprobation). It was at this time that Cocceius advanced his theory concerning the *Covenant of Grace* and the *Covenant of Works*, in which he soft-pedaled the doctrine of predestination. . . . This teaching, of course, was rejected by the Reformed Church . . . . [Then] Witsiu introduced his idea of a third covenant (later known as the *Covenant of Redemption*) which concerned God's saving purpose before the foundation of the earth. The Reformed theologians were quick to see the possibility of reconciling the doctrine of the eternal decrees with this new idea set forth by Witsius [in 1685]. Therefore, the Reformed Church did an about face and embraced the theory of the covenant."[3]   As someone has observed, Covenantism is made in Holland and not in Heaven.

---

[1] See Allis, *Prophecy and the Church*, pp. 2-3.

[2] It may also be noted that although the early church did recognize and interpret Scripture by dispensational distinctions, dispensationalism as a distinct system in systematized form did not arise until the time of John Nelson Darby (1800-82).

[3] Clarence E. Mason, Jr., "Eschatology" (Class notes, Philadelphia College of Bible, Philadelphia, 1970), p. 55.

B. The True Perspective

1. Recognition of Scriptural Distinctions.—Paradoxically, the unifying principle of Bible history and prophecy is to be seen under Scriptural distinctions. This is known as the dispensational approach to the Bible. During interpretation, the distinctions found in Scripture must be considered. The harmonizing of these distinctions leads to a unifying principle of prophecy. Some distinctions to be considered are the following:

First, Bible history does not run in an uninterrupted fashion. It comes under distinct stages, periods, and dispensations. Interpreters who study the Scriptures normally cannot avoid this basic Scriptural distinction.[1]   An interesting example of a dispensational change in Scripture is dramatically shown by Christ in Luke 4. When invited into the synagogue of Nazareth and handed the Scriptures, Christ stands up to read Isaiah 61. Then He amazes the congregation by stopping on a half-sentence, saying, "This day is this scripture fulfilled in your ears." What the Lord reads describes His first advent; what He leaves out would have described His second advent. Christ's mid-sentence stop indicates a period of time between the two advents, *viz.*, the church age or the dispensation of grace.

Second, not only is Scriptural history set under distinct periods, but under these distinct periods, God varies His procedure in dealing with man. That is, God deals with man

---

[1] The word οἰκονομία ("dispensation") comes from the Greek terms οἶκος ("house") + νέμω ("to dispense or manage"), and denotes a stewardship, management, or rule of life. A dispensation is simply "a distinguishable economy in the outworking of God's purpose" (Charles Caldwell Ryrie, *Dispensationalism Today* [Chicago, Ill.: Moody Press, 1965], p. 29).

according to the specific revelation which each group of people receives.

When the apostle Paul tells the Christians at Rome that "Ye are not under law but under grace" (Rom. 5:14), he is acknowledging the fact that Law under the Old Testament economy is to be distinguished from Grace under the New Testament. Other cases, such as the principle of revenge in the Old Testament (cf. Ps. 137:9-9) as distinguished from the principle of forgiveness emphasized in the New (cf. Rom. 12:19-21), are evidences of the fact that God deals differently with different peoples during various periods of history. "Any person is a dispensationalist," says Lewis S. Chafer, "who trusts the blood of Christ rather than bringing an animal sacrifice, . . . who observes the first day of the week rather than the seventh."[1]

Third, God has more than one people. The church is one people of God but so are Israel and the gentiles (I Cor. 10:32), and the angels (Heb. 12:22-23). Prophecy therefore should cover more than just the church, for God's program (which prophecy sets forth) does not terminate in the church. The complaint of William Kelly is well taken: "What throws all prophecy into confusion, darkness, and error, is making ourselves, the church, its object. . . . Give Christ, the true centre, His place; then everything falls into order, and shines in the light of God before our souls."[2]

2. Some Relevant Observations.—Once the interpreter acknowledges and takes into consideration all these Scriptural distinctions, God's plan of the ages will appear before him in beautiful, natural harmony. Acknowledgement of the fact that

---

[1] Lewis Sperry Chafer, *Dispensationalism* (Dallas, Tex.: Dallas Seminary Press, 1951), p. 39.

[2] William Kelly, *An Exposition of the Book of Isaiah* (4th ed.; London: C.A. Hammond, 1947), p. 35.

God's plan and program must involve the church, the nation Israel, the gentiles, and the angels, will establish the feeling that the theme of *redemption* as the sole unifying principle of prophecy is not comprehensive enough.

God's plan and program down the ages is not exclusively in view of redemption but for the grand purpose of showing forth the *glory* of His grace in Christ. The redemptive program is but one of the principle means used by God to realize the greatest demonstration of His grace and glory (Eph. 1:12-14; I Pet. 4:11).

Charles Ryrie says, "Dispensationalism alone has a broad enough unifying principle to do justice to the unity of the progress of revelation on the one hand and the distinctiveness of the various stages in the progress on the other . . . . Any seeming disunity in the dispensational scheme is superficial . . . . *Variety can be an essential part of unity.* This is true of God's creation; it is also true of God's revelation."

Thus, we would maintain that while redemption is assuredly part and parcel of God's total program, the unifying principle of the whole of God's program is *God's glory.*

Dispensational theologians have been accused by covenant theologians of splitting the Bible, since the former interpret by the distinctions found in the Scriptures. "The picture of dispensational teaching given the Christian public," observes Ryrie, "is that of a knife which not only makes hairsplitting distinctions but actually cuts away parts of the Bible."[2] This picture is not only misleading but outright unfair. The harmony of the Scripture is not preserved by forcing God's Word into an artificial mold, spiritualizing away recalcitrant parts which do not fit. When covenant theologians take one aspect of God's plan (redemption) and make all other Scriptures

---

[1] Ryrie, *Dispensationalism Today*, p. 35.
[2] *Ibid.*, p. 105.

revolve around this consideration, they themselves have split the Bible. It is therefore not surprising that Clarence Bass who, rejecting the dispensationalism he once held, should wonder aloud: "I have not found the way out of dispensationalism easy, and I sometimes wonder if even now I have left it completely."[1]

Dispensational interpreters, through normal study of the prophetic Scriptures, recognize the many-faceted program of God and seek to harmonize this program under the doxological theme of the glory of God. Dispensational distinctions are certainly not a creation of theology. They exist because a consistently normal interpretation of the Word demands it. Thus, by "rightly dividing the word of truth" (II Tim. 2:15), interpreters do honor to the Word of God.

II. ISRAEL AND THE CHURCH

A crucial area of discussion among evangelical theologians today is the relationship between Israel and the church. Covenant theologians believe that Israel and the church are one and the same people; dispensational theologians believe that Israel and the church are two distinct peoples of God.

Moreover, covenant theologians are divided into two groups: (1) covenant amillennialists, and (2) covenant premillennialists. The former sees the church and Israel in vital and total union; the latter goes halfway by affirming that the church and Israel are somewhat blended, though not fully amalgamated.

Dispensational theologians are *pretribulational* in their eschatology because pretribulationism is based on the

---

[1] Clarence B. Bass, *Backgrounds to Dispensationalism* (Grand Rapids, Mich.: Wm. B. Eerdmans Pub. Co., 1960), p. 9.

distinction between Israel and the church. Covenant premillennialists must necessarily be *post*tribulational because they see the New Testament church as part of the one-people of God and yet somewhat distinct. Covenant amillennialists are always *post*tribulational.

A. View of Covenant Theologians

Covenant theologians teach that the Old Testament Israel and the New Testament church are one people, one being the continuation and successor of the other. While some covenant theologians begin this line of people with Abraham (leaving out saints who lived before Abraham), most covenant theologians would backtrack the line to Adam. It has moreover been affirmed that the church is not to be linked with the entire ancient nation Israel but only with the *true* Israelites of that nation.[1]

This line of God's people in both Testaments is aggregately called "the Church." Albertus Pieters explains this in detail: [By Church] we mean the great community of Christians of every name . . . . composed of men, women, and children, many with true faith in their hearts, but including many others also who have only an external connection with Christ . . . . one in unbroken continuity with the Israel of patriarchs and prophets in Old Testament times . . . . This is the way we New Covenant Israelites should think of the Old Testament record, not as the story of a strange and distant people, with whom we have no connection, but as our own history, since we have been engrafted into the olive tree of the covenant."[2]

---

[1] See Louis Berkhof, *Principles of Biblical Interpretation* (Grand Rapids, Mich.: Baker Book House, 1966), Pp. 135-36.

[2] Albertus Pieters, *The Seed of Abraham* (Grand Rapids, Mich.: Wm. B. Eerdmans Pub. Co., 1950), pp. 66-67, 98.

Herman Hoeksema declares: "Israel is the Church, and the Church is Israel."[1]

The concept of one covenanted people—with Israel flowering and flowing into the church—allows for no fulfillment of Old Testament prophecy past the church. As the successor of Israel, the church has now absorbed and appropriated all Old Testament prophecies and promises. "The Christian Church in its origin was an Israelitish body fully qualified to claim the promises made to Israel."[2]

Moreover, Old Testament terms and concepts such as "Mount Zion, Jerusalem, temple and altar, sacrifices and shadows are all fulfilled in Christ and realized in the Church,"[3] say non-literalists. The denial of any fulfillment of prophecy past the church fits hand-in-glove into amillennial eschatology which sees Christ coming at the end of the church age and all things come to a close.

Covenant theologians themselves do not see eye to eye on how the promises to Israel are fulfilled in the church. One group affirms that the Old Testament promises are now being fulfilled by the church *on earth*. This is Augustinian amillennialism, and it is accepted today by the Roman Catholic church as well as by some Protestant theologians such as Berkhof and Allis. Another group affirms that the promises are being fulfilled by saints up *in heaven* in their state of blessedness. To this group belong such theologians as Duesterdieck, Kliefoth, and Warfield.

Concerning the kingdom prophecies in the Old Testament, covenant theologians affirm that the church, being the successor of Israel, has appropriated all these prophecies. The

---

[1] Herman Hoeksema, *Reformed Dogmatics* (Grand Rapids, Mich.: Reformed Free Pub. Ass'n, 1966), p. 818.

[2] Pieters, *Seed of Abraham*, p. 71.

[3] *Ibid.*

church is the "new" form of the kingdom. No other fulfillment in a future, earthly kingdom is to be expected. As theologian Archibald A. Hodge says, "the kingdom of Christ has already come . . . . The Old Testament prophecies, therefore, which predict this kingdom, must refer to the present dispensation of grace, and not to a future reign of Christ on earth in person among men in the flesh." [1]

Since the form of the kingdom prophesied in the Old Testament differs so radically from the Christian church, interpreters are forced to explain that form and essence must be distinguished in prophecy. Old Testament prophecies "received their accomplishment as regards the substance, but not as regards the form, for another state of things had entered which rendered this impracticable." [2] A.B. Davidson adds that "when the condition of the world has so greatly changed, and when the form of the kingdom of God has likewise altered, only the general idea contained in the prophecies may be expected to be fulfilled." [3]

Concerning the nation Israel, covenant theologians maintain that Israel is now cast aside because she crucified the Messiah and is now no more special to God than any other nation on earth. "In or about the spring of the year 30 A.D.," calculates Boettner, "the mass of those who then called themselves Israelites ceased to be such . . . having forfeited their citizenship in the commonwealth of Israel by refusing to accept the Messiah." [4]   John Wilmot affirms similarly:

---

[1] A[rchibald] A. Hodge, *Outlines of Theology* (New York, N.Y.: Hodder and Stoughton, 1878), p. 570.

[2] Patrick Fairbairn, *The Interpretation of Prophecy* (reprint ed.; London: Banner of Truth Trust, 1964), p. 164.

[3] A.B. Davidson, *Old Testament Prophecy*, edited by J.A. Paterson (Edinburgh: T. & T. Clark, 1903), p. 189.

[4] Loraine Boettner, *The Millennium* (Phila., Pa.: The Presbyterian and Reformed Pub. Co., 1964), p. 318.

"Jews, racially, naturally, outwardly, are not now in God's esteem, the seed or children of Abraham, any more than Ishmael and Esau; Zimran, Jokshan, Medan, Midian, and Shuah . . . . The Israel nation's service to God and the world ceased with the coming of Christ . . . ."[1]

Covenant theologians hand the Old Testament promises over to the church, and leave the threats and curses often found in the same Old Testament texts behind for Israel. The church is said to be enjoying the blessings recorded in prophecy, while the Jews collect all its curses. "For the unbelieving Jews there are prophecies which we have every reason to expect will be literally fulfilled. Those promises are of wrath and judgment, of being scattered among the nations of the world . . . . Nothing but wrath and destruction awaits the race unless they turn to Christ."[2]

No wonder George N. H. Peters clamors for honesty in this regard: "The curses pronounced, are all carefully heaped upon them [the Jews] severally and shown in their case to be sadly realized, while the blessings promised to the identically same nation and city [i.e. Israel and Jerusalem] are taken from them and carefully bestowed upon the Gentile churches. Is this honest to the Record?"[3]

Christians may properly use the Old Testament prophecies of blessings and curses on Israel in making applications to their own lives. This is application, not interpretation. Concerning the curses, we should beware lest what was literally true of Israel in history be spiritually true of us. And concerning the Old Testament blessings, we should pray that

---

[1] John Wilmot, *Inspired Principles of Prophetic Interpretation* (Swengel, Pa.: Reiner Pubs., 1967), pp. 224-25.

[2] Hamilton, *Basis of Millennial Faith*, p. 58.

[3] George N.H. Peters, *The Theocratic Kingdom* (3 vols.;

what is going to be literally fulfilled by Israel in the millennium be spiritually exemplified today in the Christian church and the spiritual lives of believers.

B. View of Dispensational Theologians

The basic test of a dispensational interpreter is his willingness to distinguish, via normal reading of the Scriptures, the difference between Israel and the church. To see the church as the Body of Christ, an organism different from Old Testament Israel, is to read Scripture dispensationally and to qualify as a dispensational interpreter.

The Scripture, when normally read, describes Israel and the church as two distinct entities. This is so apparent that even covenant theologians admit that only by spiritualizing may the fusion between Israel and the church be upheld. Albertus Pieters says: "The question whether the Old Testament prophecies concerning the people of God must be interpreted in their ordinary sense, as other Scriptures are interpreted, or can properly be applied to the Christian church, is called the question of spiritualization of prophecy."[1]

When the apostle Paul introduces the church in the New Testament as a mystery "kept secret since the world began" (Rom. 16:25), "hidden from ages and from generations" (Col. 1:26), and revealed only in New Testament times,[2]   he

---

[1] Cited by Gerrit Hendrick Hospers, *The Principle of Spiritualization in Hermeneutics* (East Williamson, N.Y.: By the Author, 1935), p. 5.

[2] The doctrine of the church is also described by Paul as "hidden in God" (Eph. 3:9). Paul does not say "hidden in Scripture," otherwise, his readers would be searching for the Christian church in the Old Testament.

is distinguishing it as an entity apart from the nation Israel. According to New Testament revelation, on the day of Pentecost, God begins to call out a people from among both Jews and Gentiles to form a new body, the church.[1] Jews and Gentiles are placed on an equal footing, the "middle wall of partition" is broken down, and believers are baptized by the Spirit into the church. This phenomenon did not take place during Old Testament times. It first occurs at the day of Pentecost. And this Body of Christ will be completed when the full number of the elect is called out into it. The Bible describes this as the "fulness of the Gentiles" (Rom. 11:25)."[2]

While the church age is in progress, Israel is not cast aside but only temporarily set aside (Rom. 11:1-5); God's promises to Israel are held in abeyance and not cancelled. Notice that even after the church begins at Pentecost, the apostle Paul still sees the nation Israel as an entity distinct from the Christian church (cf. I Cor. 10:32). Paul prays for them (in Romans 10:1) because they are still unbelievers, although they have the covenants and the promises (Rom. 10:4-5). The apostle Peter continues to address Israel as a distinct national people

---

[1] Cf. Rom. 3:9; 10:12; Gal. 3:18; Eph. 2:14; Col. 3:11; I Cor. 12:13.

[2] The *Times of the Gentiles* (mentioned by Christ in Luke 21:24) is the period of world history when political rule over the earth is vested in the hands of the Gentiles. It extends from Nebuchadnezzar's first subjugation of Israel to the time of Christ's second advent. The *Fulness of the Gentiles* (Rom. 11:25) represents the full number of people gathered out from among the nations to form the church (Acts 15:13-17). The *Fulness of the Times* (Eph. 1:7-10) refers to the final eternal state when all things are summed up in God.

even after the church has begun (Acts 3:12; 4:8). Therefore, it is right to maintain that the promises of God to Israel in the Old Testament have not been appropriated by the church but that Israel will be restored to fulfill the promises made to her.

A number of similarities of course exists between the nation Israel and the Christian church.[1] Some of these are: (1) Both have covenantal relationship with God; (2) Both are related to God by blood redemption; (3) Both are witnesses for God; (4) Both are the seed of Abraham; and (5) Both are called to walk in worldly separation. Nevertheless, the dissimilarities between these two peoples of God are very distinct. These distinctions are so overwhelmingly presented in Scriptures that there is no unanimity even in the ranks of covenant theologians on the belief that Israel *is* the church. For instance, William Hendriksen, in his treatment of Romans 9-11, allows a distinction between Israel and the church.

III. DISPENSATIONALISM AND SOTERIOLOGY

A. The Dispensations and Salvation

Interpreters who interpret the Scriptures dispensationally are often charged by their critics with teaching multiple ways of salvation. This charge is doubtless the most frequently heard objection to dispensationalism. As Clarence E. Bass warns, "the presupposition of the difference between law and grace, between Israel and the church . . . when carried to its logical conclusion will inevitably result in a multiple form of salvation—that men are not saved the same way in all

---

[1] Charles Lee Feinberg lists twelve similarities in *Premillennialism or Amillennialism?* (Wheaton, Ill.: Van Kampen Press, 1954), p. 148.

[2] William Hendriksen, *"And So All Israel Shall Be Saved"* (Grand Rapids, Mich.: Baker Book Store, 1945), pp. 16-21.

ages."[1] And John Wick Bowman attacks the *Scofield Reference Bible*, saying that "this book represents perhaps the most dangerous heresy currently to be found within Christian circles. . . ."[2]

The charge against dispensational interpreters, if true, is indeed serious and should well be heeded. To teach or even to infer more than one way of salvation is to contradict the cardinal Scriptural doctrine that there is "no other Name under heaven given among men, whereby we must be saved" (Acts 4:12).

Despite the seriousness of the charge, covenant theologians have yet to produce a case where multiple salvation is taught by any dispensational theologian. What the former usually bring into court are inferences from quotations taken out of context.[3] Obviously, it is easy to come to any conclusion when the evidences are based on inferences and statements taken out of their contexts. "Straw men are easy to create," says Ryrie, "but the huff and puff it takes to demolish them are only huff and puff."[4]

And the technique can work both ways. From the following statement of Oswald T. Allis, one may conclude that he is teaching multiple salvation: "The law is a declaration of the will of God for man's salvation. As such it manifests God's love and grace in providing a way of escape from the guilt and penalty of failure to keep the law perfectly. The priest and the altar make it possible for sinful man to obtain mercy from a righteous God."[5]

---

[1] Bass, *Backgrounds to Dispensationalism*, p. 34.
[2] John Wick Bowman, "Dispensationalism," *Interpretation*, X, No. 2 (April, 1956), 172.
[3] See Allis, *Prophecy and the Church*, p. 234.
[4] Ryrie, *Dispensationalism Today*, p. 110.
[5] Allis, *Prophecy and the Church*, p. 39.

Similarly, Louis Berkhof opens himself to misapprehension by saying: "In the Old Testament, circumcision and passover, sacrifices and purification were not simply carnal institutions pertaining to the flesh, mere shadows of a coming reality. They also pertained to the conscience; and acceptable participation in them required faith on the part of the worshipper . . . . *forgiveness for such sins was attainable through the appointed offerings* [Italics added]."[1]

Although dispensational interpreters have clearly affirmed, explained, and reiterated time and again their belief that the dispensations are not methods of salvation but rules of life, and that man has always been saved by faith through the blood of Christ in every age, these affirmations are usually ignored. "One almost gathers that antidispensationalists do not want to hear what is being said since it is more convenient to attack the so-called logical conclusions forced on dispensationalism,"[2] observes Charles Ryrie.

What dispensationalists do believe is that salvation is always by grace through faith, and that the dispensations are rules of life, never the basis or cause of salvation. Kurtaneck is clear: "The various dispensations, then, are not many ways of salvation. . . but are distinct rules of life by which man was tested to God's revealed will during a particular time."[3]

An important issue in this regard is that of salvation in the Old Testament. Covenant theologians have no real solution to this problem. The one thing they have on their side is simplicity itself. Nothing could be more simple than to say that all men are saved in exactly the same way during all ages (which is what dispensational interpreters also say). But when

[1] Berkhof, *Principles of Biblical Interpretation*, pp. 136-37.
[2] Ryrie, *Dispensationalism Today*, p. 111.
[3] Nickolas Kurtaneck, "A Survey of Dispensationalism" (Doctoral dissertation, Grace Theological Seminary, 1961), p. 204.

covenant theologians are pressed on *what* specifically did Old Testament saints believe in order to be saved, they cannot go further than "faith in the promised Redeemer, or faith in the promise of redemption through the Messiah."[1]   But the question is, how much of this did the Israelites understand?

It is true that salvation is always by grace through faith in God based on Christ's shed blood. Yet it is certainly not possible that the Israelites recognized as their Redeemer the incarnate, crucified Son, the Lamb of God. "It is very difficult if not impossible to prove that the *average* Israelite understood the grace of God in Christ."[2]   If the Israelite had insight into the finished work of Christ, then he would have stopped coming to offer the sacrifices continually. He would have rested confidently in what he saw in Christ's final sacrifice on the cross. "If the sacrifices had given a clear foreview of Christ, then the offerer would have understood the truth of a completed atonement and would not have had any conscience of sins every year."[3]

The apostle Paul, standing atop Mars' Hill, describes Old Testament times as "the times of this ignorance [which] God winked at" (Acts 17:30 ; cf. Rom. 3:25). Because of this "ignorance," God forgives the Old Testament offender but with the expectation on His own part that the basis for such forgiveness would eventually be made by the death of His Son. As Lewis S. Chafer says, "God forgave sin and renewed fellowship with them on the ground of His own certainty that a sufficient sacrifice would be made in due time by His Lamb."[4] There must therefore be two sides to the matter—

---

[1] Charles Hodge, *Systematic Theology* (3 vols.; New York, N.Y.: Charles Scribner's Sons, 1872), II, 372.

[2] Ryrie, *Dispensationalism Today*, p. 123.

[3] *Ibid.*, p. 129.

[4] Chafer, *Dispensationalism*, p. 54.

that which God sees from His side and that which man sees from his.

Perhaps there was an inherent pointer in the sacrifices themselves, *viz.*, that the sacrifices could not go on forever, and a believing and discerning worshipper could realize that there would be a final sacrifice which would deal with the entire sin question. However, it cannot be said that the average Israelite understood what that final dealing was. John L. Mitchell says: "[The animal sacrifices] were simply an evidence on the part of the sacrificer that the sovereign God would provide a complete and efficacious sacrifice which would take away sin. It is true that they possessed no perfect knowledge as to how God would do it, but their sacrifice was an evidence of their faith that He would."[1]

Dispensational interpreters therefore believe that while the dealings of God with man are different under different periods, the only basis for salvation has always been the death of Christ. Faith in God is the requirement under any and every dispensation, the content of faith varying under the progressive nature of revelation. Adam and the Old Testament saints could not have seen the Cross of Calvary under the same light as New Testament saints looking back on it can. The content of saving faith in Old Testament times thus depended on the particular revelation which God was pleased to give at that time.

In summation, the *requirement* of salvation is faith in God, the *basis* of salvation for any age is the death of Christ, and the *content* of faith varies under each dispensation.[2]

---

[1] John L. Mitchell, "The Question of Millennial Sacrifices," *Bibliotheca Sacra*, Vol. 110, No. 440 (Oct., 1953), 344.

[2] See Ryrie, *Dispensationalism Today*, p. 123.

B. Dispensationalists and World Missions

Dispensational interpreters have also been accused of harming the cause of world missions by interpreting the Scriptures dispensationally. Two cases are usually cited:

1. *First Case.*-- Revelation 14 describes a group of 144,000 persons who will be saved during the tribulation, and Revelation 7 adds that "a great multitude which no man could number" will also be saved. In other words, a great worldwide revival will occur during the tribulation period before the second coming of Christ. Normal reading of these texts in Revelation demands such an interpretation.

Detractors however wring their hands over the implication that to allow a world-wide revival *after* the church has been raptured is to remove the initiative from present world-wide evangelization. "Do you mean to say," exclaims Oswald J. Smith, "that the Jews can accomplish more in some seven years or less . . . than we have been able to accomplish in nearly two thousand years, with the Holy Spirit's aid, when it has been easy to be a Christian? Preposterous! Impossible!"[1] And in the final paragraph of *Prophecy and the Church*, O.T. Allis remarks sardonically that "the presence of the Church on earth delays its coming [i.e. world-wide revival], and that Christians should earnestly pray for the rapture of the Church in order that this better day for humanity may come."[2]

The Scripture however says nothing about the "majority" of the world's population being saved during the tribulation, or that the gospel proclamation will be "more effective"[3]

---

[1] Oswald J. Smith, *The Passion for Souls* (London: Marshall, Norgan and Scott, 1950), p. 53.

[2] Allis, *Prophecy and the Church*, p. 262.

[3] Louis Berkhof, *Systematic Theology* (4th ed. rev.; Grand Rapids, Mich.: Wm. B. Eerdmans Pub. Co., 1949), p. 698.

during the tribulation. These are but unfounded inferences and straw-man tactics of posttribulationists. What the Scripture does *not* say is that, since God has also ordained preaching of the gospel by tribulation saints, the church should give up preaching. God has ordained preaching by the church and He has also ordained preaching by tribulation saints. If God ordains to give the "latecomers" (tribulation sants) more opportunities to preach, this does not mean that the "early toilers" (church saints) need not do their job. This principle is found in Jesus' Parable of the Laborers (Matt. 20:1-16).

If it destroys the motive of world missions for one to teach that revival apart from the ministry of the church is possible, then the Old Testament should be under wraps, for it repeatedly describes how multitudes were saved without the benefit of the church's preaching ministry. The ancient city of Nineveh, from its king down, turned in repentance to God within a few days after a one-sentence proclamation by an unwilling and unworthy prophet. [1]

Some non-dispensationalists also browbeat the pretribulational implication that a "second chance" would be granted to people for salvation after the rapture. This is certainly not a strong argument and merits only a cursory reply. Even today, people are being granted "second" chances to believe in Christ, otherwise the number of the redeemed would be small indeed. Second chances *per se* are not unscriptural, although the hardening of the heart against the proferred chances will finally prove irremedial.

---

[1] Removal of the Holy Spirit with the church at the rapture (cf. II Thess. 2:1-12) does not mean that the Spirit will lose His omnipresence or His power to bring saving conviction on earth. Just like in Old Testament days, the Holy Spirit will be at work convicting sinners and filling saints at the tribulation.

It is quite possible that for those who have persistently rejected Christ, no "second" chances would be given during the tribulation, in the sense that they would become so hardened to the Gospel as to be irremedially lost. This possibility we gather from II Thessalonians 2:9-12 where the apostle Paul predicts that the Man of Sin will deceive a group of people with "the lie." The apostle says that this group will "perish" for they "received not" (aorist tense) saving truth. The use of the Greek aorist tense implies that these are people who *had* been confronted with the Gospel before the tribulation period. The apostle warns that God will send them delusions so that they will believe *the* lie (v. 11) because they "believed not the truth" (v. 12).

2. *Second Case.--* Matthew 24:14 teaches that Christ is coming after the gospel is preached throughout all the world: "And this gospel of the kingdom shall be preached in all the world for a witness unto all nations; and then shall the end come." Posttribulational interpreters, misunderstanding the context of Matthew 24, teach that Christ will come for the Christian church *after* the gospel has been preached in all the world, and no sooner. In other words, the coming of Christ hinges on the world-wide proclamation of the gospel.

As George Ladd states: "Christ is tarrying until the Church has completed its task. When Matthew 24:14 has been fulfilled, then Christ will come . . . . *Any generation which is really dedicated to the task can complete the mission.* The Lord can come in our own generation, in our life-time—if we stir ourselves and finish our task."[1] And Oswald J. Smith pleads: "Christ wants to return. He longs to reign. It is His right. Then why does He wait? He is waiting for you and me

---

[1] George Eldon Ladd, *The Blessed Hope* (Grand Rapids, Mich.: Wm. B. Eerdmans Pub. Co., 1956), p. 148.

to complete the task . . . . Many a time He must say to Himself as He sits there, 'How long, I wonder, are they going to keep me waiting? When will they let me come back?'"[1]

Although Matthew 24:14 has been used to encourage interest in missions, the context of the passage does not allow us to grant it such an interpretation. This prophecy in the Olivet Discourse of Christ (Matt. 24-25) is given with reference to the nation Israel at the tribulation. It describes the world-wide revival following the proclamation of the gospel of the kingdom just before the coming of Christ to institute the millennium.[2]

The Christian church does have the Lord's command to go "into all the world and preach the gospel to every creature" (Mark 16:15; cf. Matt. 28:19-20). This Great Commission, directed at Christians, does not tie together His second coming and the effectiveness of world evangelization in the sense of their being cause and effect. In God's foreknowledge and love, the church is spared the futile and uncommanded task of converting the world. The task is done as the Holy Spirit works through yielded Christians in calling out from the world a people chosen according to the election of grace. It is not men building the kingdom, but Christ who says that He will build

---

[1] Oswald J. Smith, *The Passion for Souls* (London: Marshall, Morgan and Scott, 1950), p. 55.

[2] The "Gospel of the Kingdom" is identical with the "Gospel of Grace" being proclaimed today. Both are based on the atoning work of Christ, which naturally includes the preaching of the cross. The difference lies in the *emphasis* of their respective preaching. The gospel ("good news") of the kingdom will emphasize the coming King (Christ) and the impending establishment of the millennial kingdom. The saved at the tribulation will be looking forward to the coming kingdom of Christ. At the tribulation period, salvation will still be through "the blood of the Lamb" (Rev. 7:14; 12:11) and under the ministry of the Holy Spirit (Joel 2:28-32).

the church (Matt. 16:18). The Lord's coming for the church is always impending and imminent, not dependent on the success or failure of world evangelization.

C. An Observation

We have heard the clamor over the alleged anti-evangelistic character and the supposed implications to salvation of dispensational teaching, and we have found the din totally uncalled for. Dispensational theology leads neither to multiple salvation nor to a weakening of the missionary thrust. On the contrary, an increased appreciation of Christ's redemption on Calvary is possible only under the light of dispensational hermeneutics. Here is what we mean:

Covenant theology, with its theory of one people and the view that the church rightfully and legally inherits Israel's chosen status, makes it that much harder for the church to possess the "boasting excluded" attitude and therefore a fuller appreciation of her blood-bought redemption in Christ (cf. Rom. 11:24-25). The true view of grace as an unmerited favor from God is weakened when the church becomes the legal successor of Israel, rightfully enjoying her promises and privileges.

This is one reason why Christians who take the Word of God literally and dispensationally have instead been in the forefront of world evangelization. Dispensationalists actually comprise the major portion of those involved in world missions today. L.S. Chafer observes that "it is the dispensationalists who are promoting Bible study movements over the whole land and they are the major factor in all evangelistic and missionary activity today." [1] Even nondispensationalists admit as much: "Celebrated missionaries such as Hudson

---

[1] Chafer, *Dispensationalism*, p. 12.

Taylor belonged to their ranks, and congregations
representative of this movement have been among the most
ardent supporters of the Church's mission program."[1]
George Eldon Ladd testifies: "It is doubtful if there has been
any other circle of men who have done more by their influence
in preaching, teaching and writing to promote a love for Bible
study, a hunger for the deeper Christian life, a passion for
evangelism and zeal for missions in the history of American
Christianity."[2]

IV. To be, or Not to be, Consistent

The issue of consistency in interpretation has been fiercely
debated and generally misunderstood. The question of the
degree of consistency, and even the possibility of being consistent, in the interpretation of prophecy has split the ranks of
interpreters down the years. While this is basically a hermeneutical issue, it has strong theological roots, and we have
chosen to discuss it under this section of the book.

A. Consistency and Figurative Language

Many interpreters assume that to be consistent one must
interpret everything—including figures and symbols—
literally. "To be thoroughly literal," supposes Bernard
Ramm, "we would have to insist that a literal (actual) woman
sat literally upon seven literal hills! that Jesus Christ has a

---

[1] C. Norman Kraus, *Dispensationalism in America* (Richmond, Va.: John Knox Press, 1958), p. 65.

[2] George Eldon Ladd, *Crucial Questions about the Kingdom
of God* (Grand Rapids, Mich.: Wm.B. Eerdmans Pub. Co., 1952),
p. 49.

literal sword coming out of his mouth! and that beasts can act and talk like men!"[1]

George Eldon Ladd similarly falters: "The Revelation, describing the second advent of Christ, pictures him riding upon a white horse, crowned with many diadems, garbed in a robe dipped in blood, accompanied by the armies of heaven on white horses, coming to smite the nations with a sword which proceeds out of his mouth. No argument is needed to prove that this is symbolic language."[2]

Consistent literal interpretation however means that the interpreter consistently acknowledges and accepts the *customary* usages of Bible language. And customary usage certainly involves both nonfigurative and figurative languages. In interpreting figurative language, one must not base his interpretation on the literal words forming the figure and symbol but on the literal sense which the figure and symbol are intended to convey. Consistent literality also allows for the interpretation of types—whenever types are properly identified.

To sum up, consistency certainly does not mean woodenheaded literalism which refuses to properly accept figures, symbols, and types. "It is not true," explains Charles Lee Feinberg, "that the premillennialists require every single passage to be interpreted literally without exception. They do hold, on the other hand, that if the language is symbolic, it is to be governed by the laws relating to symbols; if figurative, by the laws dealing with figures; if typical, by the laws connected with types; if literal, by the laws of non-figurative speech."[3]

---

[1] Bernard Ramm, *Protestant Biblical Interpretation* (3rd rev. ed.; Grand Rapids, Mich.: Baker Book House, 1970), pp. 268-69.

[2] Ladd, *Kingdom of God*, p. 137.

[3] Feinberg, *Premillennialism or Amillennialism?*, p. 27.

B. Consistency and the Kingdom

There are interpreters who fear that when consistency is followed through in prophetic interpretation, the result will be a future, literal kingdom on earth. As Hamilton says, "Now, we must frankly admit that a literal interpretation of the Old Testament prophecies gives us just such a picture of an earthly reign of the Messiah as the premillennialist pictures."[1]

In avoiding the literal earthly kingdom, interpreters use the technique of dismissing kingdom prophecies as figurative expressions borrowed from the Old Testament theocracy and colored by the life and times of the prophets. "If we survey this prophecy of the kingdom," states C. von Orelli, "we find that . . . the form of this prophecy is indeed conditioned by the views and ideas of the time of utterance."[2]   Roman Catholic theologians also follow the same technique with reference to the kingdom, saying "Catholic tradition has usually regarded this picture as a figurative adumbration in Jewish colouring of the Messianic Kingdom, the Church of Christ."[3]

Aside from the desire to dismiss the earthly kingdom, non-literalists avoid consistent literality because it gives the kingdom a *Jewish* flavor. As Oswald T. Allis warns, "For the more literally these prophecies are construed, the more thoroughly and pervasively Jewish will be the millennium."[4]

It is true that when Bible prophecy is interpreted literally, we see an earthly kingdom with Jerusalem as its centre, saved

---

[1] Hamilton, *Basis of Millennial Faith*, p. 38.

[2] C. von Orelli, "Prophecy," *International Standard Bible Encyclopedia* (5 vols.; Grand Rapids, Mich.: Wm. B. Eerdmans Pub. Co., 1939), IV, 2465.

[3] Dom Bernard Orchard, ed.; *A Catholic Commentary on the Holy Scripture* (New York, N.Y.: Thomas Nelson and Sons, 1953), p. 617.

[4] Allis, *Prophecy and the Church*, p. 242.

Israel as its nucleus, and memorial sacrifices of Christ's death instituted. But what is wrong with these elements? As Charles Feinberg incisively declares, "From Abraham to Jesus, including the disciples and the apostles . . . it was Jewish all the way. If the literal is too Jewish, where do you stop?" [1]

Suppose it is the eternal plan and will of God that the millennium should be the time when the Abrahamic and Davidic covenants will be fully realized, and when His chosen people and their land will become prominent, who are we to disapprove? Is it not logical to assume that, in the foreknowledge of God, Jewish prophets were chosen to write the kingdom prophecies precisely because the kingdom would be vitally related to God's chosen people—so long despised on the earth? Only Hebrew prophets, with their unique backgrounds, individualities, and life situations, would be able to grasp and delineate this special characteristic of the kingdom. Surely we must believe that God's choice of the Bible writers was made according to His foreknowledge of future events.

It is true that there is a paucity of description regarding the specific role of the church at the millennium. This is not because the church will not participate or will assume a secondary role in the kingdom. The reason for this apparent lack is that, in the Scripture the future hope of Christians is not anchored on a place or a period but in the person of Jesus Christ. The Scriptures present the church as waiting and looking for Christ over and above all future objects, rewards, and experiences. As the hymn writer Anne Ross Cousin so beautifully expresses it:

---

[1] Dwight L. Baker, "Bible Prophecy in the Prophets' City," *Christianity Today*, July 16, 1971, p. 29.

The bride eyes not her garment,
But her dear Bridegroom's face;
I will not gaze at glory;
But on my King of grace—
Not at the crown He giveth,
But on His pierced hand;
The Lamb is all the glory
Of Immanuel's land.

It is therefore fitting that the revelation of the church's role in the millennial kingdom should not be in elucidative detail. Christian will nevertheless actively participate in the affairs of the kingdom, for the Scripture reveals that the church will reign with Christ (cf. II Tim. 2:12; Rev. 5:10). The precise nature of this reign and other details connected with it are not given. It is possible that church saints will reign on earth in their immortal, glorified bodies (like Christ who fellowshipped bodily with the disciples after His resurrection,) while residing in the New Jerusalem which may be suspended above the millennial earth. This situation is probably analogous to angels who participate with God today in the government of the universe.

"It is probably more accurate to say that the church will reign with Christ in a different sense than saints of other ages," explains Walvoord. "An illustration is afforded in the book of Esther in the relationship of Esther and Mordecai to Ahasuerus. Esther, the queen, reigned with Ahasuerus as his wife and queen, while Mordecai reigned with Ahasuerus as his prime minister and chief administrative officer. Both Mordecai and Esther reigned with Ahasuerus but in different senses."[1]

---

[1] John F. Walvoord, *The Church in Prophecy* (Grand Rapids, Mich.: Zondervan Pub. House, 1964), pp. 156-57.

C. Consistency and Theological Systems

The connection between consistent hermeneutics and the theological systems is a real one. We shall now note how the various theological systems live up to consistent hermeneutics.

1. *Amillennialism and postmillennialism.*— The systems of amillennialism and postmillennialism must of necessity interpret prophecy very inconsistently. As George L. Murray says regarding his approach, "The plain truth is that there is not one chapter of the prophetic Scripture which can be taken with absolute literalness . . . . the only safe method of interpretation is neither strictly literal, nor strictly spiritual . . . ."[1]

Amillennialists spiritualize the "first" resurrection of Revelation 20 to mean the second birth of Christians (i.e. salvation), while accepting the second resurrection in the same verse to mean the literal raising of dead persons (i.e. resurrection). These interpreters also see the second advent of Christ as a literal advent and spiritualize away the worse aspects of the tribulation to make it more palatable to the church allegedly passing through it. Under these two non-literal theological systems, inconsistency clearly becomes a virtue and a help.

2. *Covenant premillennialism.*— The covenant premillennial position is less inconsistent in its literal hermeneutics. Perhaps "selectively inconsistent" best describes its hermeneutics. The attitude standard among covenant premillennialists is reflected in this question: "Can it be maintained that the Scriptures are *always* to be interpreted literally? This seems hardly possible."[2]   And so, the 144,000

---

[1] George L. Murray, *Millennial Studies* (Grand Rapids, Mich.: Baker Book House, 1948), p. 40.

[2] Ladd, *Kingdom of God*, p. 137.

Jews of Revelation 7 is spiritualized to mean the church,[1] while the 1,000 years of Revelation 20 is read literally as the earthly kingdom.

The danger in selective inconsistency is that, based neither entirely on the literal method nor entirely on the non-literal, the interpreter finds himself constantly struggling with the question of how far he should go spiritualizing or when he should stop literalizing. This is especially troublesome for those who wish to face eschatological issues squarely and extensively. Daniel P. Fuller, after attacking consistent literality and the dispensational system, candidly admits that "the whole problem of how far a literal interpretation of the Old Testament prophets is to be carried is still very perplexing to the present writer."[2]

The reason why covenant premillennialists are selectively inconsistent is because of their desire to be premillennial without being dispensational and pretribulational. They wish to retain the concept of the earthly millennium in premillennium while holding on to the one covenanted people idea in covenantism. They want what one writer describes as "amillennial covenantism with a premillennial topping." This mediating position however is virtually impossible to obtain Scripturally, for the Biblical systems of law and grace are irreconcilable (cf. Rom. 6:14-15).

The postmillennialist Boettner correctly sees the linkage between premillennialism and dispensationalism, saying: "There is a logical connection between Premillennialism and

---

[1] The Jehovah's Witnesses (Russellism) also allegorize the Jewish tribal names of these 144,000 persons and are thus able to interpret the group as 144,000 Jehovah's Witnesses.

[2] Daniel Peyton Fuller, "The Hermeneutics of Dispensationalism" (Doctor's dissertation, Northern Baptist Theol. Seminary, Chicago, 1957), p. 374.

Dispensationalism. Most of those who take Premillennialism seriously and become enthusiastic about it go on to adopt Dispensationalism. But, conversely, we believe that most of those who becomes convinced of the errors of Dispensationalism proceed to throw Premillennialism overboard too."[1]

And the amillennialist Berkhof also rightly connects premillennialism with dispensationalism: "The main pillars on which it [premillennialism] rests are undoubtedly the so-called literal or natural interpretation of the prophets, and the dispensational interpretation of the Bible. If this foundation is removed the building falls flat."[2]

Not only must premillennialism and dispensationalism go together, but premillennialism and pretribulationism are also inseparable. Consistent premillennialism leads to pretribulationism. The latter is the logical product of the former.

3. *Dispensationalism.*—The dispensational premillennial position is the product of consistent literal interpretation. It might even be said that to the degree one is consistently literal in prophetic interpretation, to the same degree has he approached the dispensational premillennial position.[3]

There are of course many areas of discussion among dispensational interpreters. For instance, the identity of the two witnesses of Revelation 11, the nature of the tribulation temple, the relationship of the church to the New Covenant, the "prince" of Ezekiel 34 and 37, are still being discussed among dispensationalists. There is no one-hundred percent

---

[1] Boettner, *The Millennium*, p. 158.

[2] Louis Berkhof, *The Kingdom of God* (Grand Rapids, Mich.: Wm. B. Eerdmans Pub. Co., 1951), p. 160.

[3] Oswald T. Allis calls consistent literal interpreters the "double Pre's" *(Prophecy and the Church,* p. 206). That is, believers in the *pre*tribulational rapture of the church and in the *pre*milennial coming of Christ to reign on earth.

agreement among literal interpreters on the finer points of prophecy, nor should it be expected this side of Glory. These fine points are of relative insignificance and relate to areas where the Scripture is not precise and clear. The question of consistency is usually not involved. On the other hand, dispensational interpreters are united in the framework of eschatology, as well as in a large number of prophetic details. This unity of viewpoint is the result of a consistent, normal approach to the prophetic Scripture.

We affirm that consistency of hermeneutics is far more important than the preservation of one's theological system. If attainable at all, the goal of Bible interpreters should be consistency regardless of theological systems.

XI

SOME PRACTICAL
CONSIDERATIONS

I. Literalism and the Future

Some interpreters feel that prophecy is so controversial that for answers to the question of prophecy, the best policy is to wait until Christ comes. Floyd Hamilton says, "We will *then* know who is right on these questions, anyway, so why quarrel now . . .?"[1] And Martin Wyngaarden agrees, "When we get there [to heaven], it will be early enough to find out whether these living waters from the throne of God have also a literal meaning."[2]

It is of course true that when Christ comes again, all questions of prophecy will be settled as the future becomes more fully known. But this does not mean that what has already been revealed in the Scripture should not be accepted by faith. In fact, there are good reasons why prophecy should be studied and understood in the present.

First even though a given prophecy may relate to the future and does not directly involve the present, God desires that His revelation of the future be presently comprehended.

---

[1] Floyd E. Hamilton, *The Basis of Millennial Faith* (Grand Rapids, Mich.: Wm. B. Eerdmans Pub. Co., 1942), p. 19.

[2] Martin Jacob Wyngaarden, *The Future of the Kingdom in Prophecy and Fulfillment* (Grand Rapids, Mich.: Baker Book House, 1955), pp. 77-78.

272

In Daniel 10:14, Daniel is told by the revealing angel, "I am come to make thee understand what shall befall thy people in the latter days; for yet the vision is for many days." It is apparent that God intended Daniel to *understand* future events which would not occur until the latter days.

An attitude toward Bible prophecy common among the Israelites and which greatly displeased the Lord is recorded in Ezekiel 12:27

> Son of man, behold, they of the house of Israel say,
> The vision that he seeth is for many days to come,
> and he prophesieth of the times that are far off.
> [Ezek. 12:28]

Second, the Bible is clear that God's rewards are for those who have obeyed and heeded the commands given in Scripture. Most Christians are aware of the Great Commission, "Go ye into all the world, and preach the gospel to every creature" (Mark 16:15). Strangely, not many of the redeemed are aware that Christ also commands believers to understand and keep the words of prophecy. This command is given not once but several times in Scripture.

For instance, our Lord commands concerning the Book of Daniel that "whosoever readeth, let him understand" (Matt. 24:15). On the road to Emmaus, Christ holds His disciples accountable for not listening to the Old Testament Scriptures, with this rebuke: "O fools, and slow of heart to believe all that the prophets have spoken" (Luke 24:25). Even in heaven, Christ still passes the word down concerning the Book of Revelation: "Blessed is he that readeth, and they that hear the sayings of this prophecy, and keep those things which are written in it; for the time is at hand" (Rev. 1:3).

It is obvious that there is only one order of future events, and therefore only one system of prophecy is correct. When before the Bema Seat of Christ, are we not expected to be able to say to the Lord, "Lord we took you at your word, we interpreted the future as you have literally revealed it"? Christ's words to Thomas may again be heard, "Blessed are they that have not seen, and yet have believed" (John 20:29).

It is true that, this side of heaven, we are often left with more questions than answers, and much of what is in the future is yet to be revealed in Glory. But heaven's rewards will surely belong to those who have believed and acted on the half that *has* been told.

Third, the proper understanding of prophecy will produce a life of purity (I John 3:3). The knowledge that Christ is coming for the church at any moment encourages believers to be ready in this life, looking for Him instead of to some intervening catastrophic event or death. The confidence that the future is going to be worked out according to God's plan gives patience and hope amidst the despairs and injustices of this present godless world system.[1]

Alva. J. McClain sums up this important point: "The premillennial philosophy of history makes sense. It makes a Biblical and rational basis for a truly optimistic view of human history. Furthermore, rightly apprehended, it has practical effects. It says that life here and now, in spite of the tragedy of sin, is nevertheless something worth-while; and therefore all efforts to make it better are also worth-while. Furthermore, we are encouraged in the midst of opposition and reverses by the

---

[1]Ever since the fall of man, Satan has ruled over fallen mankind. God never was able to demonstrate fully His ability to rule over those whom He created in the flesh in the beginning. If there were no future reign of God on earth, the question of God's ability to rule over the people He created in physical form would remain eternally unanswered.

assurance that help is on the way, help from above, super-natural help . . . ."[1]

II. LITERALISM AND LIBERALISM

An undeniable advantage which acceptance of literal interpretation of prophecy affords, and of which church leaders may well take note, is that the literal method has the effect of hindering the growth of liberalism and modernism in the church. It is virtually impossible to find a literal inter-preter of prophecy who is also a liberal theologian.[2]

The reason is simple. The literal method by its very nature accepts the verbal, plenary inspiration of Scripture; liberalism by its very nature does not. The basis of the literal method is the acknowledgement of the fact that the words of Scripture are inspired. The literal approach is thus consonant with the nature and fact of Bible inspiration—a doctrine which modernism utterly rejects.

It is possible of course to hold to Scriptural inspiration and not interpret prophecy literally, but it is virtually impossible to interpret prophecy literally without also accepting the doctrine of inspiration. Literal interpretation and Bible in-spiration go hand in hand. This is why liberals violently attack Christianity on the issue of the *literal* renderings of Scripture. "Fundamentalists are literalists who are militantly anti-critical," charges Robert M. Grant. "Their naive pseudo-biblical theology leads them to insist on the verbal inerrancy of

---

[1] Alva J. McClain, *The Greatness of the Kingdom* (Grand Rapids, Mich.: Zondervan Pub. House, 1959), p. 531.

[2] "One of the side effects of a proper emphasis on the doctrine of the rapture [the result of consistent literality]," observes John Walvoord, "is that it seems to have the curious result of promoting orthodoxy in theology as a whole" (*The Church in Prophecy* [Grand Rapids, Mich.: Zondervan Pub. House, 1964], p. 119).

Scripture."[1] Prophecy is rightly considered the highest evidence of the supernatural origin of the Bible. But this evidence is possible only when the Bible is literally read and interpreted.

While the literal method is an excellent barrier against the inroads of liberalism, the allegorical or spiritualized approach to Scripture easily fosters liberalism. The reason again is not hard to find. By the use of spiritualization, prophetic interpreters imply that they cannot take the entire Word of God at face value, thus weakening the case for verbal, plenary inspiration. In fact, there are evangelicals who begin by spiritualizing prophecy, then deny that every word of Scripture is inspired, and end up teaching that only the "revelational" parts or the ideas and concepts of the Bible are inspired. Such a weakened doctrine of inspiration is a welcome sign to liberalism. The reformer Martin Luther is right when he says: "I have observed this, that all heresies and errors have originated not from the simple words of Scripture, as is so universally asserted, but from *neglecting* the simple words of Scripture, and from the affectation of purely subjective tropes and inferences."[2]

Evangelicals who spiritualize Bible prophecy cannot logically forbid liberals and modernists from spiritualizing selected areas of Christology and soteriology. If evangelicals can spiritualize Christ's earthly kingdom, may not liberals spiritualize the earthly ministry of Christ, including His miracles and resurrection? The same hermeneutical principles used to spiritualize Bible prophecy can be used to spiritualize Christ's first advent. Christians who spiritualize parts of the

---

[1] Robert M. Grant, *The Bible in the Church* (New York, N.Y.: The Macmillan Co., 1948), p. 161.

[2] Quoted by Frederic W. Farrar, *History of Interpretation* (London: The Macmillan and Co., 1886), p. 327.

Scriptures, such as its prophetic portions, have forfeited a major element of their defense against liberalism.

Not surprisingly, therefore, many leading Protestant denominations (avowedly non-literal in prophecy) are now in death struggles with liberalism which has crept into their midst. The non-literal approach to prophecy has helped open the door to liberalism and fostered its growth within the church. The potent combination of literal interpretation of prophecy and verbal, plenary inspiration would have been an impregnable barrier against liberalism.

III. PROPHECY IN THE CHURCH

Prophecy in itself is not crucial to orthodoxy or salvation. It should therefore never be made an issue determining the lines of fellowship among Christians. The dividing line among believers in matters of fellowship is the cardinal doctrines of the faith, not a particular system of eschatology.

On the other hand, prophecy occupies such a sizable part of God's Word that it cannot remain for long in the side lines. Sooner or later, the teaching and preaching ministries of the church will encounter Bible prophecy. What then? There is no sadder scene than to see leaders within a church group giving forth uncertain or contradictory sounds. The seeds of confusion are soon sown.

A logical alternative under such a situation is to neglect or play down the significance of the prophetic Scripture, possibly by disclaiming full understanding of it this side of heaven. But by leaving such a large part of God's Word untouched or interpreted cursorily, church leaders will be feeding a partial diet to their flock.

From the practical standpoint, therefore, a church group or Christian organization has the right—indeed an obligation—to assure uniformity among its leadership in at least the general scheme of prophecy. This has no relationship to the issue of orthodoxy or the question of fellowship among believers, which must be maintained regardless of prophetic interpretation. Yet when the leadership of the church is united in heart and spirit on the prophetic Scriptures, it affords Satan much less occasion to discount the Word of God in the church.

The call for unity in the area of prophecy is the more pressing when one realizes that prophecy not only occupies a major portion of Scripture but tends to relate to almost all areas of God's Word. Prophecy is not confined to a specific portion of the Word. It extends its roots all over the Scripture. "Eschatological interpretations have a definite bearing upon many of the other doctrines which one holds. One's entire system of theology, view of history, interpretation of Scripture, view of the Church as an organism and as an organization in relation to other organizations, and view of Biblical theology is determined to a great extent by his view of eschatology."[1]

The question of infant baptism, for instance, is basically related to the interpretation of Bible prophecy, as seen in the explanation of Wyngaarden: "How then is this old covenant spiritualized, according to the Biblical teaching concerning the new covenant? . . . Meanwhile, these inquires are also fundamental to the question whether infant baptism should be rejected or not . . . ."[2]

Or, take the person and work of Christ. Since all major prophetic themes are related in some way either to the first or

---

[1] Robert P. Lightner, *Neo-Evangelicalism* (Des Plaines, Ill.: Regular Baptist Press, 1965), p. 102.

[2] Martin Jacob Wyngaarden, *The Future of the Kingdom in Prophecy and Fulfillment* (Grand Rapids, Mich.: Baker Book House, 1955), p. 122.

the second advent of Christ, the neglect of prophecy means the neglect of some aspects of the person and work of Christ. The importance of prophecy in the church therefore cannot be gainsaid.

XII

CONCLUSION

How one interprets prophecy determines how one's eschatology is going to be worked out. As long as the issue of interpretation remains unsettled, it is futile to debate the schemes and details of Bible prophecy. All questions of prophecy must ultimately be settled within the framework of proper hermeneutics.

We have attempted to establish in this book the case for proper interpretation of prophecy. We have shown that good and sound hermeneutics demands the literal interpretation of the entire Scriptures, including its prophecy. In addition to the fact that the literal interpretation of prophecy is based on Scriptural authority, historical fulfillments, early church precedent, and practical necessity, we have clarified the basic nature of prophecy and the prophetic processes, and have shown how they validate the literal approach. The prophetic Scriptures certainly do not originate in the human imagination but are the product of the work of the Holy Spirit in inspiration.

We have also examined the propriety of interpreting prophecy according to regular rules of hermeneutics. No special spectacles need to be worn when the prophetic Scriptures are viewed. The Scriptures, both prophetic and non-prophetic, should be interpreted according to regular rules governing normal communication among sensible men.

The proper view of the language of prophecy demands that the nonfigurative, the non-symbolical, and the non-typical, instead of the figurative, symbolical, and typical, occupy the greater portion of the prophetic Scriptures. When Bible prophecy lurks under a smoke screen of what is non-actual and unreal, it ceases to be revelation and becomes a riddle.

We have explained how prophecy, with respect to its fulfillment, generally looks forward to a given event, although foreshadowments and applications of that event are possible. Multiple fulfillments of prophecy do not truly reflect the basic outworkings of divine revelation.

In the final sections of this book, we have set forth our findings on some crucial hermeneutical and theologial issues relative to prophetic interpretation. The settlement of these issues is largely dependent on the degree of literality which one grants himself during interpretation. We have argued for the solution of these issues on the basis of consistent literal hermeneutics.

The case for the literal interpretation of prophecy has now been set forth. Its principles, procedures, applications, and implications have been presented. Blessed is the interpreter who willingly takes Bible prophecy at face value, for then will the prophetic Word be "a light that shineth in a dark place" (II Pet. 1:9). The interpreter will have a deep sense of confidence and pleasure, as he deals with facts and not fancy in unlocking the matchless treasures of God's Word.

When the interpreter has arrived at a well-based interpretation of prophecy, the next step is to apply this discovery to lives. Lives throbbing with all sorts of problems reach out for the comfort, hope, and cheer found in the sure word of prophecy. The consecrated interpreter who has diligently excavated truths from the Word of God and then prayerfully deposited them into the recesses of the minds of men may rightfully be decorated as "a workman that needeth not to be ashamed" (II Tim. 2:15).

"EVEN SO, COME, LORD JESUS"

APPENDIXES

APPENDIX I
THE NEW JERUSALEM

The prophecy of the New Jerusalem is an area on which good men have honestly struggled and bitterly fought. The most crucial question is whether the Biblical descriptions of the New Jerusalem point to an actual, material heavenly city or are intended to be a figure or symbol of something else.

I. THE NON-LITERAL APPROACH

A. Reasons for the Approach

A large number of interpreters insist that the New Jerusalem in Revelation 21 and 22 must be interpreted figuratively and symbolically. Aside from the reasoning that the description is given in a vision and is moreover found "in a highly symbolical book,"[1] several stronger reasons are given for the rejection of a material city.

One reason frequently adduced is the abnormal and phenomenal size of the city. The seer John describes the city as 12,000 furlongs long, wide, and high (cf. Rev. 21:16). This results in a city that is 1,500 miles long and wide, with its height reaching into outer space. Due to the gigantic measurements of the New Jerusalem, many interpreters forthwith

---

[1] Louis Berkhof, *Systematic Theology* (4th ed. rev.; Grand Rapids, Mich.: Wm. B. Eerdmans Pub. Co., 1949), p. 715.

jump into the non-literal camp. "Such dimensions defy imagination," sighs interpreter Swete, "permissible only in the language of symbolism."[1] Albert Barnes wryly concludes that: "The idea of a city literally descending from heaven, and being set upon the earth with such proportions. . . is absurd."[2]

There are interpreters also who find the dizzying heights of the city a dead giveaway to symbolism. Criticizing its stellar heights, P.W. Grant concludes that there is "no clearer proof . . . that all is figurative. Such a height is simply out of harmony with the constitution of our world."[3]

Moreover, the presence of material objects in the New Jerusalem does not seem right to some men. Clarke believes that "gold and jewels can have no place in the spiritual and eternal world."[4] and Grant observes that there will be "no material walls and gates, . . . All are symbolic of the exaltation and safety and glory and blessedness of the true Israel of God."[5]

The crux of the matter, however, is not whether a prophesied object or event is natural to the present scene, but whether it will be possible in the eternal state and is consonant with God's way of doing things. Regarding the size of the New Jerusalem, John Walvoord says: "Whatever its shape, a city of large dimensions would be proper, if it is to be the residence

---

[1] Henry Barclay Swete, *The Apocalypse of St. John* (London: Macmillan and Co., Ltd., 1907), p. 289.

[2] Albert Barnes, *Notes on the New Testament*, Vol. XI: *Book of Revelation* (London: Blackie and Son, n.d.), p. 481.

[3] P.W. Grant, *The Revelation of John* (London: Hodder and Stoughton, 1889), p. 593.

[4] Adam Clarke, *The New Testament with a Commentary and Critical Notes*, ed. by Daniel Curry, Vol. VI: *The Epistles and Revelation* (New York, N.Y.: Eaton and Mains, 1883), p. 630.

[5] Grant, *The Revelation of John*, p. 591.

of the saved of all ages including infants who died before reaching the age of accountability. It is not necessarily true, however, to hold that everyone will live continually within its walls throughout eternity. The implications are that there is plenty of room for everyone and that this city provides a residence for the saints of all ages."[1]

B. How the New Jerusalem is Symbolized

Once the New Jerusalem is approached non-literally, it is usually identified as a symbol of the Christian church. "A gorgeous Oriental symbol of the beautiful church which you see all around you,"[2] affirm many interpreters. Others think that it symbolizes the future of the church, *viz.*, "the Church in its later prosperity and universal increase."[3]

Another group of interpreters, while not necessarily identifying the New Jerusalem as a symbol of the church, interpret it to be a symbol of heavenly joy. In other words, what John sees of heaven is so stupendous, incomprehensible, and out-of-this-world, that he has to use symbols and figures taken from contemporary times in order that his readers might understand.

C. The Cults and the Symbolized City

A symbolical New Jerusalem is crucial to at least three major cults—Christian Science, Mormonism, and the Swedenborgians.

---

[1] John F. Walvoord, *The Revelation of Jesus Christ* (Chicago, Ill.: Moody Press, 1966), p. 324.

[2] Cited by J.A. Seiss, *The Apocalypse* (London: Marshall, Morgan and Scott, Ltd., n.d.), p. 494.

[3] Clarke, *Commentary and Critical Notes*, p. 631.

Christian Science symbolizes almost every detail of the New Jerusalem in order to fit it into the cult's teachings. To the leaders of Christian Science, the prophecy of the New Jerusalem is "the Alpha and Omega of Divine Science."[1] In other words, a big help! Thus, the phrase "no temple" in the New Jerusalem means "the real man's incorporeality,"[2] and the "Lamb's wife" describes "the spiritual unity of male and female as no longer two, but one; and this compounded spiritual idea reflects God as infinite Mind, not as a Corporeal Being."[3]

Joseph Smith, founder of Mormonism, attempted to establish the symbolized New Jerusalem ("Zion") in the State of Missouri. This was ostensibly in fulfillment of two new revelations given to him. The first revelation allegedly given in February, 1831 reads: "If thou shalt ask, thou shalt receive revelation upon revelation, knowledge upon knowledge, . . . Thou shalt ask, and it shall be revealed unto you in mine own due time, where the New Jerusalem shall be built."[4] And the other revelation in September, 1832 supposedly reveals that the New Jerusalem shall be built "in the western boundaries of the State of Missouri."[5] However, being unsuccessful and driven out of Missouri, the Mormons ultimately settled in the State of Utah.

The Swedenborgians, a small but intellectually influential sect, were organized in the British Isles in 1821. Its founder, Emmanuel Swedenborg (1688-1772), had a special revelation

---

[1] Mary Baker G. Eddy, *Science and Health with Key to the Scriptures* (Boston, Mass.: Joseph Armstrong, 1898), p. 566.

[2] *Ibid.*, p. 568.

[3] *Ibid.*

[4] *Book of Covenants and Doctrines* (Lamoni, Iowa: The Reorganized Church of Jesus Christ of Latter Day Saints, 1913), p. 80.

[5] *Ibid.*, p. 151.

that the year 1757 would mark the time when the "old church" (or Christianity in its traditional form) would pass away and all things become new. This change from the "apostolic" to the "apocalyptic" means that the New Jerusalem has arrived on earth. The Swedenborgians therefore call themselves the Church of the New Jerusalem.

Founder Swedenborg wrote voluminously, and his commentary on the Book of Revelation, *The Apocalypse Revealed*, is an example of uncontrollable hermeneutics on a rampage. The following quotation will suffice: "By the twelve thousand furlongs [in Rev. 21:16] are signified all the goods and truths of that church. That twelve thousand signifies the like as twelve, and that twelve signifies all goods and truths . . . ."[1]

II. THE LITERAL APPROACH

Dispensational premillennial interpreters believe that the account of the New Jerusalem must be interpreted literally. Here are some of the more important reasons.

First, in the description of the New Jerusalem, all the elements of an actual city—dimensions, foundations, walls, gates, streets—are indicated. The human inhabitants of the city are not in super-human forms. As McClain observes, "There is no reason for balking at the literality of the city itself. While some details of its structure may not be fully understood, none of them are wholly outside the realm of sober possibility."[2]

---

[1] Emmanuel Swedenborg, *The Apocalypse Revealed* (Phila., Pa.: J.B. Lippincott and Co., 1876), p. 1053.

[2] Alva J. McClain, *The Greatness of the Kingdom* (Grand Rapids, Mich.: Zondervan Pub. House, 1959), p. 511.

Second, although the apostle John sees this prophecy in a vision, he certainly does not resort to imagination nor indulge in exaggeration. When he sees materials which are indescribable, he takes pain to use analogies ("like jasper," and "like clear glass"). The fact that John records non-earthly things such as gate-sized pearls proves that he does not alter the form of the prophecy for the sake of reader comprehension. What was seen in the vision he dutifully records.

Third, the angel who shows John around the heavenly city is the same one who introduces the harlot sitting on a beast four chapters away (Rev. 17), In the account of the harlot on the beast, the angel, by explaining it in great detail (vs. 7-18) and ending with the interpretation "the woman whom thou sawest is that great city" (v. 18), identifies that account as a *symbol.* In the account of the New Jerusalem, however, the same angel offers not a word or clue regarding its possible symbolism. Everything is revealed as if real and actual. And when John, in pent-up gratitude and joy, is ready to worship the angel, the reply is: "See thou do it not. . . . Worship God. . . . Blessed are they that wash their robes, that they. . . may enter in through the gates into the city" (Rev. 22:9-14).

Thus, even in his parting words, the revealing angel still does not interpret the alleged symbolism of the New Jerusalem, but again mentions its pearly gates.

Fourth, in the account of the New Jerusalem, the inhabitants of the city are differentiated from the city itself. If the New Jerusalem symbolizes the church, and its inhabitants are church members, how could the church separate from itself? As we have explained in pages 161-162, a symbol cannot be seen separated from itself.

Fifth, the patriarch Abraham, tenting in the Land of Canaan, "looked for a *city* which hath foundations whose builder and marker is God" (Heb. 11:10). Moreover, the early Hebrew Christians were assured of their positional rights "unto the *city* of the living God, the heavenly Jerusalem" (Heb. 12:22). And our Lord promises the disciples, "In my Father's house are many mansions" (John 14:3). This hope of a city promised to so many people down the ages surely cannot be a symbol. It would represent deception of the highest order if the saints ultimately were to find some ethereal state of happiness or even themselves as the object of their age-long search.

Interpreter Newell is right when he says: "The sublime faith of Abraham led him to leave a city in the most remarkable civilization known on earth, and become a stranger and pilgrim, caring only for a cave in which to bury his dead . . . . Abraham will be satisfied with nothing short of a *place*, such as he looked for. And God will not disappoint him."[1]

Sixth, an actual, material city in eternity is proper and logical because of the constitution of the redeemed who will be in resurrected bodies throughout eternity. A resurrected body without any material point of reference would be highly unsatisfactory. An incorporeal and immaterial eternity does not take hold of the soul. "It is nothing but a world of shadows, of mist, of dim visions of blessedness, with which it is impossible for a being who is not mere spirit, and never will be mere spirit, who knows only to live in a body and shall live forever in a body, to feel any fellowship or sympathy."[2]

Seventh, although a literal, material New Jerusalem may be difficult for theologically trained scholars to accept, it comes naturally and logically to the thinking of most uncritical

---

[1] William R. Newell, *The Book of the Revelation* (Chicago, Ill.: The Scripture Press, 1935), p. 349.
[2] Seiss, *Apocalypse,* p. 494.

laymen. A literal eternal city seems to fulfill the longings of the soul. "In sermons, prayers, hymns, in our conversation, hopes and longings, we generally present this literal aspect, as the one most naturally suggested, and the most consonant with our desires and anticipations. Hence, the advocacy of a literal city is not so far removed from Christian feeling and concurrence, as many supposed."[1]

III. A CLARIFICATION

Perhaps we should clarify our stand on the New Jerusalem, by noting that to insist that the New Jerusalem is material and substantial is not necessarily to rule out the fact that there are spiritual applications and lessons to be derived from its structural parts and features. For instance, the "river of life" (Rev. 22:1) is a real, actual river, but it corresponds to the abundance of spiritual life which will be possessed by all in the Eternal City. "Every detail should be taken literally," says Herman A. Hoyt, "[but] everything in this city speaks of something about the glories and virtues of God, indicating that the materials serve a twofold purpose: (1) they are the substance of construction; and (2) they provide symbolism for contemplation."[2]

---

[1] George N.H. Peters, *The Theocratic Kingdom* (3 vols.; Grand Rapids, Mich.: Kregel Pubs., 1952), III, 41.

[2] Herman A. Hoyt, *The Revelation of the Lord Jesus Christ* (Winona Lake, Ind.: Brethren Missionary Herald Co., 1966), pp. 104-5.

APPENDIX II
THE MILLENNIAL SACRIFICES

In Ezekiel chapters 43 to 46, we are given a detailed account of sacrifices and offerings inside the Millennial Temple. If one interprets Ezekiel's prophecy normally, there is no escaping the fact that there will be animal sacrifices during the millennium.

But once the interpreter accepts the millennial sacrifices, he is laughed out of court under a barrage of sneers and protests. He is reminded of the New Testament teaching that Christ's one sacrifice on the cross forever superseded the Levitical sacrifices. "It is one of the plainest universal teachings of the New Testament," states Snowden, "that the sacrifices of the Mosaic economy were fulfilled in Christ and were then done away as vanishing shadows . . . ."[1] And Archibald Hughes is sarcastic: "To restore all these today, under the New Covenant, would be apostasy. But, in a millennium, under the same New Covenant, it is supposed to be according to prophecy!"[2]

The following observations, however, should lend themselves to an adequate reply on the issue of the millennial sacrifices:

---

[1] James H. Snowden, *The Coming of the Lord* (New York, N.Y.: The Macmillan Co., 1919), p. 206.

[2] Archibald Hughes, *A New Heaven and a New Earth* (Phila., Pa.: The Presbyterian and Reformed Pub. Co., 1958), p. 157.

First, the interpreter who rejects the millennial sacrifices usually also rejects the millennial kingdom. This rejection of an earthly kingdom always goes hand in hand with the rejection of the literal approach to prophecy. Conversely, once the literal approach is upheld, the millennial sacrifices shine under a new light and appear quite logical. As non-literal interpreter Loraine Boettner puts it quite aptly, "Only to a literalist does the re-establishment of the sacrificial system and temple ritual seem sensible. To a Post or Amillennialist it is too materialistic." [1]

Second, millennial sacrifices are predicted not only by Ezekiel but also by other Old Testament prophets, such as Isaiah (Isa. 56:6-7; 60:7), Zechariah (Zech. 14:16-21), and Jeremiah (Jer. 33:15-18). In fact, Jeremiah discusses the millennial sacrifices under the context of the Davidic covenant, and so places the sacrifices on a much stronger basis than does Ezekiel.

In the New Testament, Christ Himself certainly foresees the reinstitution of Jewish ritualism when He urges tribulation saints to "pray that your flight be not in the winter, neither on the sabbath day" (Matt. 24:20), for Jewish ritualistic travel regulations would hinder escape on the Sabbath. Moreover, the Abomination of Desolation is predicted to stand in the *temple* (Matt. 24:15 "the holy place") during the tribulation. The apostle Paul describes the tribulation's Man of Sin as one who "sitteth in the temple of God" (II Thess. 2:4).

Third, animal sacrifices, whether in the Old Testament, in the present dispensation, or in the kingdom age, can *never* take away sin (cf. Heb. 10:4). The blood of animals is never divinely intended to be efficacious or expiatory for salvation

---

[1] Loraine Boettner, *The Millennium* (Phila., Pa.: The Presbyterian and Reformed Pub. Co., 1964), p. 95.

(cf. Heb. 10:1-2). McClain says, "No animal sacrifice in the Bible has ever had any expiatory significance."[1] Yet, many non-literal interpreters say that sacrifices offered during Old Testament times were efficacious. Oswald T. Allis, for instance, affirms that Old Testament sacrifices". . . were expiatory [and] efficacious in the days of Moses and of David."[2]

By affirming that Old Testament sacrifices were efficacious, amillennialists are then able to back premillennialists into the corner, for the latter believe that the millennial sacrifices will be the restoration (albeit in more glorious forms and with fullest significance) of Old Testament sacrifices. Since Old Testament sacrifices were allegedly efficacious, the millennial sacrifices would be efficacious too, and this would blatantly contradict and minimize the sacrifice which Christ makes on the cross. However, in affirming the efficacious character of Old Testament sacrifices, amillennialists themselves have already minimized the cross, for if animal sacrifices were really efficacious during Old Testament days, there would have been no necessity for the cross of Christ.

The true view of the Old Testament sacrifices is that sacrifices serve to cover over sins until the cross of Christ, which once and for all perfected the saints. This is the theme of the Book of Hebrews, which is addressed to a congregation then made up mostly of Jewish converts and who had a tendency to slip back into former practices. The book argues that Christians have no more use for animal sacrifices now that Christ has already come, and that the sin question has been settled by virtue of the death of Christ.

---

[1]Alva J. McClain, *The Greatness of the Kingdom* (Grand Rapids, Mich.: Zondervan Pub. House, 1959), p. 250.

[2]Oswald T. Allis, *Prophecy and the Church* (Phila., Pa.: The Presbyterian and Reformed Pub. Co., 1964), p. 246.

Fourth, while animal sacrifices have been done away at the cross, there is no reason why some *reminders* of Christ's perfect and final sacrifice should not be allowed—both during the present church age and the millennial age.

During the present age, we have actually been given a reminder of Christ's sacrifice in the bread and wine of the Lord's Supper. Christ commands His disciples to partake "in remembrance of me" (Luke 22:19). The apostle Paul tells the Corinthians believers that the Lord's Supper is intended to "show the Lord's death till he come" (I Cor. 11:26). Why "till he come"? Because Christians will be in the immortal, resurrected state when the Lord comes again, and they will then need no outward memorials to remind them of the awful sacrifice of Christ on the cross.

However, there will be non-resurrected inhabitants of the millennium who will need *visible* reminders of Christ's sacrifice for them on the cross. According to prophecy, God has chosen to use the millennial sacrifices as reminders for those mortals in the kingdom of Christ's sacrifice.[1] "If the all-important subject of converse on the Mount of Trans-figuration was 'His decease' which He was to accomplish at Jerusalem, how much more will the merits and benefits of His death be the all-engrossing subject of discussion in that day . . . ."[2]

---

[1] Floyd E. Hamilton replies that ". . . any memorials are unnecessary when the one to be memorialized is present in person, as Christ would be after His Second Coming "(*The Basis of Millennial Faith* [Grand Rapids, Mich.: Wm. B. Eerdmans Pub. Co., 1942)], p. 40).

While this may be true in most cases when the person *himself* is to be remembered, it certainly does not apply when one's works and deeds are to be commemorated. Thus, stamps, coins, plaques, etc. bear the names and portraits of *living* personages in commemoration of their works and services.

[2] Merrill F. Unger, *Great Neglected Prophecies* (Chicago, Ill.: Scripture Press, 1955), p. 75.

Fifth, while the millennial sacrifices will commemorate and be reminders of the sacrifice of Christ, they will not be purely memorial in nature. They will relate to life under the theocracy as well.

This is what we mean. In a real sense, the millennial kingdom will be the Jewish theocracy restored. Now, under the Old Testament economy, sacrifices were brought by the worshipper for two reaons: (1) because of the consciousness or "remembrance" of sin (cf. Heb. 10:3), and (2) for theocratic adjustments. Since Old Testament individuals were corporately related to the theocracy, sins committed by an individual so related would affect his relationship to the theocracy. But as long as the offerings were made, reconciliation and theocratic adjustments were possible. Those who did not participate in the sacrifices were "cut off" from the congregation.

Because of the restoration of the theocracy at the millennium,[1] the Old Testament theocratic arrangements will remain largely in effect. Just as the sacrifices in the Old Testament serve to effect theocratic adjustments for the offender, the millennial sacrifices will also "make reconciliation for the house of Israel" (Ezek. 45:15-17; cf. 44:29), and it will be what God will gladly accept (Ezek. 43:27).

In connection with Ezekiel's temple sacrifices, a favorite text often mentioned by amillennial interpreters is Ezekiel 44:9, which reads:

> No foreigner, uncircumcised in heart or uncircumcised in flesh, shall enter into my sanctuary, of any foreigner that is among the children of Israel. [Ezek. 44:9]

---

[1] A *theocracy* is the government of a state by the immediate direction of God.

And the question from the critics is taunting: "Just what would our premillennial friends suggest that circumcision would be a 'memorial' of?"[1]

In reply, it must be noted that during Old Testament days, non-Jews were not barred from participation in the worship of Jehovah. Foreigners or non-Jews were allowed to present their offerings in the house of the Lord (cf. Lev. 17:10, 12; Num. 15:14). In this text of Ezekiel, however, the prophet is dealing with the sacrilegious and unauthorized practice of foreigners officiating in the sanctuary. Although such infringements were probably winked at before (cf. Ezek. 44:7), the prophet now predicts that the practice would be strictly banned in the millennial temple (Ezek. 44:9). The rule of the house would be that only those who are circumcized in heart and flesh may officiate in the millennial temple.[2]

The obvious significance of this house rule is to preserve the sanctity of worship in the millennium and to grant central position to the chosen people of God inside the millennial temple. This is a practical house rule, and it is gratuitous to force any far-fetched significance from it.

---

[1] Hamilton, *Basis of Millennial Faith*, p. 43.

[2] In the last verse of his book, Zechariah again prophesied that "in that day there shall be no more a Canaanite in the house of the Lord of hosts" (Zech. 14:21; cf. Ezra 8:20 and Josh. 9).

APPENDIX III
JESUS' OFFER OF THE KINGDOM

Both Jesus and John the Baptist begin their public ministries with the call: "Repent for the kingdom of heaven is at hand" (Matt. 3:1; 4:17). Jesus sends his disciples to preach with these instructions:

> Go not into the way of the Gentiles, and into any city of the Samaritans enter not; But go, rather, to the lost sheep of the house of Israel. And as ye go, preach, saying, "The kingdom of heaven is at hand." [Matt. 10:5-7]

Later on, when another group of disciples (the Seventy) returns joyfully from their preaching of the kingdom (Luke 10:9), Jesus tells them: "Blessed are the eyes which see the things that ye see; For I tell you that many prophets and kings have desired to see those things which ye see, and have not seen them" (Luke 10:23-24).

I. IDENTIFICATION OF THE PROFERRED KINGDOM

From normal reading of the Gospels, there is no other alternative—either Christ offered the kingdom prophesied by the Old Testament prophets or He offered a completely new kingdom which spiritually fulfills Old Testament prophecies.

The latter concept is espoused by non-dispensational interpreters who say that "Jesus offered a spiritual kingdom, and for that reason it was rejected."[1] When the Jews, who were expecting the earthly kingdom, refuse to accept Jesus' new concept of the kingdom, Christ then institutes the Christian church. From then on, the church becomes "spiritual Israel," replacing Israel forever as God's chosen people, and comes into existence as the legal recipient of the promises and covenants made to ancient Israel. "The kingdom which was rejected by the Jewish nation was successfully inaugurated and may be experienced even now,"[2] says George Ladd.

Normal interpretation of the Gospels, however, brings out the fact that Jesus offers the earthly, Davidic kingdom promised by the prophets, and that when the Jews reject the offer, the kingdom is postponed and the church age or intercalation is started. Three main reasons support this affirmation.

First, the Jews of Jesus' day were united in waiting for the Messiah to come and restore the Davidic throne and kingdom. This Messianic expectation was tenaciously subscribed to by both the religious and the irreligious of the nation.[3] Thus, Zacharias, the father of John the Baptist,

---

[1] Clarence B. Bass, *Backgrounds to Dispensationalism* (Grand Rapids, Mich.: Wm. B. Eerdmans Pub. Co., 1960), pp. 29-30.

[2] George Eldon Ladd, *Crucial Questions About the Kingdom of God* (Grand Rapids, Mich.: Wm. B. Eerdmans Pub. Co., 1952), p. 60. In pages 112-114, Ladd correctly points out that if Jesus *did* offer the Davidic kingdom, then the Jewish elements of the kingdom must be affirmed. But these elements are of course unacceptable to Ladd.

[3] George Peters observes: "Even the rabbis, who had already largely perverted Scriptures by allegorical and mystical interpretations, still clung with unswerving faith to the plain grammatical sense when it related to the kingdom. The testimony on this point is overwhelming" (*The Theocratic Kingdom* [3 vols; Grand Rapids, Mich.: Kregel Pubs., 1952], I, 260).

praises God for raising up the Messiah predicted "by the mouth of his holy prophets . . . that we should be saved from our enemies and from the hand of all that hate us" (Luke 1:69-71). The angel Gabriel tells Mary concerning Jesus that "the Lord God shall give unto him the throne of his father David" (Luke 1:32). The Jews at Herod's court accurately describe the coming Messiah as "a Governor that shall rule my people, Israel" (Matt. 2:6).

Amillennial interpreters admit that the Jews had waited for the fulfillment of the prophecies concerning the Messianic kingdom. But they accompany this admission by accusing the Jews of having been mistaken in their expectation. "It was this literalizing of the Jewish prophecies of the coming Messiah and his kingdom," states Snowden, "that led the Jews off into views and hopes of the Messiah that were false and cruelly disappointed . . . . It was the literal interpretation of their Scriptures that blinded the Jews to their own Messiah."[1]

Whether we believe the Jews to be right or wrong in awaiting the kingdom, it is important at this point to note that the Jews were awaiting the kingdom promised by their prophets when Jesus came to offer the kingdom.

Second, the Lord begins His public ministry by issuing an urgent call to repentance, "for the kingdom is at hand." No explanation is given by Jesus concerning the true nature of the kingdom He is offering, nor does He correct the prevailing Jewish concept of the kingdom. If Jesus were truly offering a kingdom different from the common Jewish expectations, He certainly would not mince words in telling the people about it. Even some non-dispensationalists candidly observe that: "But for all his repeated mention of the Kingdom of God, Jesus never once paused to define it. Nor did any hearer ever

---

[1] James H. Snowden, *The Coming of the Lord* (New York, N.Y.: The Macmillan Co., 1919), pp. 198-99.

interrupt him to ask, 'Master, what do these words, "kingdom of God," which you use so often, mean?' "[1]

If the Jews were wrong in expecting the restoration of the Davidic kingdom, common honesty (even apart from divine integrity) would require that Jesus first point out their error before offering them His kingdom. How could Christ in good faith ask the people to repent, and, on the condition of their repentance, offer them a kingdom radically different from what they were expecting? This would make Him guilty of misleading the people.

Jesus does not correct the prevailing Jewish concept of the kingdom but actually uses Jewish terminologies and definitions in proclaiming the kingdom. On the way to Jerusalem, Jesus mentions "Abraham, and Isaac, and Jacob, and all the prophets, in the kingdom of God" (Luke 13:28). In another instance, He foresees how many people will "sit down with Abraham, Isaac, and Jacob in the kingdom of heaven" (Matt. 8:11). Once, when the people are ascribing kingly praises to Christ at His triumphal entry into Jerusalem, saying, "Hosanna! . . . Blessed be the kingdom of our father, David, that cometh in the name of the Lord. Hosanna in the highest!" (Mark 11:10; cf. Luke 19:39), Christ enters into the ascriptions and even defends them before the scowling leaders.

The religious leaders themselves know that Jesus is offering the Davidic kingdom, and hence their constant dread is that "the Romans shall come and take away both our place and nation" (John 11:49). In rejecting Jesus and His claims, the Jewish rulers know that they are doing the right thing by

---

[1] John Bright, *The Kingdom of God* (New York, N.Y.: Abingdon-Cokesbury Press, 1953), p. 17.

their Roman overlords and for their own religious positions. Jesus puts the rulers' feelings into words in one of His parables where the shout is heard, "We will not have this man to reign over us" (Luke 19:14). The Jewish leaders apparently understand Jesus' offer of the kingdom and take it very seriously.[1]

It therefore seems hardly possible that anyone reading the Gospels normally would miss the point that Jesus offered the kingdom promised by the prophets in the Old Testament.

Third, the disciples of Jesus not only believe but go forth proclaiming the Messianic kingdom. It is Jesus who personally teaches them, sends them forth, and rejoices over their ministries (Matt. 20:20-21; Luke 9:56; 24:21). If Jesus is not prepared to set up the messianic kingdom, would He have sent them forth to preach a deception, accompanied by signs and miracles? The disciples are so convinced about their message that even after the resurrection of Christ, they still ask: "Lord, wilt thou at this time restore again the kingdom to Israel?" (Acts 1:6). "It is folly to suppose," observes George Peters, "that we know the nature of that kingdom

---

[1] Alva J. McClain in *The Greatness of the Kingdom*, pp. 286-303, describes at least six elements of the Old Testament prophesied kingdom which definitely constitute Jesus' offer of the kingdom, summarized as follows:

(1) *The Spiritual Element*—Christ emphasizes "repent," "believe," "pure in heart," etc.

(2) *The Moral Element*—Christ commands people to return good for evil. Lust and hate are equated with adultery and murder (Matt. 5). Some advances in moral standards are seen.

(3) *The Social Element*—e.g. "Who is my neighbor?" (Parable of the Good Samaritan).

(4) *The Ecclesiastical Element*—e.g. the observance of the commandments (violators are called "least in the kingdom," Matt. 5:17-19); observance of the Sabbath ("Son of Man is Lord even of

better than they did, who were expressly commissioned to hold it forth as an inducement to repentance."[1]

It has sometimes been pointed out that if Jesus really offers the Davidic kingdom, why was He at times cautions and reticent in regards to this matter? Why did He not explain it more plainly and in more detail? The answer is twofold: (1) Although Jesus on many occasions is specific regarding His Messianic claims, He exercises great prudence and caution lest it should unnecessarily arouse open hostility and persecution by the Romans. The kingdom has already been detailed and particularized in the Old Testament, and the people of the day know a lot about it. Jesus assumes that the Scriptures have already said enough about the kingdom. (2) Christ knows by foreknowledge that the Jews would reject His offer and that the kingdom would have to be postponed. An inordinate pressing of regal claims would not only be improper under the circumstances, but it might also be taken advantage of by the Jewish leaders who would charge Him as a political conspirator rather than as Saviour of sinners.

A delicate situation therefore exists which necessitates perfect discretion and absolute wisdom. Our Lord handles it flawlessly. As George Peters points out, the offer of the kingdom "was *sufficiently clear* to test the repentance and

---

the Sabbath"). and the assumption of lordship over the temple by driving away the money-changers and merchants.

(5) *The Political Element*—Christ teaches that the faithful will rule over cities (Luke 19:11-19) and that they will sit on the throne of His glory (Matt. 25:31). Christ uses political terms such as court, judge, penalty, prison (Matt. 5:23-26).

(6) *The Physical Element*—Diseases, sicknesses, and even dead persons are restored in Jesus' ministry (cf. Matt. 12:28, "If I cast out devils . . . then the kingdom of God is come"). Christ once answers John the Baptist's inquiry regarding the kingdom by working more miracles and signs (Matt. 11:2-5).

[1] Peters, *Theocratic Kingdom*, I, 270.

faith of the nation, *sufficiently distinct* for those who receive the Word of God without human additions, and *sufficiently precise* to encourage the hope of His people in His Messiahship . . ."[1]

The observation of J. Sidlow Baxter is fitting in concluding this aspect of our discussion: "Now admittedly there is a certain aesthetic appeal about this idealistic concept of the kingdom which our Lord preached; but it must be rejected because it is not true to facts. It may have its head idealistically above the clouds, but it does not have its feet realistically planted on the *terra firma* of New Testament data."[2]

II. REJECTION OF THE KINGDOM

Jesus offers the very kingdom the people were looking for, but they reject the offer. Why? The standard non-dispensational answer is that the Jews reject the offer because Jesus did not offer the kingdom of Jewish expectations but an entirely different sort of kingdom.

"Had Christ offered the Jews a political kingdom in the pomp and glory of David and Solomon, as Dispensationalism affirms that He did, they most certainty would have accepted and would have rallied to His standard. That was the very thing they wanted and were expecting. But that is what He clearly refused to offer,"[3]   says postmillennialist Boettner. Covenant premillennialist Ladd agrees: "It is very possible

---

[1] *Ibid.*

[2] J. Sidlow Baxter, *The Strategic Grasp of the Bible* (Grand Rapids, Mich.: Zondervan Pub. House, 1968), p. 212.

[3] Loraine Boettner, *The Millennium* (Phila., Pa.: The Presbyterian and Reformed Pub. Co., 1964), p. 225.

that our Lord offered the Jewish people something which they misunderstood and misinterpreted. In fact their very misunderstanding may well have been the very reason why they did not accept Him. He did not offer them the sort of kingdom they wanted. Had he offered them the earthly Davidic kingdom, they would have accepted it . . . ."[1]

Dispensational interpreters however maintain that the kingdom which Christ offers is the one promised by the prophets and awaited by the people. The reason why the Jews reject Christ's offer and so postponed the kingdom[2] is a twofold one.

First, the people go forward in droves to accept the good news of the kingdom's imminence. But when requirements are stated by Christ, the people find themselves morally unprepared and totally incapable of accepting the offer. "The new and stumbling idea in the message [of Christ] was that repentance was necessary . . . . It was new in the sense that the people of Jesus' day had expected the kingdom to come in power and without any inward change being required on their part."[3]

Second, the Jewish rulers steadfastly refuse to place their Messianic expectations on the person of Jesus Christ. While their literal approach to the Messianic prophecies certainly points to the person of Jesus Christ,[4] they reject

---

[1] Ladd, *Kingdom of God,* p. 113.

[2] The postponement of the kingdom is an important link in literal hermeneutics. If the kingdom offered by Jesus were not postponed but actually realized, then the Old Testament kingdom prophecies must be spiritualized and seen as "fulfilled" at the first advent of Christ.

[3] Charles Caldwell Ryrie, *Biblical Theology of the New Testament* (Chicago, Ill.: Moody Press, 1959), p. 73.

[4] For instance, they were able to pinpoint the location of Christ's birth in the town of Bethlehem (Matt. 2:4-6).

the fulfillment of these Messianic prophecies in Him. The crucifixion is therefore the product of unbelief and the hardness of hearts against Jesus of Nazareth. It is gratuitous for any interpreter to say that the "strongest condemnation [of the literal method] consists in its being the very method of interpretation which led to the crucifixion of Christ."[1] The fault does not lie in the hermeneutics of the Jews but in their refusal to apply its logical conclusions to Jesus whom they downgrade as "the carpenter's son" (Matt. 13:55; Mark 6:3).

So, refusing the spiritual repentance required for the institution of the kingdom, angered by the well-merited rebukes on their hypocrisy and sinful condition, and fearful of losing their position and authority, the Jewish leaders (and their people) reject Christ and His offer of the kingdom. [2]

After the withdrawal of the kingdom offer, Christ's style of preaching changes markedly. The kingdom is no longer nigh or at hand but far off. Jesus' parable of the nobleman journeying to a distant land (Luke 19:11-27) is given "because they thought that the kingdom of God should immediately appear" (v. 11). In the parables of the King's Son (Matt. 22:1-14) and of the Great Supper (Luke 14:15-24), both the "wedding" and the "supper" are postponed because the bidden guests prove to be unworthy. Jesus clearly tells the Jews, "The

---

[1] Cited favorably by Patrick Fairbairn, *The Interpretation of Prophecy* (reprinted.; London: Banner of Truth Trust, 1964), p 497.

[2] Even before the Jews officially decide to kill Him, Christ, especially in private conversations with individuals such as the woman of Samaria, the centurion, and Zacchaeus, begins to reveal the purpose of God in His coming rejection by the Jews and the subsequent calling of the Gentiles. This shows wonderfully His divine foreknowledge as well as "tact in keeping His disciples in the most favorable position and mental condition to preach the offer of the kingdom" (Peters, *Theocratic Kingdom*, I, 383).

kingdom of God shall be taken from you, and given to a nation bringing forth the fruits of it" (Matt. 21:43).[1]

III. CLARIFICATIONS ON THE KINGDOM OFFER

1. *Did Christ make a bona fide offer of the kingdom?* Critics point out that since Christ knew that the Jews would reject the offer and that the kingdom would be postponed, Christ could not have made a sincere and bona fide offer of the kingdom.

Our reply is found in the doctrine of foreordination, and like that doctrine, it may never be fully settled. On several occasions in Scripture, God offers to do certain things which He certainly knows would not eventuate. At times, He is even dissuaded from pursuing some of these actions. During the rebellion at Kadesh-Barnea, God declares that He will disinherit the Israelites and make the descendants of Moses a far greater nation than the children of Israel (Num. 14:11-20). But after Moses' fervent pleas, and in God's foreknowledge, the act is not carried through. When Jesus exclaims to the people of Jerusalem, "How often would I have gathered thy children together. . . and ye would not!" (Matt. 23:37), He is surely sincere in the offer, but He certainly knows that the desired response would not materialize.

When God is described as "not willing that any should perish, but that all should come to repentance" (II Pet. 3:9), His desire is certainly bona fide and sincere, although the number of the elect has already been foreordained. "It will be remembered that God ordained a Lamb before the foundation

---

[1] That is, the kingdom is taken from that generation of Jews and given to the remnant who will turn to Christ at His second advent.

of the world and that Lamb to be slain," cites Lewis S. Chafer. "God anticipated the sin of man and his great need of redemption. God, however, told Adam *not* to sin; yet if Adam had not sinned there would have been no need of that redemption plan which God had before determined as something to be wrought out."[1]

It should have been easy for Calvinistic theologians to accept the seeming discrepancy in the statement that Christ's offer of the kingdom is sincere, although He knows that it would be rejected and the kingdom postponed. And yet this concept seems to encounter the heaviest complaint among interpreters of Calvinistic persuasion.

Some non-dispensational interpreters insist that if Christ really offers the Davidic kingdom, it should have been instituted, whether the Jews reject it or not. "It is evident that *if* the time had come for the earthly kingdom to be restored to Israel," theorizes Mauro, *"He would have done it,* notwithstanding any opposition by the people . . . ."[2]   Our answer is that this seems to be the God-ordained way of doing things relative to the kingdom. The offer of salvation to "all the world" under the context of predestination is an analogous example.

2.   *Does it not minimize the cross of Christ?*   The charge is often made that by saying that Christ offers the literal, Davidic kingdom to the Jews, it implies that the cross is unnecessary. That is, if the Jews had accepted the offer, Jesus would not have had to die, for the kingdom would have been

---

[1] Lewis Sperry Chafer, *Systematic Theology* (8 vols.; Dallas, Tex.: Dallas Seminary Press, 1948), V, 347.

[2] Philip Mauro, *God's Present Kingdom* (New York, N.Y.: Fleming H. Revell Co., 1919), p. 218.

set up without the crucifixion. Oswald T. Allis considers this "the most serious objection to the claim of Dispensationalists,"[1] and goes on to make all sorts of implicational affirmations: "[The literal method] made the Cross unnecessary by implying that the glorious kingdom of Messiah could be set up immediately. It left no room for the Cross since Messiah's kingdom was to be without end. It led to the conclusion that had Israel accepted Jesus as Messiah, the Old Testament ritual of sacrifice would have sufficed for sin . . . ."[2]

In reply, we would affirm that if the kingdom had been accepted by the Jews, the cross would still have been necessary. An inherent element in the concept of the kingdom under the Old Testament prophets is a vicarious and suffering Messiah (cf. Isa. 53). The Old Testament prophets predict both a suffering and a reigning Messiah. Hence, even if there were no church in God's program, the cross would still have been necessary. The crucifixion is as necessary to the institution of the kingdom as it is to the building of the church. When we say that Christ offers the Davidic kingdom, we are not talking about the cross and its necessity. The kingdom offer relates primarily to God's plan of the ages, not to the necessity of the cross which is also a vital part of that plan.

Charles Caldwell Ryrie, in his section "Turning the Tables" in *Dispensationalism Today*, pages 166-68, aims the gun right back at critics, and we summarize: Suppose that Jesus *did* offer a spiritual kingdom in the hearts of men, and that repentance was the condition for receiving that kingdom, and that the people *did* repent and were born again, what then

---

[1] Oswald T. Allis, *Prophecy and the Church* (Phila., Pa.: The Presbyterian and Reformed Pub. Co., 1964), p. 230.

[2] *Ibid.*, pp. 230-1.

would have happened to the cross? Since the crucifixion had not yet taken place, does it mean that there was in those days a way of salvation different from salvation through the death of Christ?"

3. *Is there no present outworking of the kingdom?* Our answer is that there *are* present outworkings of God's kingdom. It is true that the kingdom promised by the prophets was postponed when the Messiah in the person of Jesus Christ was rejected. Nevertheless, during the present inter-advent age, the kingdom is anticipatorily present and has its present outworkings.

Actually, the kingdom has both a future and a present form. The *future* form is the Millennial Kingdom which will be instituted at the second coming of Christ. Literal interpreters generally refer to this when they mention the kingdom. However, literalists also acknowledge the *present* form of the kingdom under a twofold definition: (1) the Spiritual Kingdom where God rules in the hearts of the saved today, and (2) the Eternal Kingdom which embraces the rule of God over all creation, both saved and unsaved.

APPENDIX IV
THE CULT OF ANGLO-ISRAELISM

Critics sometimes attempt to cast the literal method in the role of a villain under the technique of "guilt by association." This is done by pointing to cults which are literal in portions of their eschatology.[1]

It is of course not necessarily true that since some fanatical groups or cults have included the second advent or the millennium in their teachings, these doctrines must become suspect and their methods of approach wrong. Arguments based on guilt by association do not truly reflect careful scholarship and appeal only to the gullible.

Among the cults most often cited by critics, Anglo-Israelism appears time and again. It is therefore fitting that this cult should be chosen for closer examination.

I. DESCRIPTION OF ANGLO-ISRAELISM

A. Theory of Anglo-Israelism

Anglo-Israelism is the cult which teaches that the English people are the descendants of the "Ten Lost Tribes" of Israel, and as such, are appropriating and fulfilling the promises made by God to Israel.

---

[1] For instance, Oswald T. Allis in *Prophecy and the Church*, (Phila., Pa.: The Presbyterian and Reformed Pub. Co., 1964), p. 48 tries to link premillennialism with Russellism because both see the Abrahamic covenant as unconditional.

DESCRIPTION

On July 14, 1930, the *Times of India* carried a whole page advertisement for the British-Israel World Federation, outlining its teachings, with these words in upper case letters:

THE ANGLO-SAXON NATION AND COMPANY OF NATIONS, AND THE UNITED STATES BRANCH OF THE SAME PEOPLE, CONSTITUTE THE NATIONAL BASIS OF THE KINGDOM OF GOD IN THE EARTH.

In more recent times, Herbert W. Armstrong, the cult's most dynamic spokesman in America, intones: "The vital key that unlocks prophecy to our understanding . . . is the identity of the United States and the British peoples in Biblical prophecy. That key has been found."[1]

B. *"Biblical" Basis of the Cult*

The Bible contains prophecies which talk about the "isles," locating them north (Jer. 3:12) and west (Isa. 24:15) of Palestine. Anglo-Israelism affirms that the British isles fit these geographical locations. It also observes that even the English language approximates the Hebrew.

For instance, words such as *berry, garden,* and *kitten* are approximate in sound to פֶּרִי (fruit), גַן (garden), and קִטֶן (kitten) respectively. And, the Hebrew word אִישׁ (man) compares phonetically and meaningfully with the English termination *-ish* (as in Brit*ish* and Span*ish* which means "man from Britian" and "man from Spain" respectively).

---

[1] Herbert W. Armstrong, *The United States and British Commonwealth in Prophecy* (Pasadena, Calif.: Ambassador College Press, 1967), p. xii.

Anglo-Israelism also teaches that the Ten Tribes of Israel are always referred to in Scripture as "Israel," never as "Jews." The Jews, they say, descend from Judah and are under the curse, while Israel is God's chosen people who later establishes the great British Empire. According to Armstrong, "true Israel" did not join in crucifying the Lord; the Jews or the descendants of the two tribes crucified Christ.[1]

In refuting the crucial dependence of Anglo-Israelism on the word "isle," *The Jewish Encyclopedia* expresses its opinion: "The whole theory rests upon an identification of the word 'isles' in the English version of the Bible unjustified by modern philology, which identifies the original word with 'coasts' or 'distant lands' without any implication of their being surrounded by the sea."[2]

Moreover, the so-called approximations between the English and the Hebrew languages, such as *fruit, kitten,* and *British* are purely verbal and merely childish quibblings on English letters. And contrary to Anglo-Israelism, the Word of God does not make a distinction between *Jews* and *Israel.* As late as the Book of Nehemiah, the same group of people is called "Jews" eleven times and "Israel" 22 times, and in the New Testament the same people is addressed as "Jews" 174 times and "Israel" 74 times.

Actually, the ten "lost" tribes of Israel are not "lost" at all. When the division of the Solomonic kingdom occurred under Rehoboam I, a large number of people from the ten

---

[1] Herbert W. Armstrong also subdivided the Ten Tribes as follows: (1) the descendants of the two sons of Joseph—Ephraim and Manasseh—are the peoples of Britain and America respectively; and (2) the other eight tribes are scattered among the northwest European nations, parts of west Germany, and Iceland.

[2] Joseph Jacobs, "Anglo Israelism" *The Jewish Encyclopedia,* 1901, I, 601.

northern tribes migrated south to escape Jeroboam's religious apostasy and innovations (cf II Chron. 11:13-15). When Nebuchadnezzar of Babylon later arrived to remove the northern tribes from the land, the "remnant" who had earlier migrated to and settled in the south was left untouched. Moreover, a portion of Nebuchadnezzar's captives did return to Palestine during the reign of the benevolent Persian monarch Cyrus and was absorbed into the population of Palestine.

C. "Historical" Basis of the Cult

It is a fact of history that the ten tribes of Israel were captured by the Assyrians under Sargon during the 8th century, B.C. It is also historical that around this time, the Scythians appeared as a conquering horde which swarmed westward into northern Europe and are (presumably) the progenitors of the Saxon invaders of England.

Anglo-Israelism, jumping on these two historical facts, links the ten "lost" tribes of Israel with the Scythians. Another jump is also made from the Scythians to the Angles and Jutes—a leap of over 1,000 years (from 700 B.C. to A.D. 500), prompting an unimpressed spectator to comment: "A bare possibility is turned into a surmise; a surmise becomes a likelihood; the likelihood becomes an extreme probability, and ends by becoming a dogmatic certainty! ! !"[1]

It is still an issue among historians where to place the historical Scythians. Herodotus places them northwest of the Black Sea. Josephus (first century, A.D.) says that the Greeks called Magog the "Scythians." If this were so, it would make the Scythians one of the principal groups composing Modern Russia, thus destroying the historical link of Anglo-Israelism.

---

[1] William C. Irvine, ed., *Heresies Exposed* (New York, N.Y.: Loizeaux Bros., Inc., n.d.), p. 42.

Moreover, the glaring diversities of language, physical type, religion, and customs between the Israelites and the progenitors of the English nation are hard for Anglo-Israelism to explain.

It is true that supporters of Anglo-Israelism have produced a genealogical table tracing the throne of England back to King David. But this has been found to be a table based on unverified historical facts and speculative inferences. Baron comments that it is "a table truly strange and wonderful, and which only shows how easy it is to prove anything if wild guesses and perverted fancies be treated as facts."[1]

II. Some Observations

The case of Anglo-Israelism has been unfairly cited as a good illustration of the literal method gone askew. *The Jewish Encyclopedia*, for instance, mistakenly calls it "an extremely literal interpretation of the Old Testament, as represented by King James' Version . . . ."[2] Of course Anglo-Israelism takes the Old Testament promises and covenants literally, but it forthwith applies these not to Israel but to a non-Jewish political hegemony. Furthermore, Anglo-Israelism appropriates the promises and leaves the curses to the Jews. This sounds more like spiritualization.

Spiritualization is apparent in the fact that descriptions of the Great Tribulation and that of the millennium are applied to the present by Anglo-Israelism. As Herbert W. Armstrong says, "Approximately 90 percent of all prophecy pertains to OUR time, in this latter half of the twentieth century."[3]

---

[1] David Baron, *The History of the Ten "Lost" Tribes* (London: Morgan and Scott, Ltd., 1915), p. 72.

[2] Jacobs, "Anglo-Israelism," p. 600.

[3] Armstrong, *United States and British Commonwealth*, p. 4.

The cult of Anglo-Israelism does not exemplify literality. It rather exemplifies the entrance of spiritualization through an initial handhold on literalism. By their radical interpretations and far-fetched exegesis (dogmatically affirmed), enthusiasts of this sect say that the rest of the church saints have been wrong in their interpretations from A.D. 70 on up to modern times.

This is what Armstrong teaches in his interpretation of the Parable of the Ten Virgins: "Yes, during more than 18 centuries, 'while the Bridegroom tarried, they all slumbered and slept.' And so, beginning the first week of January, 1945, the living Christ 'opened a door!' (Rev. 3:8). It was the 'door' of radio and the printing press, mass-media through which Christ's true Gospel [through Armstrong, i.e.] could be proclaimed to the multitudes."[1] And this has led Noel Smith to comment that all the preachings, prayings, martrydoms, and revivals of the Christian church down 18½ centuries are "nothing more than the snoozes and snores of sleeping virgins."[2]

---

[1] *Plain Truth*, Dec., 1962, p. 14, cited by Noel Smith, *Herbert W. Armstrong and His World Tommorrow* (Springfield, Mo.: Baptist Bible Tribune, 1964), p. 13.

[2] Smith, *Herbert W. Armstrong*, p. 13.

APPENDIX V

THE TEMPLE VISION OF EZEKIEL

The prophet Ezekiel devotes nine chapters of his book to one subject: the Millennial Temple and its worship.[1] The prophecy is so lengthy and detailed that regardless of one's theological persuasion, Ezekiel 40-49 simply cannot be ignored.

I. NON-LITERAL INTERPRETATIONS

Several non-literal views have been advanced by interpreters regarding the millennial temple of Ezekiel. These are:

First view—The vision was given by God for the benefit of post-exilic Jews to help them remember Solomon's temple design when they restore the old temple.

Second view— Here is an ideal blueprint of what should have been built by the Jewish remnant after their return from the Babylonian captivity.

Third view— The prophecy is a grand, complicated symbol of the Christian church. This is the standard amillennial position. As Milton Terry says, "this vision of restored

---

[1] We have already discussed sacrifices in the millennial temple (see above pp. 293-98). This section seeks to clarify the temple vision of Ezekiel as a whole.

and perfected temple, service, and land symbolizes the perfected kingdom of God and his Messiah."[1]

Fourth view— The glorious descriptions found in this
prophecy will surely be fulfilled at the millennium, but do not
fuss over the *how* of fulfillment. This is the covenant premillennial position which refuses to go into details.

II. SOME REFUTATIONS

The temple vision of Ezekiel was certainly no help to the
post-exilic Jews contemplating the restoration of Solomon's
temple, for there are great differences in structure between
Solomon's temple and Ezekiel's temple. This prophecy also
demands a topographical configuration of Palestine which
would necessitate supernatural work. Moreover, the twelve
tribes were not yet in the land of Palestine as the prophecy
predicts. The post-exilic Jews therefore never tried to build
Ezekiel's temple since it was a prophecy not intended for their
day.

Regarding the theory that the entire vision is a symbol of
the Christian church—if true—it is surely a strange and
round-about way for God to so symbolize the church. The
temple vision of Ezekiel is just a little too big and too detailed
to be waved off as a symbol.

III. THE LITERAL INTERPRETATION

Literal interpreters believe that in Ezekiel's temple vision,
God has given us a detailed picture of religious worship in the
millennium. The temple in Ezekiel's prophecy is a literal
temple to be erected, as Scripturally specified, in the land of

---

[1]Milton S. Terry, *Biblical Apocalyptics* (New York, N.Y.:
Eaton and Mains, 1898), p. 131.

Palestine during the millennium and which will serve as the center of millennial religious activity.

The location of this millennial temple is not within the city of Jerusalem but north of the city "in the midst of the holy oblation," i.e. a portion of land dedicated to Jehovah (Ezek. 45:1; 48:8, 10, 21). The temple area will be a square lot containing portions for the priests, the Levites, and the city, with the temple proper at the center of this square upon a very high mountain supernaturally raised for this purpose (Isa. 2:2-3; Zech. 14:10). The world will look up to this place as the heart and hub of the millennial earth.

IV. REASONS FOR A LITERAL TEMPLE

First, here are nine chapters of prophecy which cannot well be explained away as figurative or symbolical. The literal approach appears the most logical.

Second, the prophecy contains descriptions and measurements of the millennial temple in such detail that one may make a sketch of it just like one does with Solomon's historic temple. Moreover, God's command in Ezekiel 43:11 to "keep the whole form thereof, and all the ordinances thereof, and do them" is similar to God's command to Moses regarding the construction of the wilderness tabernacle (Exod. 25:8-9).

Third, aside from Ezekiel, other prophets also prophesy regarding this temple (cf. Isa. 2:3; 60:13; Joel 3:18; Haggai 2:7, 9; etc.).

Fourth, Ezekiel makes a clear separation between the temple and the city (Ezek. 48:8, 15). If the whole vision symbolizes the church, we would have a symbol of the church separating from itself.

Fifth, the New Testament frequently describes a future temple to be constructed during the tribulation (cf. II Thess. 2:4-5; Matt. 24:15; Rev. 11:1-2). Although this tribulational temple and the millennial temple are not identical, the New Testament record thus attests to the fact that a rebuilding of the Jewish temple in the future is to be expected.

V.   DIFFICULTIES IN LITERAL INTERPRETATION

The literal approach to Ezekiel's prophecy does not solve all difficulties. In fact, it is attended by its own set of problems. Oswald T. Allis considers these problems so insurmountable that he has called Ezekiel 40-48 "the Achilles heel of the Dispensational [literal] system of interpretation."[1] Let us defined what the problems are and offer some pertinent solutions.

(1) Once the dimensions mentioned in the prophecy are literally computed, the temple court will be larger than present-day Jerusalem! Moreover, the land portions reserved for the priests and Levites will be larger than present-day Palestine, and this is not counting "the prince's portions" on the east and west sides (Ezek. 45:7; 48:21).

The enlarged geographical dimensions of Palestine in this prophecy, however, will not only be possible but would be necessary, for millennial Palestine will be the worship centre of the whole world. In fact, according to other Old Testament prophets, more priests will be needed. Moreover, Zechariah 14:4-10 reports great topographical changes in Palestine during Christ's second advent, which may well include the enlargement of the land of Palestine.

(2) The millennial Jerusalem will be north of its present site, with the temple area still further north! But we note that Ezekiel definitely says that the temple area will *not* anymore

---

[1] Oswald T. Allis, *Prophecy and the Church* (Phila., Pa.: Presbyterian and Reformed Pub. Co., 1964), p. 248.

join the royal palace as before (Ezek. 43:7-12), and that the city will even have a new name (48:35).

(3) The stream, without tributaries, flowing from the temple, entering the Dead Sea and gushing forth healing waters is quite annoying to some interpreters. Milton Terry considers the descriptions as "insuperable difficulties in the way of any literal exposition of the vision."[1] However, as we have previously noted, the miraculous will be commonplace at the millennium. Edenic conditions will prevail over the earth.

(4) There is a "prince" in Ezekiel's temple vision who offers sacrifices for himself, have children, and is rebuked. Who is he?

Obviously, he is not the sinless Messiah. Neither is he resurrected David, for resurrected persons do not have children. This is an unglorified, mortal person serving in the millennial temple. The word "prince" is a common eschatological word, and does not necessarily have to denote the Messiah or David. Moreover, Jeremiah 33:25-26 implies that there will be mortal rulers during the millennium.

Our discussion has shown that so-called difficulties in Ezekiel's vision are not insurmountable. Of course a number of details remains unclear as to exact meanings. But once the literal approach is consistently held, difficulties begin to appear in solvent form. The doors of Ezekiel's temple, like the gates of the New Jerusalem, remain ajar only to those who come with the literal hermeneutical key.

---

[1] Milton S. Terry, *Biblical Hermeneutics* (New York, N.Y.: Eaton and Mains, 1911), p. 345.

APPENDIX VI

DANIEL 11 AND HISTORY

Daniel 11 fits the history of the Seleucids and Ptolemies[1] like a pair of tailor-made gloves. While evangelicals acknowledge the hand of God in this phenomenon, unimpressed liberals browbeat such fulfillments as a giveaway to its unauthenticity, saying that the prophecy must have been written *after* the events. Friends and foes of Daniel 11, however, are in agreement that this prophecy has been realized in history. The amazing exactness of prophetic fulfillment may be seen in the following comparison of Daniel 11 and history:

I. PARADE OF PERSIAN KINGS (v. 2)

Verse. 2.— And now will I show thee the truth. — In the third year of King Cyrus of Persia, the revealing angel was sent to Daniel to reveal what was going to happen "for sure."

Yet three kings in Persia. — The first three successors of Cyrus on the Persian throne were: (1) Cambyses who started in the Fall of 530; (b) Gautama "Pseudo-Smerdis," an usurper, who started in the Spring of 522; and (c) Darius I "Hystaspis" who began in the Spring of 521. Famed organizer of a vast empire, Darius I tried to punish the

---

[1] About 300-150 B.C.

Greek city-states for the Ionian Revolt of 499-94, but was defeated by Sparta and Athens in both land and sea at
Marathon. He is the "Darius" of Ezra 4:24.

*And the fourth . . . against the realm of
Grecia.* —The fourth successor to Cyrus was *Xerxes I
"Longimannus."* He spent four years gathering an army of
2,500,000 men from forty natons to conquer Greece. At the
Battle of Salamis (480), his fleet was ruined and at Platea
(479) his army routed. He is the "Ahasherus" of Esther 1:1.

Then follows a line of Persian kings, the last of which—
Darius III "Codomanus"—was defeated by Alexander the
Great at the Battle of Issus (333).

II.   THREE EMPIRE BUILDERS (VS. 3-5)

Ver. 3. A mighty king shall stand up.— After
the death of Darius III, Alexander the Great of Macedon
(356-23) rampaged eastward, reaching the Indus River. By
age 32, Alexander was king of Macedon, ruler of the Greek
city-states, and conqueror of the Persian realms.

Ver. 4. When he shall stand up.– At the prime
of Alexander's life.

His kingdom shall be broken.— In 323, while in
Babylon after a night of feasting and drinking, Alexander fell
ill. Within eleven days, he was dead.

Divided toward the four winds. —The crum-
bling empire was divided among four of Alexander's generals:
Ptolemy got Egypt, Antigonus was given Babylon and
Phrygia, Lysimachus had Thrace, and Cassander took
Macedon.

And not to his posterity.—Alexander's throne had
three aspirants: (a) his posthumous son, Alexander, Jr., by
Roxana; (b) his illegitimate son Herakles by Barsina; and

(c) his stupid half-brother Philip Arrhidaeus. All three did not secure the throne.

The second settlement at Triparadeisos (321) bestowed the satrapy of Babylon on *Seleucus I "Nicator"*, another of Alexander's generals. But by 316, he was fleeing the despotic Antigonus who had originally been awarded Babylon.

Ver. 5. The king of the south.— Ptolemy I *"Soter"* (or *"Lagi"*), one of the seven elite bodyguards of Alexander, got Egypt after the death of Alexander.

And one of his princes.— The fugitive Seleucus Nicator was welcomed by Ptolemy I to Egypt. In 312, both men defeated the son of Antigonus in the Battle of Gaza. Seleucus immediately force-marched into Babylon and founded the Seleucid dynasty.

He shall be strong above him. — The Battle of Ipsus (301) finally ruined Antigonus and awarded Coele-Syria and Palestine to Seleucus. Seleucus I ended up stronger than Ptolemy I.

His dominion shall be a great dominion. — Within thirty years after founding his dynasty, Seleucus I was reigning over a mammoth empire from the Punjab to the Hellespont. This was virtually the whole of Alexander's empire except Egypt.

III.   A POLITICAL MARRIAGE (v. 6)

Ver. 6. In the end of years.— This period covers about 50 years (ca. 312-250). Upon the death of Ptolemy I (285), *Ptolemy II "Philadelphus"* was placed on the Egyptian throne. His Syrian antagonist was now *Antiochus I "Sidetes."* Ptolemy II was a powerful king who amassed a military machine of 200,000 infantrymen, 20,000 cavalry, 2,000 chariots, and 400 elephants imported from Ethiopia. A couple of years' flexing of muscles left him the dominant naval power in eastern Meditteranean (First Syrian War).

They shall join themselves. — Ptolemy II and *Antiochus II "Theos"* came together after the Second Syrian War.

Daughter of the king of the south ... shall come to the king of the north. — Berenice, daughter of Ptolemy II, was given in marriage to Antiochus II. Previous to the wedding, Antiochus had fought his future father-in-law in the Second Syrian War.

To make an agreement. — The wedding was politically motivated. Antiochus signed the marriage contract, banished his first wife Laodiceia, and promised to make any child of Berenice his heir. The Egyptian princess Berenice was forthwith conducted with great pomp to him.

She shall not retain the power. — After two years, the fickle Antiochus restored Laodiceia, who in retaliation turned murderess.

Neither shall he stand ... nor his arm ... she shall be given up. — Berenice's father and his scheme did not succeed, nor did Antiochus himself survive. Laodiceia poisoned her husband, slew Berenice's son in Antioch, and killed Berenice in the temple at Daphne. The father of Berenice, Ptolemy Philadelphus died about the time of the tragedy.

IV. WARS OF REVENGE (VS. 7-9)

Ver. 7. A branch of her roots. — After his father's death and sister's tragedy, *Ptolemy III "Euergetes"* initiated the Third Syrian War.

One ... shall deal ... and shall prevail. — With an army, Ptolemy Euergetes entered Seleucia and Antioch. His antagonist, Seleucus II "Callinicus", fled to beyond the Taunus Mountains. Ptolemy then continued eastward and advanced as far as beyond the Tigris, thus occupying the entire Syrian realm. Under him, Ptolemaic power reached its zenith.

Ver. 8. Their gods ... carry captive into Egypt. — Serious insurrections in Egypt caused Ptolemy Euergetes to withdraw hurriedly, inadvertently relinquishing his claims to a now-recovering Seleucus Callinicus. Nevertheless, Ptolemy did pocket 40,000 talents of Syrian silver and 2,500 mixed Syrian and Egyptian idols. The idolatrous Egyptians fondly nicknamed him "Euergetes" or Well-doer."

Ver. 9. Come into the realm of the king of the south. — In 242, two years after Ptolemy's wide-ranging Syrian conquests, Seleucus II retaliated in turn by launching a two-pronged land-sea attack on Egypt.

Return into his own land. — But Selecus' fleet was ruined in a storm and his army returned to Antioch decimated. Both kings finally decided on a ten-year truce (240).

V. A TIRELESS WARRIOR (vs. 10-19)

Ver. 10. His sons shall war.—After the death of Seleucus II and the expiration of the truce of 240, *Seleucus III "Ceraunus"* expended three years of his short reign waging wars in Asia Minor. Upon his death, the army summoned *Antiochus III "the Great"* to the Seleucid throne. Antiochus the Great, who was then a teenager, started a long 37-year regal career characterized as "one of unwearied warfare."

Shall assemble a multitude.- In 221, Antiochus the Great advanced westward and crushed the rebellion of Molon and Alexander. Letting Achaeus' insurrection in Asia Minor simmer, Antiochus prepared to attack Egypt in three major campaigns.

Certainly come and overflow.— Antiochus gathered an army of 72,000 soldiers, 6,000 horses, and 102 elephants and took the Egyptian fortresses of Seleucia, Tyre, Ptolemais, and colonies in north Syria. The First Egyptian Campaign had begun.

Shall return . . . even to his fortress.— While besieging the fortress of Dora, Antiochus was bamboozled into a four-month winter truce and retired to Seleucia (or Ptolemais).

Ver. 11. The king of the south shall move with choler.—The Spring of 218 found Antiochus the Great in Palestine picking off the fortresses of Sidon and Gaza in the Second Egyptian Campaign. This finally provoked the indolent *Ptolemy IV "Philopater."* Ptolemy Philopater, a dilettante-voluptuary, is credited with slaying his father, mother, and brother, marrying his sister Arsinoe, falling madly in love with a lute-player Agathoclea, and starting the Ptolemaic kingdom in a spiraling decline.

Shall set forth . . . given into his hand. — Ptolemy Philopater personally led his 73,000 men, 5,000 cavalry, and 73 elephants to Raphia. Antiochus the Great, losing 10,000 men, 300 cavalry, 4,000 prisoners, and 5 elephants, fled through the desert.

Ver. 12. But he shall not be strengthened. — The victorious Ptolemy however was satisfied only to make peace with the Seleucid and returned to Egypt. This gave Antiochus another chance to attack Egypt in later years.

Ver. 13. The king of the north shall return.– After his defeat at Raphia (214), Antiochus the Great headed eastward in a long expedition (212-204), following the footsteps of Alexander the Great into India and then down the Persian Gulf to the Arabian coast. Then with a much seasoned army, a supply of Indian elephants, the support of Philip of Macedon, several Egyptian insurrections in the air, and a weak infant king *Ptolemy V "Epiphanes"* in Egypt, he prepared to attack in the Third Egyptian Campaign (198).

Ver. 14. Shall many stand up against the king of the south. – The arming of Egypt for the battle of Raphia led to a series of native revolts in Egypt for the next 30 years. The rebel stronghold was Lycopolis.

Ver. 15. The king of the north shall . . cast up a mount. – In the Third Egyptian Campaign, the Egyptian general Scopas met Antiochus the Great in Palestine. Antiochus sent Scopas fleeing from Paneas into the fortress of Sidon with a decimated army of 10,000. Sidon was forthwith besieged.

The arms of the south shall not withstand. – When three ranking Egyptian generals (Eropus, Menocles, and Hamoxenus) could not lift the siege of Sidon, Scopas surrendered.

Ver. 16. He shall stand in the glorious land. — Antiochus the Great became the undisputed conqueror of Palestine. Henceforth, the land of Judea was to remain under the Seleucidae until its brief independence in 142 under Simon Maccabees.

Ver. 17. Upright ones with him . . . give him the daughter of women. – The treaty of 198 following the victory at Paneas gave Coele-Syria and Palestine to the Seleucids. It also provided for a political marriage between the conqueror's daughter Cleopatra and the defeated seven-year-old Ptolemy Epiphanes. Ptolemy and Cleopatra were married at Raphia (193), with Coele-Syria and Palestine promised her as dowry.

She shall not stand, neither be for him. — The couple apparently were happily married. When the bride's father was routed at Thermopylae (191) and then soundly defeated at Magnesus (190), Cleopatra joined her husband in sending congratulations to the Roman senate!

Ver. 18. Turn his face unto the isles. — Right after the treaty of 198, Antiochus the Great continued to advance along the Mediterranean coastline, and by the Summer of 197, the coast of Asia Minor was subjugated under him. In the Spring of 197, Antiochus conquered Macedon, Hellas, and Thrace, and became vocally reproachful of the Romans.

A prince shall cause the reproach ... to cease. — Rome went into action. After a series of victories led by the Roman general Lucius Scipio Asiaticus, the Romans saddled Antiochus the Great with the peace treaty of Apamea (188).

Ver. 19. He shall stumble and fall. — In 187, this tireless Seleucid warrior was killed trying to plunder the temple of Belus (or Jove) in Elymais by night.

VI.   A KING IN DEBT (v. 20)

Ver. 20. Then shall stand in his estate. — Antiochus the Great was succeeded by *Seleucus IV "Philopator"* famed for his unambitious policy. Jerome gibed that he "performed no deeds worthy of Syria or of his father, but perished ingloriously without fighting a single battle." It is fair to note, however, that he was compelled by heavy war indemnities imposed on his late father under the Peace of Apamea to pursue an inactive program.

One that shall cause an exactor to pass. — Saddled with bills, Seleucus Philopator sent his finance minister Heliodorus to plunder the temple treasury at Jerusalem.

He shall be destroyed. — Seleucus died in the Winter of 163 at Tabae in Persia after exhibiting mental derangement and was probably poisoned by Heliodorus.

VII.   A SCHEMING UNCLE (vs. 21-28)

Ver. 21. And in his estate ... a vile person. — Seleucus Philopator left three aspirants to the Seleucid throne: (a) Demetrius, the legitimate heir but a hostage in Rome; (b) Seleucus' baby in Syria; and (c) Antiochus Epiphanes, the late king's brother. The third aspirant finally got the throne by usurpation.

Ver. 22. With the arms of a flood shall they be overflown. — Antiochus IV "Epiphanes" was in Athens on his way home after fourteen years as friendly hostage in Rome when the news of his brother's death reached him. He rushed to Antioch, ousted Heliodorus and Seleucus Ceraunus the young puppet-king, and got the throne.

Ver. 23. He shall work deceitfully. — When Cleopatria I's sons, *Ptolemy VI "Philometor"* and *Ptolemy VII "Physcon"* brashly and immaturely demanded from their Seleucid uncle Antiochus Epiphanes the lands of Coele-Syria and Palestine as their mother's promise dowry, the aroused uncle went to war. Antiochus defeated the Egyptians between the Casian Mountains and Pelusium, took Pelusium, captured Ptolemy Philometor in Egypt, crowned himself king at Memphis, and befriended Philometor against Physcom. But when Antiochus besieged Alexandria—where Physcom had been crowned king by the Alexandrians—the siege was unsuccessful.

Ver. 24. Enter peaceably even upon the fattest places. — This prediction probably points to the campaigns of Antiochus Epiphanes in lower Egypt.

Ver. 25. Against the king of the south. — Refers to either the First (173) or the Second (170?) Egyptian Expedition of Antiochus.

Ver. 27. And both these kings. — Can refer to Antiochus Epiphanes and Ptolemy Philometor against Ptolemy Physcom.

Ver. 28. Then shall he return. — The news of a revolt in Cilicia, plus rumors circulating among the riffraff of Jerusalem that he had died, sent Antiochus Epiphanes rushing back through Palestine, amidst great carnage and plunder of the Jerusalem temple.

VIII. THE ILLUSTRIOUS MADMAN (vs. 29-35)

Ver. 29. Shall return and come toward the south. — With the sudden withdrawal of Antiochus Epiphanes from Egypt, his two Egyptian nephew-kings agreed to reign cojointly for the sake of solidarity. Roman support was also sought. Antiochus Epiphanes, enraged by his nephews' machinations, again invaded Egypt in the Third Egyptian Expedition (168).

But it shall not be as the former. — This time, however, Antiochus Epiphanes (called "the Madman" by the Jews) was not as unopposed as before.

Ver. 30. Ships of Chittim shall come against him. — Antiochus Epiphanes was besieging Alexandria when the Roman C. Popillius Laenus confronted him. Refusing his hand of greetings, the Roman general gave Antiochus a letter from the Roman senate which peremptorily forbade war with the Ptolemies. Then with a vine stick, the Roman drew a circle around the Syrian with the curt command: "Decide there!"

Return . . . against the holy covenant. — Furious and frustrated, Antiochus Epiphanes stumped back to Palestine and vent his venomous fury on the Jews.

Ver. 31. Pollute the sanctuary . . . place the abomination that maketh desolate. — Amidst the carnage created by him and his lieutenant Apollonius in Jerusalem, Antiochus erected the idol Zeus Olympus inside the temple. Hellenization with its concomitant idolatrous worship was foisted on the hapless Jews. A blood bath ensued.

Ver. 34. They shall be holpen with a little help. — As the madman stiffened in his diabolical works, the militant Maccabees and the religious Asidaeans rose in defense of their faith. Their action, though helpful, was never totally successful.

Ver.35. Even to the time of the end. – That is, to the time of the appointed end of the Jews' sufferings.

NOTE: Verses 36-45 belong to events in eschatology.

IX. TEXT OF DANIEL 11:2-35

²And *now will I shew thee the truth.* Behold, there shall stand up *yet three kings in Persia;* and *the fourth* shall be far richer than they all: and by his strength through his riches he shall stir up all *against the realm of Grecia.*

³And *a mighty king shall stand up,* that shall rule with great dominion, and do according to his will. ⁴And *when he shall stand up, his kingdom shall be broken,* and shall be *divided towards the four winds* of heaven; and *not to his posterity* nor according to his dominion which he ruled: for his kingdom shall be plucked up, even for others beside those. ⁵And *the king of the south* shall be strong, and *one of his princes;* and *he shall be strong above him,* and have dominion; *his dominion shall be a great dominion.*

⁶And *in the end of years* they shall *join themselves* together; for the *king's daughter of the south* shall come *to the king of the north* to make *an agreement:* but *she shall not retain the power* of the arm *neither shall he stand, nor his arm:* but *she shall be given up,* and they that brought her, and he that begat her, and he that strengthened her in these times.

⁷But out of *a branch of her roots* shall *one* stand up in his estate, which shall come with an army, and shall enter into the fortress of the king of the north, and *shall deal* against them, *and shall prevail:* ⁸And shall also *carry captives into Egypt their gods,* with their princes, and with their precious vessels of silver and of gold; and he shall continue more years than the king of the north. ⁹So the king of the south shall come into his kingdom [or And he shall *come into the realm of the king of the south*], and shall *return into his own land.*

¹⁰But *his sons shall be stirred up,* and *shall assemble a multitude* of great forces: and one shall *certainly come, and overflow* and pass through: then *shall* he *return,* and be stirred up, *even to his fortress.* ¹¹And *the king of the south shall be moved with choler,* and shall come forth and fight with him, even with the king of the north: and he *shall set forth* a great multitude; but the multitude shall be *given into his hand.* ¹²And when he hath taken away the multitude, his heart shall be lifted up; and he shall cast down many ten thousands: but *he shall not be strengthened* by it. ¹³For *the king of the north shall return,* and shall set forth a multitude greater than the former, and shall certainly come after certain years with a great army and with much riches. ¹⁴And in those times there shall *many* stand up *against the king of the south:* also the robbers of thy people shall exalt themselves to establish the vision; but they shall fall. ¹⁵So *the king of the north shall* come, and *cast up a mount,* and take the most fenced cities: and *the arms of the south shall not withstand,* neither his chosen people, neither shall there be any strength to withstand. ¹⁶But he that cometh against him shall do according to

his own will, and none shall stand before him, and *he shall stand in the glorious land*, which by his hand shall be consumed. [17]He shall also set his face to enter with the strength of his whole kingdom, and upright ones with him [or *equitable conditions*]; thus shall he do: and he shall *give him the daughter of women,* corrupting her: but *she shall not stand* on his side, *neither be for him* [18]After this shall he *turn his face unto the isles*, and shall take many: but *a prince* for his own behalf *shall cause the reproach* offered by him *to cease;* without his own reproach he shall cause it to turn upon him. [19]Then he shall turn his face toward the fort of his own land: but *he shall stumble and fall*, and not be found.

[20]Then shall *stand up in his estate* a raiser of taxes in the glory of the kingdom [or *One that shall cause an exactor to pass*] : but within a few days *he shall be destroyed* , neither in anger, nor in battle.

[21]And *in his estate* shall stand up *a vile person*, to whom they shall not give the honour of the kingdom: but he shall come in peaceably, and obtain the kingdom by flatteries. [22]And *with the arms of a flood shall they be overflown* from before him, and shall be broken; yea, also the prince of the covenant. [23]And after the league made with him *he shall work deceitfully:* for he shall come up, and shall become strong with a small people. [24]He shall *enter peaceably even upon the fattest places* of the province; and he shall do that which his fathers have not done, nor his fathers' fathers; he shall scatter among them the prey, and spoil, and riches: yes, and he shall forecast his devices against the strongholds, even for a time. [25]And he shall stir up his power and his courage *against the king of the south* with a great army; and the king of the south

shall be stirred up to battle with a very great and mighty army; but he shall not stand: for they shall forecast devices against him. ²⁶Yes, they that feed of the portion of his meat shall destroy him, and his army shall overflow: and many shall fall down slain. ²⁷And *both these kings'* hearts shall be to do mischief, and they shall speak lies at one table; but it shall not prosper: for yet the end shall be at the time appointed. ²⁸Then *shall he return* into his land with great riches; and his heart shall be against the holy covenant; and he shall do exploits, and return to his own land.

²⁹At the time appointed *he shall return,* and come *toward the south;* but *it shall not be as the former,* or as the latter. ³⁰For the *ships of Chittim shall come against him:* therefore he shall be grieved, and *return,* and have indignation *against the holy covenant:* so shall he do; he shall even return, and have intelligence with them that forsake the holy covenant. ³¹And arms shall stand on his part, and they shall *pollute the sanctuary* of strength, and shall take away the daily sacrifice, and they shall *place the abomination that maketh desolate.* ³²And such as do wickedly against the covenant shall he corrupt by flatteries: but the people that do know their God shall be strong, and do exploits. ³³And they that understand among the people shall instruct many: yet they shall fall by the sword, and by flame, by captivity, and by spoil, many days. ³⁴Now when they shall fall, *they shall be holpen with a little help:* but many shall cleave to them with flatteries. ³⁵And some of them of understanding shall fall, to try them, and to purge, and to make them white, even *to the time of the end:* because it is yet for a time appointed.

APPENDIX VII

THE PRETRIBULATIONAL RAPTURE

I. THE PRETRIBULATIONAL POSITION

Pretribulationists believe that the church will be raptured to meet the Lord in the air just before the start of the tribulation on earth. According to I Thessalonians 4, Christians who have died will be resurrected (v. 16) and believers living at the time of the rapture will be translated without having to die (v. 17). This entire company of saints will then appear before the Judgment Seat of Christ (Rom. 14:10) for examination as to works and rewards (I Cor. 3:12-15). Then will follow two heavenly events: the presentation of the "bride" (the church) who is arrayed "in fine linen, clean and white" and the "marriage of the Lamb" (Rev. 19:7,8).

If one accepts the literal nature of these events of Scriptures, a period of time must be allowed. The Judgment Seat of Christ, for instance, will not occur "in an instant, in the twinkling of an eye, as part of the downward sweeps of the Lord to earth, with no preview of heaven."[1] The only possible time period for these blessed experiences is between the rapture of the church to heaven and Christ's return again to earth.

---

[1] Gerald B. Stanton, *Kept from the Hour* (London: Marshall, Morgan and Scott, 1964), p. 262.

II. Reasons for Pretribulationism

Many strong arguments exist in support of the doctrine of the pretribulational rapture. The following seem to be more significant:

First, the nature of the tribulation demands that the church be kept from it. When the tribulational prophecies are read literally, one sees a period of tribulation "such as was not since the beginning of the world to this [Jesus'] time, no, nor ever shall be" (Matt. 24:21). The Scripture reports that special protection will be afforded Israel through this awful period (cf. Isa. 26:20-21), but in no instance is the church promised protection. The church is promised to be "kept from the hour of temptation which shall come upon all the world, to try them that dwell upon the earth" (Rev. 3:10).

The analogies of Noah and Lot may be elucidative. Noah and his family went through the great flood, being protected inside the ark. Lot and his daughters were snatched away from the raining brimstones because, as the angel says to Lot, "I cannot do anything till thou be come there" (Gen. 19:22). Noah and his family typify Israel going through the tribulation; Lot and his daughters typify the church being caught away from the tribulation.

Second, while signs of the second coming of Christ are given to the nation Israel (Matt. 24-25), the church is given no signs in passages on the resurrection of the dead in Christ and the translation of believers (cf. John 14:1-3; I Thess. 4:13-18; I Cor. 15:51-58). For the church, the command is always to watch for the Lord, not for signs (I Thess. 5:6; Titus 2:13; Rev. 3:3). The implication is clear: the church, which will not go through the tribulation, needs no intervening signs. The coming of the Lord for the church is always imminent; the time of the church's rapture is at any moment. Gerald Stanton observes: "The placing of even a seven year period such as the tribulation, with its impressive personages and clearly scheduled events between the present hour and the rapture, just as certainly destroys the Biblical concept of an imminent return."[1]

The events of the tribulation period do cast an adumbration before it, and the church may tell the closeness of her Lord's coming by signs of the tribulation made to Israel. But, for the church itself, the coming of the Lord is always impending and imminent.[2]

Third, the Scripture is clear that when Christ returns to set up the millennial kingdom, the saints will have glorified bodies and the unrighteous will be consumed in judgment (Matt. 13:30, 40-42; II Thess. 2:8-12; Rev. 19:15). A literal interpretation of millennial passages however makes it certain that there will be family life, children, and mortal people in the millennial kingdom. Since glorified saints who enter the kingdom obviously cannot propagate children (Matt. 22:30), who then are going to propagate children in the millennium? If no time period is allowed for a group of mortals to be born or born-again after the rapture of the church, and who will enter the kingdom in their mortal bodies, the Scriptures cannot be reconciled. The following response of critics would then be legitimate: "Since no wicked nations exist on earth at the beginning of the alleged millennium, having all been sent to eternal punishment; since the righteous cannot fall into sin and cannot bear children; and since the wicked dead have not yet been raised according to the premil-

---

[1] Stanton, *Kept from the Hour,* p. 109.

[2] Posttribulationism cannot really support the imminent return of Christ, for even posttribulationists admit that once the tribulation period begins its end can approximately be known (see J. Barton Payne, *The Imminent Appearing of Christ* (Grand Rapids, Mich.: Wm. B. Eerdmans Pub. Co., 1962), p. 96).

lennialists, just whom could Satan gather to war against the saints?"[1]

The pretribulational rapture is therefore essential to the interpretation of the millennial prophecies. One necessitates the other. Harmony of the prophetic Scriptures is possible only when an interval between the rapture of the church and Christ's second coming in glory is recognized.

Fourth, interestingly, posttribulationists do allow an interval—whether long or short—between the rapture and the second coming. George L. Rose in *Tribulation till Translation* speculates between "forty days . . . a full year, or . . . the same day."[2] George Ladd argues that the interval need not be "considerable."[3] and J. Barton Payne affirms that "in no case need His appearing be greatly postponed."[4] In view of these conjectures, we are tempted to inquire if seven years will stretch the "considerable" length of time too "greatly"? The thing is, once an interval is admitted, it is only a few steps to the pretribulational position.

Fifth, a normal interpretation of II Thessalonians 2:1-12 makes it apparent that the apostle Paul teaches pretribulationism. Someone in Thessalonica had taught the believers that the great tribulation was already present and that they had therefore been left behind (II Thess. 2:1-2). The apostle Paul challenges that teaching by assuring the Thessalonians: "that day shall not come, except there come a [the] falling away first, and that man of sin be revealed" (v. 3). Since both events obviously had not yet occurred, the apostle says that they have no reason to fear.

---

[1] Floyd E. Hamilton, *The Basis of Millennial Faith* (Grand Rapids, Mich.: Wm. B. Eerdmans Publ. Co., 1942), p. 135.

[2] Cited by Stanton, *Kept from the Hour,* p. 263.

[3] George Eldon Ladd, *The Blessed Hope* (Grand Rapids, Mich.: Wm. B. Eerdmans Pub. Co., 1956), p. 91.

[4] Payne, *Imminent Appearing of Christ,* p. 136.

In II Thessalonians 2, the apostle gives us the impression that he is assuming a lot of things. At least three times, he reminds the Thessalonians of his previous teaching on the subject—"Remember ye not that, when I was yet with you, I told you these things?" (2:5), "ye know . . ." (2:6), and "for you yourselves know perfectly that the day of the Lord so cometh . . ." (5:2). The Thessalonians believers apparently had been taught a lot of eschatology. Their tutor Paul had moreover previously written to them about the rapture event (I Thess. 4). The apostle, assuming the underlying fact of pre-tribulational rapture, advances in II Thessalonians to deal with specific questions and misunderstandings regarding the implications of this event.[1]

What precisely does Paul mean when he says that "*the* falling away" (2:3) must come before the tribulation? The definite article "the" denotes that this will be a definite event, an event distinct from the appearance of the Man of Sin. The Greek word for "falling away", taken by itself, does not mean religious apostasy or defection.[2] Neither does the word mean "to fall," as the Greeks have another word for that. The best translation of the word is "to depart." The apostle Paul refers here to a definite event which he calls "the departure," and which will occur just before the start of the tribulation. This is the rapture of the church.

---

[1] There is no basis for Oswald T. Allis statement that "Certainly, if Paul held the any moment rapture doctrine, it is passing strange that he did not expound it here (In II Thess. 2)" *(Prophecy and the Church* [Phila., Pa.: Presbyterian and Reform Publ. Co., 1964], p. 197).

[2] The apostle Paul uses this word in I Timothy 4:1, "Some shall *depart* from the faith." The necessity for qualifying the word with the phrase "from the faith" shows that the word taken by itself has no such connotation.

Moreover, the apostle reveals that someone is hindering or restraining the appearance of the Man of Sin, and that after he is "taken out of the way" (v. 7), the tribulational Man of Sin will be "revealed" (v. 8). It is logical to assume that one able to hinder or restrain the Satan-motivated Man of Sin must be stronger than the Man of Sin. And there can be none stronger and mightier except God Himself.[1] Thus, just before the tribulation, God the Spirit who has been indwelling the church will go with the church.[2] This will release the Man of Sin for his maniacal activities in the tribulation.

Sixth, Throughout the Scriptures, celestial beings such as angels, cherubims, and seraphims (Isa. 6), and other marvelous beings (Ezek. 1) appear time and again. But just before the start of the tribulation in Revelation 6-19, there appear on the pages of Scriptures (in Rev. 4) an entirely new group of heavenly beings the 24 elders.

Literal interpreters believe that the 24 elders represent the saints who are raptured before the tribulation. The description of their being crowned and laying their crowns at Jesus' feet certainly fits that of redeemed saints. If we take Revelation 2-3 as the history of the Christian church from the first century on to just before the rapture, Revelation 4 would then describe the close of church history (Note: "Come up here" v. 1). And the 24 elders make their debut at this precise moment of the close of church history.

Seventh, the pretribulational rapture agrees with the Biblical revelation concerning the number of resurrections. If living as well as dead believers are raptured *before* the

---

[1] Many pretribulationists identify the Restrainer as the Holy Spirit, for the Holy Spirit is also God.

[2] The Holy Spirit, being omnipresent, will not be excluded from earth. His presence and power will still be felt in filling saints and convicting sinners at the tribulation, just as in Old Testament times.

tribulation, this will rightly add one more resurrection event to the eschatological scheme. Posttribulationists adamantly insist that Revelation 20:4-6 depicts only *one* general resurrection of the just and of the wicked. However, the "first" resurrection of Revelation 20 was certainly preceded by other resurrections (such as that of the two witnesses in Rev. 11:1-12), and the apostle Paul calls the resurrection of Christ "the first fruits" (I Cor. 15:23), denoting a harvest scene of many "fruits" (resurrections). The Scriptural concept of the resurrections can therefore admit the resurrection of saints at the rapture before the tribulation.[1]

III. A CONCLUSION

The pretribulational position is based not so much on simple texts or arguments but on the accumulation of evidences and texts. A consistent literal approach to prophecy makes the pretribulational rapture inescapable. Interestingly, once the truth of the pretribulational rapture is seen, the entire prophetic Word seems to fall into place and a harmonious picture of God's dealing with the church in redemptive grace is granted.

---

[1] For a comprehensive listing of the reasons for the pretribulational rapture, *see* "Fifty Arguments for Pretribulationism" in John F. Walvoord, *The Rapture Question* (Findlay, Ohio: Dunham Pub. Co., 1957, pp. 191-99.

APPENDIX VIII
THE UNPRECEDENTED TRIBULATION

One of the most significant and interesting themes of prophecy in both the Old and the New Testaments is that of the tribulation period. It is the period when the rebellions, apostasies, and sufferings of this sin-cursed world are brought to a head.

I. DURATION OF THE TRIBULATION

The length of the tribulation period is not difficult to ascertain under the literal method of interpretation. Daniel's prophecy of the 70 "weeks" is the starting point. The first 69 "weeks," when interpreted as "week of years," equals 483 years—the exact length of time from the decree of Artaxerxus to rebuild Jerusalem (Neh. 2:1-6) in 445 B.C. to the triumphant entry into Jerusalem of Jesus the Messiah! This gives us assurance to take the final 70th "week" (the tribulation period) as a period of seven literal years. The mid-point of the 70th week, properly called the Great Tribulation since sin and suffering then will be unprecedented, is revealed even in days and in months (Rev. 11:3; 12:6 and 11:2; 13:5).

II. POWER PLAY AMONG GENTILE NATIONS

The tribulation period will affect both Gentile nations and the nation Israel in the throes of time prior to Christ's second event. For Gentile nations, it will be the culmination of the so-called "Times of the Gentiles" which begins when Jerusalem first fell into the hand Nebuchadnezzar.

The prophet Daniel gives the fullest account of the times of the gentiles and predicts that four earthly kingdoms will follow one another before the coming of messiah's glorious kingdom. A number of revelations regarding the *fourth* kingdom in its final form are given in both the Old and New Testaments. Let us go into this in more detail.

A. Eschatological Personages

Many conservative interpreters agree that eschatological persons are real-life persons. At least five eschatological personages frolick in prophecy: (1) The "Beast" or head of the revived Roman Empire; (2) The False Prophet; (3) The King of the North; (4) The King of the South; and (5) Kings from the East.

The "beast" is by far the most famous end-time person. He is described in the Bible as "the beast" (Rev. 13:1-10), "the little horn (Dan. 7:8, 24), "the prince that shall come" (Dan. 9:26-27). There is some discussion as to whether "the king of fierce countenance" (Dan. 11:40-42) refers to the beast or to the King of the North, and whether "the antichrist" (I John 2:18, 22) and "the man of sin, the son of perdition, the lawless one" (II Thess. 2:3-8) refer to the beast or to the False Prophet. After his emergence as ruler of the 10-nation Roman confederacy,[1] the "beast" will virtually dominate the tribulational scene.

The "false prophet" mentioned in Revelation 19:20; 20:10; 13:11-17 is a person distinct from the apostate world

---

[1] History will repeat itself. The phenomenal rise of the antichrist will be comparable to Alexander the Great who, at age 22, crossed the Hellespont as prince of a small Grecian state, but four years later, founded an empire which wrote subsequent history.

church described and destroyed in Revelation 17. This false religious leader will play lackey to the uncaged "beast" throughout the tribulation.

The other eschatological personages—the King of the North, the King of the South, and the Kings of the East—play politics around the beast and over the land of Palestine before being defeated at the middle of the tribulation.

B. The Ten-nation Confederacy

Literal interpreters see a ten-nation confederacy in existence during the end-times. The reason is, Daniel visionally sees the fourth kingdom which will immediately precede the Messianic kingdom as a *ten*-horned beast (Dan. 7:7). Nebuchadnezzat's four-sectional image logically contains *ten* toes in its final stage,[1] and Daniel interprets the number "ten" as *ten* kings (Dan. 7:24). In Revelation 13:1 and 17:12, the "ten kings" are seen as still future by the apostle John. The ancient Roman Empire (Daniel's fourth world kingdom) will be revived to run its course in the final "toe" stage in the person of rulers who will reign simultaneously under one supreme ruler just before the second coming of the Messiah. The same literal principles which demand the restoration of the Jews to their ancient land necessitates our placing the ten-nation confederacy in the region where the ancient Roman Empire once held sway.

---

[1] Ten toes in Nebuchadnezzar's image seems most natural, despite Milton Terry's foot dragging: "Not a few interpreters have put great stress upon the import of the ten toes of Nebuchadnezzar's image . . . and have searched to find ten kings to correspond; whereas, from aught that appears to the contrary, the image may have had twelve toes, like the giant of Gath" (*Biblical Hermeeutics* (New York, N.Y.: Eaton and Mains, 1911), p. 323.

This ten-nation Roman confederacy will be headed by the "beast" who will make a treaty of peace and protection with the nation Israel during the beginning of the tribulation (Dan. 9:27). The treaty or covenant, made for purposes of political expediency, will however be short-lived and will beguile Israel into a fatal false security during the first 3-½ years of the tribulation. The prophet Isaiah calls it an "agreement with hell" (Isa. 28:18).

C. Crises Events at Middle of Tribulation

At the middle of the tribulation period, a movement of forces in and about Palestine will result in the worldwide rulership of the beast.

This movement starts when the king of the south (allied with that of the north) invades Palestine (Dan. 11:40). The king of the north also attacks Palestine, a "land of unwalled villages . . . those who are at rest" (Ezek. 38:11).

The beast (or the European confederacy) then lands in Palestine, ostensibly to fulfill treaty commitments with Israel. The beast is first defeated (Rev. 13:3), but the northern confederacy is supernaturally annihilated (Ezek. 39:1-4; Dan. 11:45), and the beast becomes the world ruler (Rev. 13:7). With world rulership assured, he abrogates the covenant with Israel (Dan. 9:27), destroys apostate Christendom (Rev. 17:16), and goes all out to persecute those opposing his Satanic rule. This terrible period is properly known as the Great Tribulation.

III. TIME OF TROUBLE FOR ISRAEL

The tribulation will definitely be a part of Israel's sorrowful and tragic history. The Bible describes the tribulation as the "time of Jacob's trouble" (Jer. 30:4-7; Dan. 12:1; Matt. 24:21). The unbelief and failures of Israel are pruned and punished through the unparalleled fires of the tribulation. The Jewish remnant entering the millennium at the end of the tribulation will thus have been purified for the kingdom.

Perhaps the most systematic New Testament description of Israel in the tribulation is given by the Lord in His Olivet Discourse. The discourse is prompted by and given in answer to the disciples' two-fold question: "Tell us, when shall these things be? [i.e. the destruction of the temple]; and what shall be the sign of thy coming, and of the end of the world?" (Matt. 24:3).[1]

The answer to the disciples' first question is given in Luke 21:20-24. The disciples' second question is covered by Matthew 24. The account of Matthew 24 strikes a surprising harmony with the tribulation scenes of Revelation 6-19. The correspondences are as follows:[2]

> Matthew 24:4-8 - Revelation 6-11 (first half of tribulation)
> Matthew 24:9-28 - Revelation 12-18 (second half of tribulation)[3]
> Matthew 24:29-31 - Revelation 19 (Christ's second coming)

According to prophecy, there is also a bright side to Israel's journey through the tribulation. The Scripture promises that God will raise up a remnant who will preach the gospel of the kingdom to the ends of the world (Matt. 24:14). The number of these evangelists will be 144,000 (Rev. 7), and the Holy

---

[1] In the disciples' minds, "thy coming" and "the end of the world" are one complex of events (cf. Matt. 13:40-41; 19:28) occuring for Israel at the end of the tribulation.

[2] The mid-point in Matthew 24 is verse 8 (note the "then" of verse9). Other interpreters place it at verse 15.

[3] Note the "time, times, and half a time" in 12:14 and 11:2 where the second half of the tribulation is yet future.

Spirit will so empower them so that they will be like "144,000 Jewish Billy Grahams turned loose on the earth."[1] The world has never seen such a period of evangelistic activity. The Spirit will be poured upon the nation Israel and many Gentiles will also be saved (Rev. 7:9-17). But martyrdom will be the lot of most tribulational saints as the beast and the false prophet maintain total control over the lives of the people.

IV. THE BATTLE OF ARMAGEDDON

Although, by the latter half of the tribulation period, the beast will have extensive control over the entire world, his political organization will not be strong enough to knit the world into a tight hegemony. And so, just before the second coming of Christ with the saints, major sections of the world will be in rebellion against the beast, advancing their forces towards the land of Palestine.

Armageddon (Rev. 16:16) is apparently the focal terrain of the conflicting forces, although the battle will spread over a wider area (cf. Isa. 34:1-6; 63:1-6; Joel 3:2, 12; Zech. 12:2-10). The Holy Land will be crowded with the armies of the world as Christ and His saints return to institute the millennial kingdom. The armies of the world then unite against the coming Christ, but do not stand a chance for they are destroyed by a word from His mouth.

V. THE REVELATION OF JESUS CHRIST

The New Testament mentions the coming of Christ over 300 times. This is about once in every 25 verses. In the Old Testament, there are 20 times as many references to the

---

[1] Hal Lindsey, *The Late Great Planet Earth* (Grand Rapids, Mich,: Zondervan Pub. House, 1970), p. 111.

second coming as to the first coming of Christ. If anything is found in prophecy, it is His coming again.

The term "Second Coming" is commonly loosely used of the two phases of Christ's coming, either as one concept or separately. When we say Christ is coming, we may mean either the rapture or the revelation, or both as one concept. For purposes of clarity, we have described the *second* phase of His coming (i.e. *after* the Tribulation) as "the revelation."

Chronologically, this second phase of Christ's coming will be "immediately after the tribulation" (Matt. 24:29). It will be sudden (Matt. 24:27), although preceded by signs (Matt. 24:4-26), and evident to all (v. 30). The chronology of Revelation 19:11-20:15 shows also that the revelation of Jesus Christ will be *before* the millennium. The revelation of Christ *with* the saints will therefore be after the tribulation and before the millennium.

With regard to the Jews, as the coming of the Lord draws near, there will be a regathering back to the land of Palestine (Matt. 24:31). The nation will be "born in a day" (Zech. 12:10) as they recognize and acknowledge Him "whom they had pierced" (Zech. 12:10). After His coming, Israel will be judged (Ezek. 20:33-38) and prepared for entrance into the millennial kingdom.

With regard to the Gentiles, the Lord's coming will be seen and mourned (Rev. 1:7). The nations will be gathered for judgment (Matt. 25:31-46) and only the righteous will be allowed to enter the kingdom.

Of the tribulation's evil trilogy—the beast, the false prophet, and Satan—the first two will be cast permanently into the Lake of Fire (Rev. 19:20), while the last one is temporarily chained in the bottomless pit (Rev. 20:1-3). This will happen after the seven-year tribulation period when Christ and the saints return to earth to reign (Rev. 19).

With His enemies thus disposed of, Christ with the saints sets up the millennial kingdom on earth (Dan. 7:13-14; Zech. 14:9).

APPENDIX IX
THE MILLENNIAL KINGDOM

When discussing the millennium, the literal inter-preter, encounters a peculiar hardship, not of searching for, but of sifting through mountains of millennial prophecies. As Thiessen notes: "When once we adopt the view that the Bible means what it says, and that it should be interpreted literally, we find ourselves overwhelmed with material concerning the future [kingdom]."[1]

Literal interpretation of millennial prophecies presents the hope of a future kingdom of Christ on the earth where peace, righteousness, and blessing will ensue as Satan is bound for a thousand years. The elect Jews, the righteous Gentiles, and the glorified Church will all participate in the glories of the millennium. The wicked dead are not raised until after the thousand years when they will be judged at the Great White Throne. A more detailed description of the millennium now follows.

I. ITS NATURAL SETTING

Our Lord describes the millennial period as "the regenera-tion" (Matt. 19:28), and truly the creation will be

---

[1] Henry Clarence Thiessen, *Introductory Lectures in Systematic Theology* (Grand Rapids, Mich.: Wm. B. Eerdmans Pub. Co., 1949), p. 510.

regenerated during the millennium. As the curse is lifted and Edenic conditions exist, the entire earth will become extremely fruitful (Isa. 29:17; Ezek. 34:26-27; Joel 2:22-27; Amos 9:13; Zech. 14:4). There will be geographical changes (Isa. 35:1-2; 55:13; Zech. 14:4-10), such as the elevation of the Dead Sea, which will be stocked with lively fish   and skirted with luxuriant growths of shade and fruit trees (Ezek. 47).

The animal creation, will live under Edenic conditions. Wild beasts will become tame (Isa. 11:5-9; 35:9; Ezek. 34:25) and even their dietary habits altered. "The wolf and the lamb shall feed together, and the lion shall eat straw like the bullock . . . . They shall not hurt, nor destroy in all my holy mountain, saith the Lord" (Isa. 65:25).

II.   ITS SPIRITUAL ATMOSPHERE

Critics of the millennium on earth presuppose that an earthly kingdom cannot be spiritual. As Loraine Boettner would have it: "We believe that the principle of literal interpretation . . . leads to serious error in that it fails to recognize the truly spiritual nature of the kingdom in this world as manifested in the Church and sets forth instead an earthly, political kingdom." [1]

Despite the reservations of critics, Old Testament prophets do predict that the millennial kingdom will be the greatest outpouring of the Spirit, with joy, gladness, and peace in the Holy Spirit (Isa. 35:10; 51:11; Ezek. 11:19; Joel 2:18-32). The earth will be filled with the knowledge of God (Isa. 11:9) as an increase in illumination is divinely granted (Isa. 2:3). "If anything is obvious from the literal interpretation of passages concerning the Millennial Kingdom,"

---

[1] Loraine Boettner, *The Millennium* (Phila., Pa.: Presbyterian and Reformed Pub. Co., 1964), p. 375.

observes Charles Ryrie, "it is that the period will be a rule of God which includes the highest ideals of spirituality." [1]

Incidentally, the large scale rebellion of the unrighteous will not occur until the end of the millennium when Satan will be let loose to incite the nations. Allis' sardonic picture of a millennium (which he forthwith rejects) is not complete: "It is not pleasing to think of the Messianic King, the Prince of Peace, sitting enthroned as it were on a smouldering volcano; of a reign of Messiah, peaceful on the surface but seething with hate and muttered rebellion." [2] The rebellion of the unrighteous will not happen until Satan is let loose at the end of the millennium. There can hardly be "seething rebellion" in the millennium to destroy millennial bliss under an omniscient Messiah.

III. Its Inhabitants

The millennium will be quickly populated by two helping factors: a mighty increase in population and an extraordinary prolongation of human life (Isa. 49:19-20; 65:20; Jer. 30:18-20; Mic. 4:1-5; Zech. 8:4-6). A hundred-year-old person will be considered "a child" (Isa. 65:20). [3] The prolongation of life will not exclude the attrition of death

The millennial inhabitants need not worry about sicknesses, wars, or famines, for these will be removed (Isa. 33:24; 35:5-6; Ezek. 36:29-35; Isa. 2:4). There will be great prosperity and security such as was never seen on earth (Zech. 8:12; Mic. 4:2-5). An increase in human intelligence

---

[1] Charles Caldwell Ryrie, *Basis of the Premillennial Faith* (New York, N.Y.: Loizeaux Brothers, 1953), p. 174.

[2] Oswald T. Allis, *Prophecy and the Church* (Phila., Pa.: Presbyterian and Reformed Pub. Co., 1964), pp. 240-41.

[3] This has no reference to second childhood!

and learning (Jer. 31:34; Isa. 54:13) and a unity of language (Isa. 32:4; Zech. 3:9) will prevail.

Since only the righteous enter the millennial kingdom, the millennium will begin with righteous Jews and Gentiles (aside from glorified Christians).[1] The children of these unglorified people however are born with sinful natures. They will choose or reject the Messiah in their hearts, although any evidential sin will mean immediate punishment (Zech. 14:16-19).

IV. ITS THEOCRATIC GOVERNMENT

If the age of a nation is measured by the continuity of its political institutions, the United States would be the world's second-oldest nation (next to Britain). The thousand-year theocratic kingdom of Christ however will, by far, surpass that of today's superpower. It will be the longest continuous political institution ever to be set up on earth.

A theocracy is a government under the immediate direction of God. God ruled through His chosen rulers during the Old Testament theocracy. But the millennial kingdom will be a much more glorious one in that a visible Messiah-King rules in perfect righteousness, exercising direct sovereignty over the affairs of the kingdom. No one has ever seen such a phenomenon. The perfect nature of the theocracy will then be exhibited in all its original beauty and excellency.[2]

In a very real sense, the theocratic kingdom in the millennium may be said to be Jewish in nature. Old Testament

---

[1] See above "The Church in the Millennium," pp. 266-67.

[2] Some interpreters contend that a risen and glorified Christ cannot reign over earthly people. But did not the risen Christ walk on earth and live its life? Even after the ascension, Christ did not give up His theanthropic person, and is seen in heaven as "the Lamb slain" (Rev. 13:8).

prophets link this future kingdom to the Jewish common-wealth because the former will largely be the Old Testament theocracy restored, with the theocratic personage Jesus Christ on the Davidic throne. During this thousand-year period, promises made under the Abrahamic, Palestinian, Davidic, and New Covenants will be fulfilled by the Jewish remnant. The New Testament[1] as well as the Old Testament describes the millennium under these terms.

---

[1]See above, p. 231n.

APPENDIX X

WORLD WITHOUT END

And I saw a new heaven and a new earth; for the
first heaven and the first earth were passed away,
and there was no more sea. . . . And he that sat upon
the throne said, Behold, I make all things new,
Write; for these words are true and faithful. [Rev.
21:1,5]

I. Eternal Abode of Saints

There is a paucity of Scriptural revelation regarding the
Eternal State. The Bible does reveal that after the millennial
reign of Christ and the Great White Throne judgment, there
will appear "a new heaven and a new earth" (Rev. 21:1),
with the New Jerusalem as its probable crown and capital. Of
the new heaven and earth's configuration, size, and appearance, we know nothing. Doubtless, these will be regions of
eternal bloom and beauty.

Saints in eternity will enjoy a totally new kind of existence—"no more death, neither sorrow, nor crying, neither
shall there be any more pain; for the former things are passed
away" (Rev. 21:4). The service of God out of pure love and
pleasure (Rev. 22:3-4) and the enjoyment of God and His
new creation will be the eternal occupation of the redeemed.

II. Final Destiny of Sinners

The Biblical revelation regarding the destiny of the lost is
indeed tragic. The Great White Throne judgment at the end of

357

the millennium will confirm the eternal destiny of unbelievers. Their final, eternal destination is the Lake of Fire (Rev. 19:20; 20:10, 14-15; 21:8). This is an actual place—as actual as heaven—and not a mere state of mind. The tragic thing about this is that man was not destined to be in the Lake of Fire. It was "prepared for the devil and his angels" (Matt. 24:21).

The sufferring in the Lake of Fire will be conscious and unending. It is significant to note that the word "everlasting" is used *both* of heaven and of hell in the Bible. Hell will be as lengthy as heaven. No wonder Christ told Judas that "it had been good for that man [the betrayer] if he had not been born" (Matt. 26:24).

111.   How Long is Eternity?

The eminent Dutch historian, Hendrick Van Loon, in *The Story of Mankind* thus describes the length of eternity: High up in the North, in the land called Svitjod, there stands a rock. It is one hundred miles high, and one hundred miles wide. Once every thousand years, a little bird comes to this rock to sharpen its beak. When the rock has thus been worn away, then a single day of Eternity will have gone by!

We have another illustration:

When a baby is born, he is—

0 YEARS OLD

If properly cared for, he becomes—

10 YEARS OLD

If *very* properly cared for, we add another zero—

100 YEARS OLD

Now, suppose we continue to add zeros:

1,000, 000, 000, 000, 000, 000, 000, 000, 000, 000, 000,
000, 000, 000, 000, 000, 000, 000, 000, 000, 000, 000, 000,
000, 000, 000, 000, 000, 000, 000, 000, 000, 000, 000, 000,
000, 000, 000, 000, 000, 000, 000, 000, 000, 000, 000, 000,
000, 000, 000, 000, 000, 000, 000, 000, 000, 000, 000, 000,
000, 000, 000, 000, 000, 000, 000, 000, 000, 000, 000, 000,
000, 000, 000, 000, 000, 000, 000, 000, 000, 000, 000, 000,
000, 000, 000, 000, 000, 000, 000, 000, 000, 000, 000, 000,
000, 000, 000, 000, 000, 000, 000, 000, 000, 000, 000, 000,
000, 000, 000, 000, 000, 000, 000, 000, 000, 000, 000, 000,
000, 000, 000, 000, 000, 000, 000, 000, 000, 000, 000, 000,
000, 000, 000, 000, 000, 000, 000, 000, 000, 000, 000, 000,
000, 000, 000, 000, 000, 000, 000, 000, 000, 000, 000, 000,
000, 000, 000, 000, 000, 000, 000, 000, 000, 000, 000, 000,
000, 000, 000, 000, 000, 000, 000, 000, 000, 000, 000, 000,
000, 000, 000, 000, 000, 000, 000, 000, 000, 000, 000, 000,
000, 000, 000, 000, 000, 000, 000, 000, 000, 000, 000, 000,
000, 000, 000, 000, 000, 000, 000, 000, 000, 000, 000, 000,
000, 000, 000, 000, 000, 000, 000, 000, 000, 000, 000, 000,
000, 000, 000, 000, 000, 000, 000, 000, 000, 000, 000, 000,
000, 000, 000, 000, 000, 000, 000, 000, 000, 000, 000, 000,
000, 000, 000, 000, 000, 000, 000, 000, 000, 000, 000, 000,
000, 000, 000, 000, 000, 000, 000, 000, 000, 000, 000, 000,
000, 000, 000, 000, 000, 000, 000, 000, 000, 000, 000, 000,
000, 000, 000, 000, 000, 000, 000, 000, 000, 000, 000, 000,
000, 000, 000, 000, 000, 000, 000, 000, 000, 000, 000, 000,
000, 000, 000, 000, 000, 000, 000, 000, 000, 000, 000, 000,
000, 000, 000, 000, 000, 000, 000, 000, 000, 000, 000, 000,
000, 000, 000, 000, 000, 000, 000, 000, 000, 000, 000, 000,
000, 000, 000, 000, 000, 000, 000, 000, 000, 000, 000, 000,
000, 000, 000, 000, 000, 000, 000, 000, 000, 000, 000, 000,
000, 000, 000, 000, 000, 000, 000, 000, 000, 000, 000, 000,
000, 000, 000, 000, 000, 000, 000, 000, 000, 000, 000, 000,
000, 000, 000, 000, 000, 000, 000, 000, 000 **YEARS OLD**

If we should fill the remaining pages of this book with zeros, and cover the earth and universe with zeros — and then comprehend its total value — we shall have discovered the length of one day in Eternity.

GLOSSARY

GLOSSARY *

OF PROPHETIC TERMS

ALLEGORIZATION. — A method of interpretation based on the assumption that the Scripture contains multiple sense.

ALLEGORY. — A figure of speech which, by expressing one thing under the image of another, conveys a moral truth. An allegory is an extended metaphor.

AMILLENNIALISM. — A system of eschatology which, among other things, interprets the millennium as symbolical of present life in heaven.

ANALOGY OF FAITH. — The principle that any interpretation of the Scripture must conform and harmonize with the whole teaching of Scripture on that given subject.

APOCALYPTICS. — Prophecies which have to do with end-time events.

APPLICATION. — The deduction of truths, principles, and concepts from that which has been literally interpreted.

CANON OF SCRIPTURE. — The complete listing of the sixty-six books of the Bible.

CHILIASM. — The belief in a thousand-year reign of Christ on earth.

CHURCH. — The entire body of believers who are saved by believing in Christ, from the day of Pentecost and up to the Rapture event.

---

*Some definitions are based on usages only in this book.

COMPREHENSION. — The state of understanding reached when both the speaker or writer and the listener or reader fix the same meaning to that which is being spoken or written.

CONSERVATIVE INTERPRETER. — An interpreter who believes in the cardinal doctrines of the Christian faith, although not necessarily in the literal interpretation of prophecy.

CONSISTENT LITERAL INTERPRETATION. — Interpretation which consistently follows the customary and normal usages of Bible language.

COVENANT PREMILLENNIALISM. — A system of eschatology which attempts to reconcile premillennialism with covenantism while avoiding dispensationalism and pretribulationism.

COVENANT THEOLOGY. — A system of theology which, among other things, explains all relationship between God and man from the beginning to the end of time under the Covenant of Works, the Covenant of Grace, and (sometimes) the Covenant of Redemption.

DISPENSATIONAL THEOLOGY. — A system of theology which, among other things, believes that God varies His procedure in His dealings with man under the various dispensations, and that history and prophecy in the Scripture should be interpreted under this light, particularly under the distinction between Israel and the Church.

DOUBLE SENSE.—A theoretical concept which affirms that the written words of prophetic Scripture are shallow and superficial and that the hidden and deeper sense behind the literal is the true sense.

DUAL HERMENEUTICS. — A method of interpretation whereby non-prophetic Scripture is interpreted literally and prophetic Scripture is interpreted non-literally.

EARLY FATHERS. — Leaders of the Christian Church during the first three centuries after Christ.

ECSTASY.—The highest gradation of the prophetic state when the prophet is elevated above the sphere of mundane sense producing absolute concentration and perception of divine revelation.

ESCHATOLOGICAL SYSTEM.—A theological system which systematizes Biblical revelations of end-time events.

ESCHATOLOGY.—Doctrine of last things; the period of time relating to Christ's second coming and events preceding and following it.

ETERNAL KINGDOM. — One aspect of the concept of the Kingdom which comprehends the rule of God over all creation—saved and unsaved—down the ages.

EXEGESIS.—The study of the basic, originally intended meaning of Scripture; interpretation.

EXPOSITION.— The deduction of spiritual truths, principles, and concepts from that which has been literally interpreted.

FIGURATIVE INTERPRETATION. — An erroneous method whereby plain, actual language is figuratively interpreted.

FIGURATIVE LANGUAGE.— The legitimate expression of an original literal idea in a figure of speech or figurative act.

FIGURE.—A valid grammatical device which serves to convey more graphically an originally intended literal concept or idea.

FOREORDINATION. — "God from all eternity did by the most wise and holy counsel of his own free will freely and unchangeably ordain whatsoever comes to pass" (Westminster Confession).

FULFILLMENT.— A fulfillment occurs when the event predicted in a prophecy actually takes place. Fulfillments are different from foreshadowments and applications.

HERMENEUTICS. — The skill or art of interpretation.

HISTORY PREWRITTEN. — The belief that the main outlines of future history—with a surprising number of details—have been revealed and will take place under regular progressions of time.

HYPERBOLE. — A figure of speech involving an exaggeration.

ILLUMINATION. — A work of the Holy Spirit which enables Christians to understand the written revelation of Scripture.

IMMINENCY. — The doctrine that no intervening prophesied event stands between the Church and the Lord's coming and that Christ may come at any moment.

INSPIRATION. — The supernatural work of the Holy Spirit on human writers in producing the Scripture which stands inerrant in all its parts and embraces God's complete revelation to man.

INTERCALATION. — The age between the first and second advents of Christ.

INTERPRETATION. — The art of explaining the original sense of a speaker or writer.

ISRAEL. — Physical descendants of Abraham; the Jews.

ISRAEL'S PROMISES. — Promises made by God to Israel and found especially in the Old Testament covenants and prophecies. These promises will be fulfilled at the millennial kingdom.

KINGDOM. — A term indicating (in this book) the future Davidic and earthly reign of Christ as promised by Old Testament prophets and New Testament writers.

KINGDOM OF GOD and *KINGDOM OF HEAVEN.* — Non-technical terms used interchangeably to denote either the earthly or the eternal kingdom, depending on the context.

KINGDOM PROPHECIES. — Old Testament prophecies which relate to the institution and glories of the future Davidic kingdom on earth under the Messiah.

LANGUAGE OF PROPHECY. — The linguistic expression of prophecy.

LEXICOGRAPHY. — The study of individual words.

LIBERAL INTERPRETER. — Interpreters who reject the cardinal doctrines of the Christian faith, including the inspiration of Scripture.

LITERAL. — Customary, natural, normal, plain; (sometimes) nonfigurative, earthly.

LITERAL INTERPRETATION. — The art of explaining the original meaning of Scripture according to the normal and customary usages of its language.

LITERAL INTERPRETERS OF PROPHECY or LITERAL PROPHETIC INTERPRETERS. — Interpreters who are consistently literal in prophetic interpretation, and are thus premillennial, dispensational and pretribulational in eschatology.

MILLENNIUM. —A term which indicates the thousand-year reign of Christ on the earth.

NATURAL ISRAEL. — Physical descendants of Abraham; the Jews.

NON-LITERAL PROPHETIC INTERPRETERS or NON-LITERALISTS —— Interpreters who are not consistent in literal prophetic interpretation, and are thus amillennial, postmillennial, posttribulational, and covenant premillennial in eschatology.

144,000. — The number of saved Jewish evangelists who will be used by God to proclaim the Gospel of the Kingdom during the tribulation period and help bring about a world-wide revival.

PARABLE. —A figure of speech intended to reveal as well as conceal truths. A parable is more extended than a simile or metaphor.

PARALLELISM. — A device of Hebrew poetry which repeats or states the same thing in a different way.

PERSONIFICATION. — A figure of speech which describes inanimate objects as if animate.

PERSPECTIVE OF PROPHECY. — A phenomenon of prophecy which sees two or more future events—widely separated in time—under a single profile or side by side.

POSTMILLENNIALISM. — A system of eschatology which, among other things, sees the millennium ushered in through a gradually Christianized world. Christ comes at the end of this "millennium."

POSTTRIBULATIONISM. — A system of eschatology which sees the Church passing through the Tribulation and which pictures the Rapture and the Revelation as one single event in Christ's second advent, with hardly a break in between. Covenant theologians are almost always posttribulational.

PREMILLENNIALISM. — A system of eschatology which interprets prophecy literally and believes in the thousand-year reign of Christ on the earth following Christ's second advent.

PRETRIBULATIONISM. — A system of eschatology which sees the Church raptured before the start of the Tribulation and then returning with Christ after the Tribulation to institute the Millennial Kingdom on the earth. Dispensational theologians are pretribulational.

PROGRESSIVE REVELATION. — The doctrine which teaches that the complete revelation of God to man was given not all at once in complete, final form, but unfolded in gradual fashion.

PROPHECY. — The oral or written message of a prophet, especially related to future events.

PROPHET. —A person to whom the will of God has been revealed under inspiration in order that it might in turn be communicated to man.

PROPHETIC COLORATION. — The theory that the written words and form of prophecy are colored by the thoughts and life forms of the prophets and their contemporaries, and that prophecy rises out of the historical experiences and backgrounds of the prophets.

PROPHETIC STATE. — The state of absolute and supernatural concentration by the prophet under which revelation is communicated from God.

RAPTURE. — The event just before the Tribulation when the Church is caught up—dead saints being resurrected and living saints "changed"—to meet the Lord in the air prior to the Second Coming to institute the Millennial Kingdom.

REVELATION. — A truth made known by God to man which man would otherwise not be able to discover or discern; the Second Coming of Christ with His saints to institute the Millennial Kingdom.

RIDDLE. — A statement that is designed to puzzle and to hide.

SEED OF ABRAHAM. — A term which embraces the following groups of people: Natural Israel, Spiritual Israel, and the Church.

SIMILE. — A figure of speech which compares two dissimilar objects or concepts with the use of adverbs such as "like" and "as."

SPIRITUAL ISRAEL. — Physical descendants of Abraham who through faith are also Abraham's spiritual children; the Remnant.

SPIRITUAL KINGDOM. — The present form of God's kingdom where God rules in the hearts of all saved persons.

SPIRITUALIZATION. — A method of interpretation which explains the written words of prophetic Scripture non-literally.

SYMBOL. — A representative and graphic delineation of an actual event, truth, or object.

SYMBOLICAL INTERPRETATION. — A method of interpretation (to be avoided) which explains a symbol symbolically and thus never arrives at the literal meaning intended behind the use of the symbol.

SYMBOLICAL SIGNIFICANCE. — An acceptable element in prophecy which sees applicational and representative meanings in prophetic objects without negating their actuality.

SYNTAX. — The study of word relationships.

TRIBULATION. — The seven-year period before the second advent of Christ when divine judgment is poured on the earth in an unprecedented manner and when sin comes to a head in the person of the Antichrist.

TYPOLOGICAL INTERPRETATION. — The literal interpretation of types.

VISION.—A supernatural presentation of future events before the mind of the prophet whether in actual or symbolical language.

BIBLIOGRAPHY

I. BOOKS

Achtemeier, Paul J. *An Introduction to the New Hermeneutic.* Phila., Pa.: Westminster Press, 1964. Pp. 190.

Alexander, Joseph Addison. *Isaiah.* 2 vols. New York, N.Y.: John Wiley, 1852.

Alford, Henry. *The Greek Testament.* 4 vols. London: Logmans, Green, and Co., 1894.

Allen, Stuart. *The Interpretation of Scripture.* London: Berean Publishing Trust, 1967. Pp. 60.

Allis, Oswald T. *Prophecy and the Church.* Phila., Pa.: Presbyterian and Reformed Pub. Co., 1964. Pp. x+339.

Anderson, Robert. *The Coming Prince.* 14th edition. Grand Rapids, Mich.: Kregel Pubs., 1954. Pp. liv+311.

————. *Daniel in the Critics' Den.* New York, N.Y.: Fleming H. Revell Co., n.d. Pp. xiv+186.

Angus, Joseph. *The Bible Handbook.* 2nd ed. revised. New York, N.Y.: Nelson and Phillips, 1873. Pp. ix+781.

Armstrong, Herbert W. *The United States and British Commonwealth in Prophecy.* Pasadena, Calif.: Ambassador College Press, 1967. Pp. xii+226.

Barndollar, W.W. *Jesus' Title to the Throne of David.* Findlay, Ohio: Dunham Pub. Co., Pp. xvii+151.

Barnes, Albert. *Notes on the New Testament.* Vol. XI: *Book of Revelation.* London: Blackie and Son, n.d. Pp. 464.

373

Baron, David. *The Ancient Scriptures and the Modern Jew.* London: Hodder and Stoughton, 1900. Pp. xi+342.

————.*The History of the Ten "Lost" Tribes.* London: Morgan and Scott, Ltd., 1915. Pp. 85.

Bass, Clarence B. *Backgrounds to Dispensationalism.* Grand Rapids, Mich.: Wm. B. Eerdmans Pub. Co., 1960. Pp. 184.

Baxter, J. Sidlow. *The Strategic Grasp of the Bible.* Grand Rapids, Mich.: Zondervan Pub. House, 1968. Pp. 405.

Beecher, Willis Judson. *The Prophets and the Promise.* New York, N.Y.: Thomas Y. Crowell Co., 1905. Pp. xiv+427.

Berkhof, Louis. *The Kingdom of God.* Grand Rapids, Mich.: Wm. B. Eerdmans Pub. Co., 1951. Pp. 177.

————. *Principles of Biblical Interpretation.* Grand Rapids, Mich.: Baker Book House, 1966. Pp. 169.

————. *Systematic Theology.* 4th ed. revised. Grand Rapids, Mich.: Wm. B. Eerdmans Pub. Co., 1949. Pp. 784.

Blackstone, W.E. *Jesus is Coming.* New York, N.Y.: Fleming H. Revell Co., 1908. Pp. 252.

Boettner, Loraine. *The Millennium.* Phila., Pa.: Presbyterian and Reformed Pub. Co., 1964. Pp. iv+380.

Book of Doctrine and Covenant. Lamoni, Iowa: The Reorganized Church of Jesus Christ of Latter Day Saints, 1913. Pp. 296.

Boyer, James L. *For a World Like Ours: Studies in I Corinthians.* Winona Lake, Ind.: BMH Books, 1971. Pp. 153.

————. *Prophecy: Things to Come.* Winona Lake, Ind.: Brethren Missionary Herald Co., 1950. Pp. 79.

Bradbury, John W., ed. *The Sure Word of Prophecy.* New York, N.Y.: Fleming H. Revell Co., 1943. Pp. 318.

Briggs, Charles Augustus. *General Introduction to the Study of Holy Scripture.* New York, N.Y.: Charles Scribner's Sons, 1899. Pp. xxii+688.

Bright, John. *The Kingdom of God.* New York, N.Y.: Abingdon-Cokesbury Press, 1953. Pp. 288.

Broomall, Wick. *Biblical Criticism.* Grand Rapids, Mich.: Zondervan Pub. House, 1957. Pp. 320.

Bullinger, E.W. *The Apocalypse.* London: Eyre and Spottiswoode, 1935. Pp. xix+741.

_____. *Figures of Speech Used in the Bible.* Grand Rapids, Mich.: Baker Book House, 1968. Pp. xlvi+1104.

Buswell, James Oliver. *A Systematic Theology of the Christian Religion.* 2 vols. Grand Rapids, Mich.: Zondervan Pub. House, 1963.

Buttrick, George Arthur, ed. *The Interpreter's Bible.* 12 vols. New York, N.Y.: Abingdon Press, 1957.

Calvin, John. *Commentaries on the Epistle of Paul the Apostle to the Hebrews.* Translated by John Owen. Grand Rapids, Mich.: Wm. B. Eerdmans Pub. Co., 1948. Pp. xxx+448.

Campbell, Roderick. *Israel and the New Covenant.* Phila., Pa.: Presbyterian and Reformed Pub. Co., 1954. Pp. xiii+336.

Carnell, Edward John. *The Case for Orthodox Theology.* Phila., Pa.: Westminster Press, 1959. Pp. 162.

Case, Shirley Jackson. *The Millennial Hope.* Chicago, Ill.: University of Chicago Press, 1918. Pp. ix+253.

Chafer, Lewis Sperry. *Dispensationalism.* Dallas, Tex.: Dallas Seminary Press, 1951. Pp. 108.

_____. *Systematic Theology.* 8 vols. Dallas, Tex.: Dallas Seminary Press, 1948.

Chafer, Rollin Thomas. *The Science of Biblical Hermeneutics.* Dallas, Tex.: Bibliotheca Sacra, n.d. Pp. 92.

Charles, R.H. *The Revelation of St. John.* Vol. XLVII of *The International Critical Commentary.* Edited by C.A. Briggs, S.R. Driver, and Alfred Plummer. 47 vols. New York, N.Y.: Charles Scribner's Sons, 1920. Pp. viii+497.

Cheyne, T.K. *The Prophecies of Isaiah.* 2 vols. New York, N.Y.: Thomas Whittaker, 1895.

Clarke, Adam. *The New Testament with a Commentary and Critical Notes.* Edited by Daniel Curry. Vol. VI: *The Epistles and Revelation.* New York, N.Y.: Eaton and Mains, 1883. Pp. 633.

Cox, William E. *Amillennialism Today.* Phila., Pa.: Presbyterian and Reformed Pub. Co., 1972. Pp. vii+143.

Criswell, W.A. *Why I Preach that the Bible is Literally True.* Nashville, Tenn.: Broadman Press, 1969. Pp. 160.

Culver, Robert D. *Daniel and the Latter Days.* Chicago, III.: Moody Press, 1954. Pp. 224.

Dana, H.E. *Searching the Scriptures.* New Orleans, La.: Bible Institute Memorial Press, 1936. Pp. 253.

Davidson, A.B. *Old Testament Prophecy.* Edited by J.A. Paterson. Edinburgh: T. & T. Clark, 1903. Pp. xi+507.

Davidson, Samuel. *Sacred Hermeneutics.* Edinburgh: Thomas Clark, 1843. Pp. xii+747.

Davis, John J. *Biblical Numerology.* Winona Lake, Ind.: BMH Books, 1968. Pp. 174.

————. *The Birth of a Kingdom: Studies in I-II Samuel and I Kings I-II.* Foreword by S. Herbert Bess. Winona Lake, Ind.: BMH Books, 1970. Pp. 209.

————. *Conquest and Crisis: Studies in Joshua, Judges, and Ruth.* Introduction by John C. Whitcomb, Jr. Winona Lake, Ind.: BMH Books, 1969. Pp. 176.

Delitzsch, Franz. *Biblical Commentary on the Prophecies of Isaiah.* Translated by James Martin. 2 vols. Grand Rapids, Mich.: Wm. B. Eerdmans Pub. Co., 1950.

Douty, Norman F. *Another Look at Seventh Day Adventism.* Grand Rapids, Mich.: Baker Book House, 1962. Pp. 224.

Dusterdieck, Friedrich. *Handbook to the Revelation of John.* Vol. XI of *Commentary on the New Testament.* Edited by Heinrich A.W. Meyer. 11 vols. New York, N.Y.: Funk and Wagnalls, Pubs., 1887. Pp. viii+494.

Eddy, Mary Baker G. *Science and Health with Key to the Scriptures*. Boston, Mass.: Joseph Armstrong, 1899. Pp. xii+663.

Edersheim, Alfred. *Prophecy and History*. Grand Rapids, Mich.: Baker Book House, 1955. Pp. xxiv+391.

Ehlert, Arnold D. *A Bibliographic History of Dispensationalism*. Grand Rapids, Mich.: Baker Book House, 1965. Pp. 110.

Elliott, Charles and William Justin Harsha. *Biblical Hermeneutics*. New York, N.Y.: Anson D.F. Randolph and Co., 1881. Pp. xvi+282.

Ellis, E. Earle. *Paul's Use of the Old Testament*. Grand Rapids, Mich.: Wm. B. Eerdmans Pub. Co., 1957. Pp. xi+204.

English, E. Schuyler. *Re-Thinking the Rapture*. Travelers Rest, S.C.: Southern Bible Book House, 1954. Pp. xii+123.

Fairbairn, Patrick. *An Esposition of Ezekiel*. Evansville, Ind.: Sovereign Grace Pubs., 1960. Pp. 504.

————. *Hermeneutical Manual*. Edinburgh: T. & T. Clark, 1858. Pp. xi+478.

————. *The Interpretation of Prophecy*. Reprint edition. London: Banner of Truth Trust, 1964. Pp. xxiii+532.

————. *The Typology of Scripture*. Grand Rapids, Mich.: Zondervan Pub. House, n.d. Pp. vii+484.

Farrar, Frederic W. *History of Interpretation*. London: Macmillan and Co., 1886. Pp. li+553.

Feinberg, Charles Lee. *Israel in the Spotlight*. New York, N.Y.: American Board of Missions to the Jews, Inc., 1964. Pp. viii+159.

————. *Premillennialism or Amillennialism?* Wheaton, Ill.: Van Kampen Press, 1954. Pp. xx+354.

————, ed. *Prophecy and the Seventies*. Chicago, Ill.: Moody Press, 1971. Pp. 255.

————. *The Prophecy of Ezekiel: The Glory of the Lord*. Chicago, Ill.: Moody Press, 1969. Pp. 286.

Freeman, Hobart E. *An Introduction to the Old Testament Prophets*. Chicago, Ill.: Moody Press, 1968. Pp. 384.

Gaebelein, Arno C. *The Prophet Ezekiel*. New York, N.Y.: By the Author, 1918. Pp. 346.

Gardiner, F. *The Book of the Prophet Ezekiel*. Vol. V of *Elliocott's Commentary on the Whole Bible*. Edited by Charles John Ellicott. 8 vols. Grand Rapids, Mich.: Zondervan Pub. House, n.d. Pp. 199-353.

Gerstner, John H. *The Theology of the Major Sects*. Grand Rapids, Mich.: Baker Book House, 1960. Pp. 206.

Girdlestone, Robert Baker. *The Grammar of Prophecy*. Grand Rapids, Mich.: Kregel Pubs., 1955. Pp. xiii+192.

Grant, P. W. *The Revelation of John*. London: Hodder and Stoughton, 1899. Pp. xii+636.

Grant, Robert M. *The Bible in the Church*. New York, N.Y.: Macmillan Co., 1948. Pp. 194.

Hamilton, Floyd E. *The Basis of Millennial Faith*. Grand Rapids, Mich.: Wm. B. Eerdmans Pubs. Co., 1942. Pp. 160.

Hamilton, Gavin. *Maranatha!* N.p.: By the Author, 1953. Pp. 123.

Harrison, Everett F., ed. *Baker's Dictionary of Theology*. Grand Rapids, Mich.: Baker Book House, 1960. Pp. 566.

Harrison, Norman B. *The End: Re-Thinking the Rapture*. Minneapolis, Minn.: Harrison Service, 1941. Pp. 239.

Harrison, William K. *Hope Triumphant*. Chicago, Ill.: Moody Press, 1966. Pp. 153.

Hartill, J. Edwin. *Biblical Hermeneutics*. Grand Rapids, Mich.: Zondervan Pub. House, 1947. Pp. 123.

Hendriksen, William. *"And So All Israel Shall be Saved."* Grand Rapids, Mich.: Baker's Book Store, 1945. Pp. 36.

————. *Bible Survey*. 2nd ed. Grand Rapids, Mich.: Baker Book House, 1947. Pp. 485.

————. *More Than Conquerors*. Grand Rapids, Mich.: Baker's Book Store, 1940. Pp. 285.

Hengstenberg, E. W. *Christology of the Old Testament*. 4 vols. Grand Rapids, Mich.: Kregel Pubs. 1956.

Heslop, William G. *Riches from Revelation*. Butler, Ind.: Highley Press, 1932. Pp. 161.

Hodge, A [rchibald] A. *Outlines of Theology*. New York, N.Y.: Hodder and Stoughton. 1878. Pp. 678.

Hodge, Charles. *Systematic Theology*. 3 vols. New York, N.Y.: Charles Scribner's Sons, 1872. Pp. viii+880.

Hoekema, Anthony A. *The Four Major Cults*. Grand Rapids, Mich.: Wm. B. Eerdmans Pub. Co., 1963. Pp. xiv+447.

Hoeksema, Herman. *Reformed Dogmatics*. Grand Rapids, Mich.: Reformed Free Pub. Ass'n, 1966. Pp. xvii+917.

Horne, Thomas Hartwell. *An Introduction to the Critical Study and Knowledge of the Holy Scriptures*. 4 vols. Boston, Mass.: Littell and Gay, 1868.

Hospers, Gerrit Henrick. *The Principle of Spiritualization in Hermeneutics*. East Williamson, N.Y.: By the Author, 1935. Pp. 52.

Hoyt, Herman A. *Biblical Eschatology*. Winona Lake, Ind.: By the Author, 1966. Pp. 290.

————. *The End Times*. Chicago, III. Moody Press, 1969. Pp. 256.

————. *The Revelation of the Lord Jesus Christ*. Winona Lake, Ind.: Brethren Missionary Herald Co., 1966. Pp. 108.

Hughes, Archibald. *A New Heaven and a New Earth*. Phila., Pa.: Presbyterian and Reformed Pub. Co., 1958. Pp. 233.

Ironside, Harry A. *The Great Parenthesis*. Grand Rapids, Mich.: Zondervan Pub. House, 1943. Pp. 131.

————. *The Lamp of Prophecy*. Grand Rapids, Mich.: Zondervan Pub. House, 1940. Pp. 159.

————. *Lectures on the Book of Revelation.* Neptune, N.J.: Loizeaux Bros., 1920. Pp. 366.

————. *Wrongly Dividing the Word of Truth.* Neptune, N.J.: Loizeaux Bros., Inc., n.d. Pp. 66.

Irvine, William C., ed. *Heresies Exposed.* New York, N.Y.: Loizeaux Bros., Inc., n.d. Pp. 225.

Jennings, F.C. *Studies in Isaiah.* New York, N.Y.: Loizeaux Bros., n.d. Pp. 784.

Kaplan, Jacob H. *Psychology of Prophecy.* Phila., Pa.: Julius H. Greenstone, 1908. Pp. xii+148.

Keil, Carl Friedrich. *Biblical Commentary on the Prophecies of Ezekiel.* Edinburgh: T. & T. Clark, 1876. Pp. vii+434.

Kelly, William. *An Exposition of the Book of Isaiah.* 4th ed. London: C.A. Hammond, 1947. Pp. 400.

————. *Lectures on the Book of Revelation.* London: G. Morrish, n.d. Pp. lxiv+502.

Kent, Homer A., Jr. "Matthew." *The Wycliffe Bible Commentary.* Edited by Charles F. Pfeiffer and Everett F. Harrison. Chicago, III.: Moody Press, 1962. Pp. 929-85.

————. *Ephesians: The Glory of the Church.* Chicago, III.: Moody Press, 1971. Pp. 128.

Kraus, C. Norman. *Dispensationalism in America.* Richmond, Va.: John Knox Press, 1958. Pp. 156.

Kromminga, D. H. *The Millennium.* Grand Rapids, Mich.: Wm. B. Eerdmans Pub. Co., 1948. Pp. 121.

————. *The Millennium in the Church.* Grand Rapids, Mich.: Wm. B. Eerdmans Pub. Co., 1945. Pp. 360.

Kuyper, Abraham. *The Revelation of St. John.* Translated by John Hendrick de Vries. Grand Rapids, Mich.: Wm. B. Eerdmans Pub. Co., 1935. Pp. 360.

Ladd, George Eldon. *The Blessed Hope.* Grand Rapids, Mich.: Wm. B. Eerdmans Pub. Co., 1956. Pp. 167.

————. *A Commentary on the Revelation of John.* Grand Rapids, Mich.: William B. Eerdmans Pub. Co., 1972. Pp. 308.

————. *Crucial Questions about the Kingdom of God.* Grand Rapids, Mich.: Wm. B. Eerdmans Pub. Co., 1952. Pp. 193.

Lange, John Peter. *Revelation.* Edited by E.R. Craven. In *A Commentary on the Holy Scriptures: Critical, Doctrinal and Homiletical.* Edited by J.P. Lange. Translated by Phillip Schaff. Grand Rapids, Mich.: Zondervan Pub. House, 1949-51. Pp. vii+446.

Lenski, R.C.H. *The Interpretation of St. John's Revelation.* Columbus, Ohio: Wartburg Press, 1957. Pp. 675.

Leupold, H.C. *Exposition of Isaiah.* 2 vols. Grand Rapids, Mich.: Baker Book House, 1968.

Lightfoot, J.B. *St. Paul's Epistle to the Galatians.* Andover, Mass.: Warren F. Draper, Pub., 1885. Pp. viii+398.

Lightner, Robert P. *Neo-Evangelism. Des Plaines, Ill.: Regular Baptist Press, 1965. Pp. 190.*

Lindblom, J. *Prophecy in Ancient Israel.* Phila., Pa.: Fortress Press, 1962.

Lindsey, Hal. *The Late Great Planet Earth.* Grand Rapids, Mich.: Zondervan Pub. House, 1970. Pp. 192.

Lockhart, Clinton. *Principles of Interpretation.* 2nd ed. rev. Kansas City, Kansas: Central Seminary Press, 1901. Pp. 260.

McClain, Alva J. *Daniel's Prophecy of the Seventy Weeks.* Grand Rapids, Mich.: Zondervan Pub. House, 1969. Pp. 62.

————. *The Greatness of the Kingdom.* Grand Rapids, Mich.: Zondervan Pub. House, 1959. Pp. xvi+556.

————. *The Jewish Problem and its Divine Solution.* Winona Lake, Ind.: Brethren Missionary Herald Co., Inc., 1944., 1944. Pp. 31.

MacIntosh, C.H. *Papers on the Lord's Coming.* New York, N.Y.: Loizeaux Bros., n.d. Pp. 111.

Manley, G.T. *The Return of Jesus Christ.* Chicago, III.: Inter-Varsity Press, 1960. Pp. 104.

Martin, Walter R. *The Kingdom of the Cults.* Grand Rapids, Mich.: Zondervan Pub. House, 1965. Pp. 443.

————. *The Truth about Seventh Day Adventism.* Grand Rapids, Mich.: Zondervan Pub. House, 1960. Pp. 248.

Martin, Walter R. and Norman H. Klain. *Jehovah of the Watch Tower.* 6th ed. rev. Grand Rapids, Mich.: Zondervan Pub. House, 1963. Pp. 221.

Mauro, Philip. *God's Present Kingdom.* New York, N.Y.: Fleming H. Revell Co., 1919. Pp. 270.

————. *The Patmos Vision.* Boston, Mass.: Scripture Truth Depot, 1925. Pp. 576.

Mickelsen, Anton Berkeley. *Interpreting the Bible.* Grand Rapids, Mich.: Wm. B. Eerdmans Pub. Co., 1963. Pp. xiv+425.

Milligan, William. *Lectures on the Apocalypse.* London: Macmillan and Co., 1892. Pp. xxiii+239.

Murray, George L. *Millennial Studies.* Grand Rapids, Mich.: Baker Book House, 1948. Pp. 207.

Neufeld, Don F., ed. *Seventh Day Adventist Encyclopedia.* Washington, D.C.: Review and Herald Pub. Ass'n, 1966. Pp. 1452.

Newell, William R. *The Book of the Revelation.* Chicago, Ill.: Scripture Press, 1935. Pp. ix+404.

Oehler, Gustav Friedrich. *Theology of the Old Testament.* Revised and translated by George E. Day. New York, N.Y.: Funk and Wagnalls Pubs., 1883. Pp. xix+593.

Orchard, Dom Bernard, ed. *A Catholic Commentary on the Holy Scripture.* New York, N.Y.: Thomas Nelson and Sons, 1953. Pp. xvi+1312.

Orelli, C. von. *Old Testament Prophecy.* Edinburgh: T. & T. Clark, 1885. Pp. viii+472.

Orr, James. *The Problem of the Old Testament.* New York, N.Y.: Charles Scribner's Sons, 1907. Pp. lii+562.

──────. *The Progress of Dogma.* London: Hodder and Stoughton, 1908. Pp. xxviii+365.

Ottman, Ford C. *The Unfolding of the Ages.* Fincastle, Va.: Scripture Truth Book Co., 1967. Pp. xxx+510.

Pache, Rene. *The Return of Jesus Christ.* Translated by William Sanford LaSor. Chicago, Ill.: Moody Press, 1955. Pp. 448.

Payne, J. Barton. *The Imminent Appearing of Christ.* Grand Rapids, Mich.: Wm. B. Eerdmans Pub. Co., 1962. Pp. 191.

──────. *The Theology of the Older Testament.* Grand Rapids, Mich.: Zondervan Pub. House, 1962. Pp. 554.

Pentecost, J. Dwight. *Things to Come.* Introduction by John F. Walvoord. Findlay, Ohio: Dunham Pub. Co., 1958. Pp. xxx+633.

Peters, George N.H. *The Theocratic Kingdom.* 3 vols. Grand Rapids, Mich.: Kregel Publications, 1952.

Pettingill, William L. *History Foretold.* Findlay, Ohio: Fundamental Truth Pubs., n.d. Pp. 117.

Pieters, Albertus. *The Seed of Abraham.* Grand Rapids, Mich.: Wm. B. Eerdmans Pub. Co., 1950. Pp. 161.

Pink, Arthur W. *Interpretation of the Scriptures.* Grand Rapids, Mich.: Baker Book House, 1972. Pp. 137.

Plummer, Alfred A. *Revelation.* In *The Pulpit Commentary.* Edited by H.D.M. Spence and Joseph S. Exell. New York, N.Y.: Funk and Wagnalls Co., n.d. Pp. xxvii+585.

Pusey, E.B. *Daniel the Prophet.* New York, N.Y.: Funk and Wagnalls, Pubs. 1885. Pp. lxxiii+519.

Rad, Gerhard von. *Old Testament Theology.* Translated by D.M.G. Stalker. 2 vols. New York, N.Y.: Harper and Row, Pubs., 1965.

Ramm, Bernard. *Protestant Biblical Interpretation.* 3rd rev. ed. Grand Rapids, Mich.: Baker Book House, 1970. Pp. xvii+298.

384 BIBLIOGRAPHY

Redpath, Henry A. *The Book of the Prophet Ezekiel.* New York, N.Y.: Edwin S. Gorham, 1907. Pp. xlii+276.

Reid, R.J. *Amillennialism.* New York.: Loizeaux Bros., 1943. Pp. 103.

Rhodes, Arnold Black, ed. *The Church Faces the Isms.* New York, N.Y.: Abingdon Press, 1958. Pp. 304.

Roberts, Alexander and James Donaldson, eds. *The Ante-Nicene Fathers.* American reprint of the Edinburgh edition. 9 vols. Grand Rapids, Mich.: Wm. B. Eerdmans Pub. Co., 1951.

Ryrie, Charles Caldwell. *The Basis of the Premillennial Faith.* New York, N.Y.: Loizeaux Bros., 1953. Pp. 160.

————. *The Bible and Tomorrow's News.* Wheaton, Ill.: Scripture Press Pubs., Inc., 1969. Pp. 190.

————. *Biblical Theology of the New Testament.* Chicago, Ill.: Moody Press, 1959. Pp. 384.

————. *Dispensationalism Today.* Chicago, Ill.: Moody Press, 1965. Pp. 221.

Sauer, Erich. *The Dawn of World Redemption.* Grand Rapids, Mich.: Wm. B. Eerdmans Pub. Co., 1953. Pp. 206.

Schaff, Philip. *History of the Christian Church.* 7 vols. New York, N.Y.: Charles Scribner and Co., 1884.

Schep, J.A. *The Nature of the Resurrection Body.* Grand Rapids, Mich.: Wm. B. Eerdmans Pub. Co., 1964. Pp. 252.

Scofield, C.I., ed. *The New Scofield Reference Bible.* New ed. Edited by E. Schuyler English and others. New York, N.Y.: Oxford Univ. Press, Inc., 1967. Pp. xvi+1392.

————. *The Scofield Bible Correspondence School.* 3 vols. Los Angeles, Calif. Bible Institute of Los Angeles, 1907.

Scott, Walter. *Exposition of the Revelation of Jesus Christ.* London: Pickering and Inglis, Ltd., n.d. Pp. 456.

Seiss, J.A. *The Apocalypse.* London: Marshall, Morgan and Scott, Ltd., n.d. Pp. xiii+536.

Shedd, William G.T. *Dogmatic Theology.* Classic reprint ed. 3 vols. Grand Rapids, Mich.: Zondervan Pubs. House, n.d.

Silver, Jesse Forest. *The Lord's Return.* New York, N.Y.: Fleming H. Revell Co., 1914. Pp. 311.

Simpson, A.B. *Heaven Opened.* Nyack, N.Y.: Christian Alliance Pub. Co., 1899. Pp. vi+299.

Smith, J.B. *A Revelation of Jesus Christ.* Scottsdale, Pa.: Herald Press, 1961. Pp. xiii+369.

Smith, Noel. *Herbert W. Armstrong and His World Tomorrow.* Springfield, Mo.: Baptist Bible Tribune, 1964. Pp. 61.

Smith, Oswald J. *The Passion for Souls.* London: Marshall, Morgan and Scott, 1950. Pp. ix+124.

Smith, Uriah. *The Prophecies of Daniel and the Revelation.* Wash., D.C.: Review and Herald Pub. Ass'n, 1944. Pp. 830.

Smith, Wilbur. *The Biblical Doctrine of Heaven.* Chicago, Ill.: Moody Press, 1968.Pp. 317.

Smith, Wilbur. *The Biblical Doctrine of Heaven.* Chicago, Ill.: Moody Press. 1968. Pp. 317.

————. *Profitable Bible Study.* Boston, Mass.: W.A. Wilde Co., 1953. Pp. 227.

Snowden, James H. *The Coming of the Lord.* New York, N.Y.: Macmillan Co., 1919. Pp. xxi+288.

Spurgeon, Charles H. *Lectures to My Students.* 3 vols. Reprint (3 vols. in 1). Grand Rapids, Mich.: Associated Publishers and Authors, 1971.

Stam, Cornelius. *Things That Differ.* Chicago, Ill.: Berean Bible Society, 1959. Pp. 279.

Stanton, Gerlad B. *Kept from the Hour.* London: Marshall, Morgan and Scott, 1964. Pp. 320.

Stoner, Peter W. *Science Speaks.* Chicago, Ill.: Moody Press, 1968. Pp. 128.

Strombeck, J.F. *First the Rapture.* Moline, Ill.: Strombeck Agency, Inc., 1950. Pp. 197.

Strong, Augustus Hopkins. *Systematic Theology*. Phila., Pa.: Judson Press, 1907. Pp. xxviii+1166.

Stuart, M. *Hints on the Interpretation of Prophecy*. Andover, Mass.: Allen, Morrill & Wardwell, 1842. Pp. 146.

Swedenborg, Emmanuel. *The Apocalypse Revealed*. Phila., Pa.: J.B. Lippincott and Co., 1876. Pp. 1202.

Swete, Henry Barclay. *The Apocalypse of St. John*. London: Macmillan and Co., Ltd. 1907. Pp. ccix+338.

Tenney, Merrill C. *Interpreting Revelation*. Grand Rapids, Mich.: Wm. B. Eerdmans Pub. Co., 1957. Pp. xi+220.

Terry, Milton S. *Biblical Apocalyptics*. New York, N.Y.: Eaton and Mains, 1898. Pp. 513.

———. *Biblical Hermeneutics*. New York, N.Y.: Eaton and Mains, 1911. Pp. 511.

Thiessen, Henry Clarence. *Introductory Lectures in Systematic Theology*. Grand Rapids, Mich.: Wm. B. Eerdmans Pub. Co., 1949. Pp. 574.

Todd, James H. *Principles of Interpretation*. Chicago, Ill.: Bible Institute Colportage Ass'n., 1923. Pp. 62.

Trench, Richard Chenevix. *Notes on the Parables of Our Lord*. 1948. Reprint. New York, N.Y.: Dover Pubs., 1964.

Unger, Merrill F. *Great Neglected Prophecies*. Chicago, Ill.: Scripture Press, 1955. Pp. 167.

Urquhart, John. *Wonders of Prophecy*. 3rd ed. London: Pickering and Inglis, Ltd., 1950. Pp. 195.

Vos, Geerhardus. *Biblical Theology*. Grand Rapids, Mich.: Wm. B. Eerdmans Pub. Co., 1948. Pp. 453.

Walvoord, John F. *The Church in Prophecy*. Grand Rapids, Mich.: Zondervan Pub. House, 1964. Pp. 183.

———. *Daniel: The Key to Prophetic Revelation*. Chicago, Ill.: Moody Press, 1971. Pp. 317.

———. *Israel in Prophecy*. Grand Rapids, Mich.: Zondervan Pub. House, 1962. Pp. 138.

————. *The Millennial Kingdom.* Findlay, Ohio: Dunham Pub. Co., 1959. Pp. xxiv+373.

————. *The Nations in Prophecy.* London: Pickering and Ingles Ltd., 1967. Pp. 176.

————. *The Revelation of Jesus Christ.* Chicago, Ill.: Moody Press, 1966. Pp. 347.

Warfield, Benjamin Breckinridge. *Biblical and Theological Studies.* Phila., Pa.: Presbyterian and Reformed Pub. Co., 1952. Pp. xlviii+580.

Weiss, Bernhard. *Biblical Theology of the New Testament.* Translated by David Eaton. 2 vols. Edinburgh: T. & T. Clark, 1885.

West, Nathaniel. *The Thousand Years in Both Testaments.* Chicago, Ill.: Fleming H. Revell, 1880. Pp. xxii+493.

Whitcomb, John C., Jr., and Morris, Henry M. *The Genesis Flood.* Foreword by John C. McCampbell. Grand Rapids, Mich.: Baker Book House, 1961. Pp. xxxii+518.

Whitcomb, John C., Jr. *The Origin of the Solar System.* Phila., Pa.: Presbyterian and Reformed Pub. Co., 1964. Pp. 34.

————. *Solomon to the Exile: Studies in Kings and Chronicles.* Winona Lake, Ind.: BMH Books, 1971. Pp. 182.

Wilmot, John. *Inspired Principles of Prophetic Interpretation.* Swengel, Pa.: Reiner Pubs., 1967. Pp. 290.

Winthrop, Edward. *The Characteristics and Laws of Prophetic Symbols.* 2nd ed. New York, N.Y.: Franklin Knight, 1854. Pp. xiv+191.

Wyngaarden, Martin Jacob. *The Future of the Kingdom in Prophecy and Fulfillment.* Grand Rapids, Mich.: Baker Book House, 1955. Pp. 211.

Young, Edward J. *My Svrvants the Prophets.* Grand Rapids, Mich.: Wm. B. Eerdmans Pub. Co., 1952. Pp. 231.

————. *The Prophecy of Daniel.* Grand Rapids, Mich.: Wm. B. Eerdmans Pub. Co., 1949. Pp. 330.

II. ARTICLES AND PERIODICALS

Baker, Dwight L. "Bible Prophecy in the Prophets' City." *Christianity Today*, July 16, 1971, pp. 29-30.

Bess, S. Herbert. "The Office of the Prophet in Old Testament Times." *Grace Journal*, I, No. 1 (Spring, 1960), 7-12.

Bowman, John Wick. "Dispensationalism." *Interpretation*, X. No. 2 (April, 1956), 170-87.

Boyer, James L. "The Office of the Prophet in New Testament Times." *Grace Journal*, I, No. 1 (Spring, 1960), 13-20.

Campbell, Donald K. "The Interpretation of Types." *Bibliotheca Sacra*, CXII, No. 447 (July, 1955), 248-55.

Childs, Brevard S. "Prophecy and Fulfillment." *Interpretation*, XII, No. 3 (July, 1958), 259-71.

Cohen, Gary G. "Some Questions Concerning the New Jerusalem." *Grace Journal*, VI, No. 3 (Fall, 1965), 24-29.

Culver, Robert D. "The Difficulty of Interpreting Old Testament Prophecy." *Bibliotheca Sacra*, Vol. 114, No. 455 (July, 1957), 201-5.

Darby, George. "Dispensationalism and the Bible." *The Discerner*, III, No. 11 (July-Sept., 1961), 5-9.

Franzmann, Martin H. "The Hermeneutical Dilemma: Dualism in the Interpretation of Holy Scripture." *Concordia Theological Monthly*, XXXVI, No. 8 (Sept., 1965), 502-33.

Hughes, Edward. "On the Holy Road to Mecca." *Reader's Digest*, Oct., 1971, pp. 27-36.

"Israel: The Beginning of the End." *Campus Life*, Aug-Sept., 1971, pp. 13-16.

Jackson, Robert Summer. "The Prophetic Vision." *Interpretation*, XVI, No. 1 (Jan. 1962), 65-75.

Jacobs, Joseph. "Anglo-Israelism." *Jewish Encyclopedia*. 1901. I, 600-601.

Kent, Homer A., Jr. "Matthew's Use of the Old Testament." *Bibliotheca Sacra*, Vol. 121, No. 481 (Jan.-Mar., 1964), 34-43.

Kubo, Sakae. "The Principle of Equivalency." *Andrews University Seminary Studies*, VIII, No. 2 (July, 1970), 144-67.

McNally, R.E. "Medieval Exegesis." *New Catholic Encyclopedia.* 1967. V,707-712.

Michaels, J. Ramsey. Review of *The Gospel of the Kingdom*, by George Eldon Ladd. *Westminster Theological Journal*, XXIII, No. 1 (Nov., 1960), 47-50.

Miller, Russell Benjamin. "Sermon on the Mount." *International Standard Bible Encyclopedia.* 1939. IV, 1732-36.

Mitchell, John L. "The Question of Millennial Sacrifices." *Bibliotheca Sacra*, Vol. 110, No. 440 (Oct., 1953), 342-61.

Newport, John P. "Biblical Interpretation and Eschatological-Holy History." *Southwestern Journal of Theology*, IV, No. 1 (Oct., 1961), 83-110.

Orelli, C. von. "Prophecy." *International Standard Bible Encyclopedia.* 1939. IV, 2459-66.

Pentecost, J. Dwight. "The Sermon on the Mount." *Bibliotheca Sacra*, Vol. 115, No. 458 (April, 1958), 128-92.

Pickering, Ernest. "Distinctive Teachings of Ultra-Dispensationalism." *The Discerner*, CXI, No. 11 (July-Sept., 1961), 10-15.

Smith, Neil Gregor. "Imagination in Exegesis." *Interpretation*, X, No. 4 (Oct., 1956), 420-26.

Unger, Merrill F. "The Character of Old Testament Prophecy." *Bibliotheca Sacra*, Vol. 108 (April-June, 1951), 167-71.

Walvoord, John F. "The New Covenant with Israel." *Bibliotheca Sacra*, Vol. 110, No. 439 (July, 1953), 193-205.

Vawter, Bruce. "The Fuller Sense: Some Considerations." *Catholic Biblical Quarterly*, XXVI, No. 1 (Jan., 1964), 85-96.

Zimmerli, Walther. "Promise and Fulfillment." Translated by James Wharton. *Interpretation*, XV, No. 3 (July, 1961), 310-38.

Zimmerman, Charles. "To This Agree the Words of the Prophets." *Grace Journal*, IV, No. 3 (Fall, 1963), 28-40.

III. UNPUBLISHED MATERIALS

Fuller, Daniel Payton. "The Hermeneutics of Dispensationalism." Unpublished Th. D. dissertation, Northern Baptist Theological Seminary, 1957. Pp. x+403.

Kurtaneck, Nickolas. "A Survey of Dispensationalism." Unpublished Th. D. dissertation, Grace Theological Seminary, 1961. Pp. iii+361.

INDEXES

INDEX OF AUTHORS

II
INDEX OF SCRIPTURE

Double sense. *See also* Allegorization; Mystical interpretation; Sense
according to allegorists, 37, 38
according to Aquinas, 52
according to Augustine, 50-51
according to Origen, 49-50
according to Philo, 47
answers to, 61, 213-16
and Berkhof's definition, 212, 215-16
in comprehension, 30, 59-60, 118-19. *See also* Principle of Comprehension
definition of, 364
and depth of Scripture, 35, 61, 211-13, 213-16
and double reference, 181-82
in music compositions, 30
rejected by *Westminster Confession of Faith*, 119
in spiritualization, 32-33, 35, 38, 215-16
its supposed reasons, 35, 53, 60, 211-13
and typology, 35, 169, 181-82, 216
Dreams, 82-83, 91. *See also* Revelational dreams
Duesterdieck, 248
Dual hermeneutics
and Augustine, 50-51
defined, 364
and the Reformers, 54, 117-18
and the Roman Catholics, 54, 118
and today, 38, 57-58, 59, 73-74, 118, 276-77

E

Ecstasy, 83, 85, 90-91, 365. *See also* Prophetic mind
Eden, Garden of, (61), 157-59, 214n, 238, 239
Edenic Covenant, 240
Edom, 224
Egypt, 140, 153, 163, 324
Elam, 224
Eli, 190
Eliezer, 43
Elijah the Prophet
coming in the future, 153, 185-87
person of, 78, 80, 186
prophesied by Malachi, 178, 185, 186
typified by John the Baptist, 178, 185-87
Ellicott, Charles J., 57
Emmaus, Road to, 19, 273
Encounter, revelational, 84
England, 312-17, 355
Enigma, 59, 77, 93
Equivalents. *See* Principle of Equivalents
Ernesti, John Augustus, 55
Eschatology. *See* Prophecy
Eternal kingdom, 184n, 234, 311, 365. *See also* Kingdom earthly
Eternal State, 357-60
Ethiopia, 22, 43, 224, 325
Eucherius, 52
Euphrates, River, 37, 127, 127n
"Every Promise in the Book is Mine," 120, 120n
Exegesis, 119, 120, 121-23,

365. *See also* Interpretation
and application
Exposition, 40-41, 119, 120,
121-23, 365. *See also* Interpretation and application
Ezra, 40, 41, 42

F

Fables, 49, 141
False Prophet (tribulation),
345-46, 349, 351
False prophets, 78-82
Fathers. *See* Church fathers
Feelings, 25, 130, 272
Figurative interpretation, 143,
365
Figurative language. *See also*
Actual language; Form of
prophecy
and consistent hermeneutics,
263-64
and context, 137-38
defined, 365
and figurative interpretation,
143, 323
and form of prophecy, 83-84,
222-23, 226, 287
and historical studies, 102,
103n
identification of, (135-36),
137-38, 142-43
interpretation of, 31, 142-43,
264
and literal method, 20, 30-31,
36, 132-33
and non-literal interpreters,
131-32, 285-89
reasons for, 138-39
and visions, 89-91, 134

Figures of speech. *See also*
Symbol; Type
classified, 140-42
confused with symbols, 164
defined, 31, 91, 137, 365
described, 137-38
and the literal method, 31,
158
in poetry, 146
First Coming of Christ
and conditional prophecies,
189
and Elijah, 185-87
and fulfillment, 63, 176, 306
in typology, 105, 114, 173
First resurrection. *See* Resurrection, first
Flying Roll, The (Zech. 5), 165-
66
Foreordination. *See* God, foreordination of
Foreshadowing
case of Antichrist, 182
case of Bethlehem infants,
182
case of Joel's prophecy, 183-
85
case of John the Baptist, 185-
87
described, 180, 182
of millennial kingdom, 183-84
not fulfillment, 180-81
in prophecy, 182-87
in typology, 172-73, 180, 181
Foreshortening. *See* Perspective
of prophecy
Foretelling, 75-76. *See also*
Prophecy
Form of prophecy. *See also*
Prophetic mind

and interpreter, 25, 26-28

and issues in hermeneutics, 201-36

and issues in theology, 237-71

of kingdom offered by Christ, 299-311. *See also* Kingdom, earthly

limits of, 30, 31, 32-33, 44-45, 60-61

of millennial sacrifices, 293-98. *See also* Millennial Temple

of New Jerusalem, 283-92. *See also* New Jerusalem

of parables, 147-51. *See also* Parable

principles of prophetic, 96-130

of symbols, 152-66. *See also* Symbolical language

of types, 166-74. *See also* Type

Interpretation and application
latter depends on former, 34, 35, (52), 118-20

  affirmed by Calvin, 34

  affirmed by Spurgeon, 50

  affirmed by *Westminster Confession*,, 119

  in literal interpretation, 34

  as primary and secondary application, 119

  in Sermon on Mount, 121-23

Interpreter (conservative and evangelical), 38, 39, 55-56, 57, 58, 120, 120n, 364

Interpreter, qualifications of 25-28, 132-33, 171

Interval (gap)
in prophecy, 91-95, 337, 350

and mortals at millennium, 95, 111, 339

in resurrections, 94-95

in second advent of Christ, 95, 109, 111, 350

Irenaeus (church father), 71-72, 72n

Irony (figure of speech), 141

Isaac, 302

Israel. *See also* Church; Remnant; Restoration of Israel; Seed of Abraham

ancient enemies of, 64-65, 224-26

in Anglo-Israelism, 313-14

blessings and curses of, 120, 187, 191, 236, 248, 250, 262, 300, 312, 316, 366

definition of, 366

described as Natural Israel, 198, 367

described as Spiritual Israel, 198, 369

in God's program, 66-67, 190, 191, 243-46, 251-53, 298

in millennium, 352, 354-56

and New Covenant, 190, 195-97

not cast aside, 192, 232-33, (249-50), 252-53

and Olivet Discourse, 109, 261

as people of God, 198, 243, 244-45

restoration of, 66-67, 177, 232-33, 253, 346, 350

restrictive use of word, 199-200, 200n

similarities with church, 253, 253n